Born in Eastbourne, the author aspired, at an early age but for no obvious reason, to go to sea, being accepted as a Cadet to the HMS *Conway* pre-sea nautical College on the Isle of Anglesey at the tender age of 15. Acceptance as a Cadet Apprentice to the mighty P & O. S.N. Co followed two years later, rising through the Officer ranks to eventually gain his Master Mariner qualification, and a Commission as a Royal Naval Reserve Officer. Marriage happily retrieved him from assumed bachelorhood, and shortly after to a decision to "swallow the anchor", and seek a career ashore, which rather explains his choice of book title!

Please join him, as you travel his adventures from the relative safety of seagoing, through those deeper waters ashore, where buoyancy was never guaranteed!

To my beloved wife Anna, better known to friends and colleagues by her preferred Dutch name, Ankie. Her love, loyalty, laughter, and pragmatism brought to this adventure from a sea-going career into the unknown challenges of a business life ashore a degree of success that would otherwise never have happened. The twenty-plus peripatetic years portrayed, through the United Kingdom, the Netherlands, Greece/Eastern Mediterranean, India and associated twelve new homes, all the while bringing up two much-loved sons, seeks to underline her extraordinary contribution, and enthusiasm. In its way, it is a story of love, but not a love story, and it belongs to Ankie!

John William Perry

THE DEEPER WATER IS ASHORE

AUSTIN MACAULEY PUBLISHERS
LONDON • CAMBRIDGE • NEW YORK • SHARJAH

Copyright © John William Perry 2023

The right of John William Perry to be identified as author of this work has been asserted by the author in accordance with sections 77 and 78 of the Copyright, Designs and Patents Act 1988.

All rights reserved. No part of this publication may be reproduced, stored in a retrieval system, or transmitted in any form or by any means, electronic, mechanical, photocopying, recording, or otherwise, without the prior permission of the publishers.

Any person who commits any unauthorised act in relation to this publication may be liable to criminal prosecution and civil claims for damages.

All of the events in this memoir are true to the best of the author's memory. The views expressed in this memoir are solely those of the author.

A CIP catalogue record for this title is available from the British Library.

ISBN 9781398484931 (Paperback)
ISBN 9781398484948 (ePub-e-book)

www.austinmacauley.com

First Published 2023
Austin Macauley Publishers Ltd®
1 Canada Square
Canary Wharf
London
E14 5AA

There are times when memory requires some assistance, or indeed clarification, and one has been blessed with ex-colleagues and friends from around the world that have been happy to oblige. Of particular note are Dick McGregor in Charleston Carolina, P. Narayan in Cochin (now Kochi) India, Jaap Verbeek in Oud Beijerland, Holland, George Callitsis in Athens, Greece, Esther Dougan in Polmont, Scotland, and Claire Noye in Felixstowe, England. Sons Duncan and Darren, themselves growing stars during the adventure, have corrected in places, their memories remaining sharp. Special mention must also be made of good neighbour in Woodbridge, Peter Skeet, whose photographic skills and IT knowledge have proved invaluable.

Foreword

In June 1966, and at the age of 29, he may, had he thought about it, which he hadn't, seen himself as a confirmed bachelor, reasonably content with his maritime career which, to that point, he had applied himself for some fourteen years. Two were spent as a Cadet at the pre-sea College H.M.S Conway from the tender age of 15, and the balance becoming an Officer with the P & O Company (later to become P & O-Orient Line), and Commissioned within the Royal Naval Reserve (List One), reaching the dizzy heights of Senior Second Officer with his Masters Licence aboard 'Orcades', with the former, and Lieutenant RNR, the latter.

It would be fair to describe the career duality to that point as having presented the very best of two different maritime worlds, with promotion potential within each as a reasonably foregone conclusion, albeit dependent upon continued professional application, recognition of diplomacy as a required skill to be continually honed, and not, definitely not, fouling one's own nest while serving with either the P & O, or the Royal Navy. (Purists will recognise that P & O in this context and time relates to the P & O. Steam Navigation Company, and not to P&O as a brand name of the American owned Carnival Cruise Company, as sadly it was eventually to become.)

In that same month of June 1966, his halcyon state of reasonable maritime bliss was to be, totally unforeseen or anticipated, nudged. Or, to give it its dictionary definition, 'touched or pushed, gently or gradually'. So gentle was the nudge as to be un-noticed by him, deeply involved as he was, as the vessel's Navigator, in the Season's Mediterranean Cruise programme, and having little time or indeed interest in pondering P & O's philosophy as to the employment of Purser staff aboard their vessels.

To digress slightly, P & O had decided, as a function of its marketing approach relative to customer care, to employ a number of Women Assistant Pursers (WAPS as they were so kindly referred) aboard their Liners, acknowledging in so doing increased interest in attracting European passengers seeking to travel to or from Australia and New Zealand, or indeed the Far East, P & O's other main trade lane. To qualify, applicants for these posts were required to have fluency in spoken and written English, Dutch, and German, as well as in shorthand. Anticipating the absence of any British applicants, P & O turned to the Netherlands, and lo and behold, were able to employ as many as were required.

Let us, at this stage, forego the use of the first person singular, 'he', and put name to the navigator in question, as bestowed on him at birth. Actually, not immediately at birth, as his mother was desperately hoping for a girl, and when asked, "What shall we call him?", came the response, "I don't care, call him anything you like", or words to that effect. Discussion then evinced the information that the child's grandfather bore the names William John, so in thoughtful haste, he became John William, and was thus, despatched into the world.

In that same June, in 1966, a 26-year-old Dutch woman, born in the town of Baarn in 1941, and having passed the P & O's application with flying colours, joined P & O and, more importantly, was in due course appointed to join 'Orcades' – further, she was to be assigned to assist the Navigator in the typing of voyage planning, passenger information as related to the vessel's progress, and such nautical bric-a-brac as deemed necessary or appropriate on matter of fact or interest as the Cruise Season, or main-line voyage, unfolded. As part of her induction, she was given copy of a small black book, being 'Regulations Instructions and Advice' for Officers in the service of P & O S N Co.

Her name was Ankie. Actually, it wasn't, because at birth, she had been registered as Anna Petronella, Anna from her father's side, and Petronella from her mother's side, but her mother much preferred the name Ankie, so one has to question who registered the birth. Notwithstanding, everyone knew her as Ankie, which pleased her mother no end. De facto, Anna Petronella joined 'Orcades', and was known as Ankie. Veni, vidi, vici. Or, as she might have said in her native tongue, "Ze kwam, Ze zag, Ze overwon!" She was proudly Dutch. We will uncover her maiden name as we progress.

When they were introduced, he and she, it may have occurred to him subconsciously, had he thought about it, which he didn't, that his bachelor status was possibly threatened, and if so, would life at sea remain sustainable? Thankfully, and with much to otherwise ponder, such as courses and distances, clock changes, sunsets and sunrises, high and low waters and careful avoidance of shoals, reefs, and other potentially damaging slices of terra firma, subconscious was overridden by need for active planning. Even thought that he (John) would feel some affection for her (Ankie, geregistreerd als Anna), this would have been put aside as being the result of undigested beef or cheese, to lightly plagiarise from Dickens 'Christmas Carol', "The die was cast! Or to stay with the more appropriate, indeed prescient verb, nudged!"

P & O Motto 'Quis Nos Separabit' (Who Shall Separate Us?)

'Reflections and Reminiscence'

Extract From P & O Regulations (Reflections)

"Our traditions are rooted in the past, but we must see that they are growing in the present and out into the future, and the career of every individual Officer adds something, good or bad, to this growth. For the traditions – standards – atmosphere of the Company is the sum of our careers in the Company, whoever we may be."

During the summer of 1966, 'Orcades' was scheduled for a series of cruises in and around the Mediterranean, and here it must be pointed out that this would bring about a considerably increased workload for, in particular, the Navigating Officer and his junior Watch-Keeping Officer, as well as the Purser's Bureau staff.

In the matter of navigating and planning, it was that paper charts alone were in full-time use, requiring both pre-voyage assembly, occasional correction as directed by Notices to Mariners, and course plotting prior to the commencement of each cruise/voyage leg. The present-day routine availability and use of GPS, which has taken over and become virtually indispensable for any sort of marine navigation, was a luxury as yet unknown in 1966, and voyages had to be planned well in advance, and in P & O submitted to Head Office (for Passenger ships) by the ship's Captain (who had himself approved the content) for approval. Altogether, a substantial project that left no room for error, but in every way professionally very satisfying. (N.B. the pronoun 'himself' is indicative of the fact that at that time, there were no female Captains in the P & O-Orient Line)

Thus, and whilst the Cruise Season programme, in all its complexity, had been completed during the previous voyage to/from Australia, planning and preparation for the next deep-sea (round the World) voyage scheduled post the

Med cruises had to be done <u>during</u> said cruises, a period covering a multiplicity of port calls which, in itself, would keep the Navigator extremely busy – think too of the Purser Officers, with the then interminable port-by-port calls for passenger lists, and no computers.

Not in 1966 were leather seats available for the Officers of the Watch, in front of GPS screens, but rather a severe telling-off if found sitting on the wooden high stool provided for Pilots. Mark1 eyeball prevailed, assisted by radar, sextants, parallel rulers, dividers and, hopefully, a chart pencil. Oh, and not to forget the hand-lead, when proceeding up the Hoogli river towards Calcutta, but that would not, thankfully, involve 'Orcades'.

Pausing for a moment to broadly identify the next deep-sea programme, and therefore, the preparation to be achieved, it was to be as follows:

SW'ly to Trinidad, thence Cartagena, transit the Panama Canal, thence Acapulco (Mexico), Los Angeles, San Francisco, Vancouver, Honolulu, Suva Fiji, Auckland, Sydney, (then a cruise through Wellington, Auckland and Brisbane and return Sydney) Hobart, Melbourne, Adelaide, Fremantle, Singapore, Colombo, Sri Lanka (Ceylon as was then), Bombay, and homeward through the Red Sea and Suez Canal, Naples, Barcelona, Marseilles and finally, London; three months and a week in all.

This preparation would prove to be a major workload, and the Navigator, together with his 4th Officer junior Watch-Keeper, Keith Robertson (who would himself rise to be the Senior Second Officer aboard P & O's 'Chusan'), had their work cut out but were to be ably assisted in the typed presentation of their efforts by someone appointed to thus assist, by the Purser. In the event, fate had intervened, and whilst the WAP so designated had originally been scheduled to join another vessel, once the Cruise programme was finally allowed to proceed, she had instead been appointed to 'Orcades'.

In saying 'finally allowed to proceed', thereby hangs a substantial negative tale in that on or about the May 17th, 1966, the Seamans Union called a country-wide strike which lasted for 47 days, ending July 1st, during which time the then Prime Minister, Harold Wilson, roundly berated the Union leaders as being Communists seeking to bring his Labour Government down, all to absolutely no avail. On an equally substantial benefit side, Woman Assistant Purser Ankie (and, it is promised, we will get to her surname eventually) was chosen by the Purser to assist the Navigator, tasked to give as much of her time as required, in addition to her Bureau duties. Thus was the dice given a further slight nudge, unnoticed as such by the Navigator, who was probably pondering the impact of crossing the International Date Line during the RTW, for him, a first as Navigator.

With Captain Harris RD, RNR in Command, and occasionally supported by Staff-Captain Harrison RNR, the Orient Line line-up of Officers was completed by Chief Officer McCarthy, and First Officer Free, whilst from the Senior Second Officer down, the balance were of P & O origin, a cheery bunch to be sure, including Jnr Second Officer Cawthorne, Third Officer Knight, fourth Officer Robertson, and Jnr. Fourth Officer Beavington. Oh, and not to forget Cadet Carr, previously noted for leaving cocktail sticks on charts, and who eventually rose to Command such as 'Canberra', and the new 'Oriana' among others, thus confirming his excellent training, particularly aboard 'Orcades'.

Extract From P & O Regulations (Discipline)

"Any Senior Officer….is to take action toward any Junior Officer whom he sees or hears to be behaving when off duty which, in the opinion of the Senior Officer, is unbecoming to an Officer, or liable to be injurious to the good name of the Company. Duty of the Senior Officer is, without fuss, to send for him and tell him in private what he thinks. This action must not be taken in public."

(N.B. For female Officers, the pronoun 'she' or 'her' was used in correspondence, and the collective pronoun 'them' for any singular gender, (male or female) had yet to sully the English lexicon!)

In pondering the 'cause and effect' to 'Quis Nos Separabit', it is relevant to note that during the voyage to Australia that preceded the cruise season that was now 'finally allowed to proceed', the Second Officer aka the Navigator, had been summoned to the cabin of Staff Captain Harrison, who at that time was off-duty sick; the summons, therefore, coming as both unusual and unexpected. Knocking on 'Staffie's' cabin door, and bid to enter, was to find the Staff Captain in dressing gown, and sitting in his armchair, with two young and attractive female passengers standing next to him. Without further ado or introduction, the Second Officer listened to the following:

"It has been reported", began Harrison, "that at yesterday's Gala Dance, you were wearing Mess Kit trousers with a silk stripe down the sides. That is not correct uniform." Both girls giggled loudly, and he went on. "So, what do you intend to do about it?"

Despite the appalling behaviour of the Senior Officer, and recognising the need for continued diplomacy honing, the Navigator responded, hoping his balanced response would not be contradicted by facial expression, "It is a common P & O practice, Sir, to have light-weight Mess Kit trousers made, when possible, in Hong Kong, and the very thin strips have never before been adversely commented upon, aboard 'Canberra', 'Oriana', or 'Arcadia', just three of my previous appointments. That aside, and as we are in the middle of the Indian Ocean, not much I can do to change the trousers." Again, both girls giggled loudly, clearly enjoying the scene. Assuming that the resultant, and petulant, "dismissed" from Staffie suggested that facial expression (contemptuous) had contradicted diplomacy efforts, the Second Officer turned on his heel, and returned to the matter of fixing the ship's noon position.

This incident did not necessarily bode well for any working relationship with the Staff Captain, and the 12–4 Watch and Navigator's work otherwise demanded professional attention, but at least no further mention of Mess Kit trousers arose thereafter. Other things, yes, but not trousers.

And so, it began, a near three-month hectic medley of cruise port calls, now so well known by cruising enthusiasts, all commencing from Southampton. They mostly covered the Mediterranean and Adriatic seas, but also embraced Madeira and the Canary Islands, together with Lisbon, and it has to be said that 1966 heard no complaints by Cities such as Barcelona, Valetta, and Venice as to the massive disembarkation of passengers (sorry, guests) on to the finite attractions of their cities and surrounding areas as today experienced, and now so feared by the local population, other than perhaps pick-pockets. Or, in the case of Venice, the near parking of massive cruise ships in St Mark's Square!

To touch upon each port call might well induce a degree of reader boredom, but some moments, or departures from the anticipated norm, should not go unmentioned. Forerunner of one such incident was the fact that shortly after commencement of the cruise programme, a 'first-trip' Nursing Sister, by name of Jenny, was to join, and as 'Orcades' cut through calm seas between ports during the Second Officer's 12-4 Watch, he observed her (as it turned out) sitting on the ship's rail of the Boat Deck. He despatched his junior Watch Officer forthwith to administer a very sharp reminder that it was both foolhardy, and an extremely poor example to set passengers, and so was the message delivered.

In early 1970, these two were to marry, and enjoy many happy and fulsome years together, before finally settling in Cornwall, so perhaps sitting on the ship's rail was fate, to be eventually feted!

Woman Assistant Purser Ankie was also finding her sea legs, as well as dividing her time between Bureau duties, and those associated with assisting the Navigator, as the flow of papers to be typed appeared from time to time from the direction of the Bridge. There also came an invitation to join a small group of fellow-Officers invited to a pre-lunch drink in port with the Second Officer, albeit that the invite was issued via another Bureau invitee, casually issued as "oh, and by the way, why not bring the new Dutch WAP along too, if she's not busy", such ploy having absolutely nothing to do with fact that he had observed her sun-bathing on deck whilst the ship was at anchor, and had sent her a glass of chilled orange juice from the Bridge, carried thereto by the much put upon Fourth Officer! It is possible that he was noticing the nudge of fate, mentioned heretofore. Fact of the matter, he was!

Extract From P & O Regulations (Discipline)

"No Officer is to entertain a lady by herself in his cabin."

Coming under the sub-title of 'Mixing with Passengers', this regulation was clearly designed to address the issue of entertaining female passengers by Officers, and in view of the need for occasional closer professional liaison between the Navigator and Ankie, (geregistreerd als Anna), it would occasionally happen that as the 12-4 Watch at sea was over, they would meet in his cabin at about 1630 to talk, whilst partaking of afternoon cups of tea, and perhaps a sandwich, brought thereto by the Steward. It also happened occasionally that work to be typed, not well dictated over the telephone, would require amplification, and if the Second Officer was on Watch, she would make her way to his cabin, there to find his scribbled notes, and with that, clarity. En passant, she also corrected spelling, punctuation, and any errors of addition/subtraction found, (extremely rare as they were!) possessing an acute mathematical mind and having been inculcated at and from school with correct English grammar and spelling.

This activity appeared to disturb the Staff Captain, who took it upon himself to upbraid the Second Officer (although this time without a passenger audience) raising question as to the nature of the 1630 liaison, with scarcely hidden inference, and therefore accusation, that it must had sexual overtones.

"So just what is going on?" he questioned, his mind clearly made up. The Second Officer, by now increasingly aware that for some unknown reason he had become the object of 'Staffie's' dislike or antagonism, was nevertheless tiring of the role, and diplomacy was substituted by unbridled plain speaking.

"Sir," he commented, "if in the twenty or so minutes that it takes for Miss (and here he used Ankie's surname, which will indeed be revealed soon) and me to enjoy our afternoon tea, you would be capable of undressing, having sex, and re-dressing, then you are more accomplished, or desperate, than am I." This response was retrospectively regretted as being not exactly appropriate, and on discussing it later with Ankie, she was to mention, by no means for the last time, her English translation from a Dutch expression that 'one gains more with honey than with vinegar!'

Much reference to increased workload during the cruise season (and we are talking 1966, not 2020!) was true, but time ashore was available from time to time, and indeed as the season progressed, so was a trip ashore planned during a Lisbon call. Second Officer John together with Ankie, now seeking to spend more leisure time together, were to travel to Estoril accompanied by Fourth Officer Keith and Nursing Sister Jenny; there to enjoy part of the day in the sunshine and sea as tourists, away from shipboard pressures and concerns. Having worn little but naval uniform since the age of 15, the male eye for colour co-ordination was not of the best, but nevertheless, John strode toward the gangway proud of his assembled greens and blues, long white socks, and brown chukka boots. Ankie took one astonished look, followed by the ultimatum that unless he returned to his cabin and changed, the trip to Estoril was off! Whilst perhaps not realising it at the time, from then on, he became (as far as Ankie was concerned) 'work in progress'!

Change he did, to Estoril the four went, and as time would substantiate, the excursion was to prove a major building block in the friendship between the four that was to extend a lifetime, with much laughter and camaraderie enjoyed that happy day.

Extract From P & O Regulations (Discipline – Mixing with Passengers)

"Officers on board ship have a full day's work to do, and they must be fit to do it. The Management has no wish to deny them unnecessarily, the opportunity to mix with passengers, but it must be remembered that passengers have no work to do and bear no responsibility on board. What is suitable when one is on holiday is often quite unsuitable when one has to be on watch in a few hours' time."

The freedom which various Officers are entrusted is a recognition that they are responsible persons who can be trusted to behave. But they must realise that it holds out certain dangers to their career which would be avoided if they were not to mix socially with passengers…for (continued) service in the Company requires the ability of an Officer to mix socially with passengers and yet to stand up to any problem which this may involve."

In effect, Officers were indeed encouraged in those days to mix socially with passengers (why not today one wonders or does discipline no longer prevail?) and quite apart from the customary 'Captain's Cocktail Party' held each cruise, or during Line voyages, when Officers were required to assist as hosts, this enabled Officers to both use the public rooms, and to attend such as Gala or Fancy-Dress nights. This, of course, was privilege better utilised by non-watch keeping officers, and indeed it was to be strictly observed that the so-referred 'Deck Officer' watch-keepers had to be off decks by 2100 hours latest each evening, i.e. those keeping the 12–4, and 4–8-night watches.

It was thus made able for the Second Officer (John, as you will recall) to meet up with Ankie and others to occasionally enjoy together the entertainment laid on for passengers which, whilst by no means similar in quality to that available on board cruise ships now, nevertheless had progressed beyond ships' Bands of the '50s, such as the so-referred 'Prickly Heat Trio' aboard the P & O Liner 'Strathaird'! Thus, also aboard for the 1966 cruises of 'Orcades' was the boyband 'The Atlantics' which strove mightily to emulate (and indeed well succeeded) 'The Beatles', to the great enthusiasm and pleasure of all. In many ways, this brought light relief from the highly demanding navigating duties for both the Second Officer, and his junior assistant, the Fourth Officer, now pursuing First Aid instruction from Nursing Sister Jenny.

As the season progressed, however, the Second Officer found himself increasingly nursing depression. Not on account of the workload, or indeed the apparent, but continued, interest of the Staff Captain in seeking (but not finding!) fault. It was a function of emotional stress, as slowly but surely, he was having to come to terms with fact that he had at some stage, developed a heart condition heretofore unknown with, therefore, no previous experience as to how he should react. The object of this emotional turmoil was indeed she who so capably expedited the required navigational paperchase into professional format for presentation, and whose perfectly spoken English was so delightfully spiced with her Dutch accent which, incidentally, she was never to lose. 'Twas, of course, Ankie, and by now, the Second Officer had become proficient in pronouncing her surname, Breeschoten, pronounced as spelt, and now offered, as promised!

His amateurish reaction was to occasionally avoid any off-duty evening functions in public rooms, nursing his depression to no obvious conclusion, and it was on these occasions that the Fourth Officer and Jenny would despatch Ankie to rouse out the Second Officer from his cabin, which she would do with her customary good humour and resolve. Work in progress? The future would suggest it was thus!

Extract From P & O Regulations (Uniform)

Stenographers; (by 1966, re-classified as Woman Assistant Pursers)
"The uniform to be worn by Officers in (the Company's) service. Cold Climate.
Jacket – as worn by W.R.N.S. Officers
Skirt – As worn by W.R.N.S. Officers
Shirt – White, long-sleeved, with collar and black tie.
Cap – Tricorn, with Company's Badge on black mohair band
Black leather shoes, and black stockings."

Whilst, sadly, obliged to purchase her own Uniform herself (as did all Officers) Ankie nevertheless made the most of it in appearance terms, to the extent that she could well have been mistaken for someone modelling, on behalf of the retailer. That said, she had an aversion to wearing the Tricorn hat (as worn by W.R.N.S. Officers) purely because of her total dislike for any head covering. However, and along with other Bureau staff, she would often walk out on deck to watch as the ship approached the port of call – Malta as example, being a prime example of such a magnificent approach vista. Invariably, the Staff Captain would see her from the Bridge, and invariably shout to the Second Officer, "Tell your bloody girlfriend to put her Uniform hat on," to the general amusement of the duty quartermasters, and occasional passenger that had been invited to the Bridge by Captain Harris for the occasion. One began to wonder if he, the Staff Captain, was openly demonstrating a form of jealousy, rather than a display of appalling behaviour for an Officer of his seniority.

It is a matter of record that Anna Petronella Breeschoten wore her Uniform hat but once, and that was on the Bridge of 'Orcades', together with the Second Officer, posing together for the occasion, for the photograph that was to be treasured over many years thereafter, but as then, still unforeseen.

Extract from P & O Regulations (Navigation)

"Pilots – In ports where it is compulsory to employ regular Pilots, Commanders are not to consider themselves released from responsibility, nor are they to pay any less attention to navigation and safe handling of their ships."

Istanbul was one such port where compulsory pilotage was necessary, and during the one cruise port-call there, a Pilot was taken aboard in preparation accordingly, during the 8–12 night watch, the Watch of the Junior Second Officer. It was, therefore, in anticipation of meeting with the Pilot that the Second Officer took over the Bridge watch at midnight, but he, the Pilot, was nowhere to be seen. Peter Cawthorne was found in close adjacence to the starboard bridge-wing compass repeater, and on questioning, he confirmed the Pilot had gone to bed, to be awakened before final approach to Istanbul. Fortunately, Captain Harris had total confidence in his watch-keeping Officers, and so 'Orcades' proceeded, the course clear on the chart. 'Any shipping about' was the next question, at which Peter pointed dramatically to his right, and downwards toward the sea. Puzzled, the Second Officer went to investigate, only to find a Turkish warship less than a hundred metres from 'Orcades' and maintaining station there by dint of maintaining identical course and speed, almost as if escorting the Liner. "Just reachable if you chuck an ashtray onto her deck," reported Peter, apparently having tried just that, and took himself off to write up the logbook, and thence to bed! This was indeed one of the more unusual approaches to a port, and fortunately the warship peeled away shortly after, but not before a cautionary instruction to the fresh watch Quartermaster from the Second Officer, "Nothing to starboard, please," and echoed by the helmsman, "Nothing to starboard, Sir." Never a dull moment!

Incidentally, a similar situation had developed during the previous Line voyage when, and during some close pilotage through the Torres Strait, the Australian Pilot turned to the Second Officer with the words, "Keep her running along the line of sticks, mate, I'll be back soon," at which he departed the Bridge and made his way to a passenger cabin on A Deck (as was discovered later) to rendezvous with his girlfriend who had boarded in Sydney! The line of sticks was indeed closely, nay religiously, followed, and to the Second Officer's relief, the Pilot did indeed return, looking quite pleased with himself. Never a moment of dullness!

Quite apart from throwing ashtrays at Turkish warships, Peter Cawthorne also had a mischievous nature when not fulfilling his duties, as noted at a night club in one of the Spanish port calls when, recognising that the strip-tease artiste was less than enthusiastic as to her showbiz calling, he offered vocal encouragement. "Give 'em Gibraltar," he shouted, "but get 'em off!"

With the cruise season coming to a close September 18th in Southampton, and departure for the next so-called deep-sea voyage scheduled for October 5th, 'Orcades' Officers could look forward to some well-earned leave, with Dock Staff Officers relieving them during that time. (Dock Staff being duty allocated to Officers that were awaiting appointment to sea-going vessels themselves). Relief, therefore, from the full volume, daily at 1800 hours rendition from Peter's cabin of the then hugely popular No 4 in the UK singles chart of a male lament for his dead dog, and his descent into madness accordingly, to the 'funny farm'. 'They're Coming to Take Me Away, Ha, Ha'. Much enjoyed by all though, as a simple reflection of the general camaraderie that existed – simple souls, really!

Oh, and with some off-duty moments increasingly stirred (or nudged?) by thoughts of other than matters navigational, the Second Officer a.k.a. John, had sought to bring some sort of poetic acknowledgement to that which 'Orcades' had been guided through during the six cruises that had been successfully discharged, (hopefully to passengers' pleasure), and as now follows:

"To A Cruising Liner"

"Near sleek, near white, and bounds and pounds,
Not in Sterling, but in weather weight
Not young, gets older, pushing time, seeking people, turning round
In circles great or steers a line not too defined for one to sea,
Involved in keeping Watch and time, livelihood, near sanity.
Within the bowels, vast movements form, passing miles whilst up above
For want of womb, the bearing comes from land and eye caused not by love

But pure necessity.
In alley veins, her life blood lives, formed with cells of human bode
Some First, more not, in some all one, injected there by different mode
But oft as not by plasma drip of honeyed words from practised lips
Of advertising housemen!
In calmer waters bounding on, by stern all trimmed and mouth a'foam
Sometimes ensnared by Nature's shroud, and gives two-minute moans
Of mournful dirge, cacophony, decreed by Law and Ministry.
The end must come deprived of life, her lines all out umbilical
In death re-joined to Mother Earth for few short hours, at least until
Adrenaline in human form, intent in seeking garlic sun
Pours to her heart which, in its turn, responds and takes her out again"

'Orcades', then, was a happy ship – one can always tell, as soon as boarding a ship, for reasons hard to explain. Easier perhaps to recognise the reason why the Navigator John, and WAP Ankie, had decided to take leave together, themselves to better explore or confirm their attraction to each other, and whether it was something to nurture, or abandon as just two ships that pass in the night. To quote Mahatma Gandhi, "You may never know what results from your action, but if you do nothing, there will be no result!"

Shore Relief

The plan was simple, assisted by fact that the Second Officer's car, a Wolsley saloon, had made its usual appearance, delivered to the ship by stepfather (to all intents and purposes, father) in whose tender care it would usually reside whilst owner was sea-borne. They were Devon bound, and to say that Ankie was enthralled by England's countryside would be an understatement, in that in common with most of her Dutch contemporaries, their perception of the UK was little short of Blake's view of the Black Country, 'with its dark, Satanic mills'. She, therefore, found the reality, that sun-filled September, both astonishing and wonderful, all of which boded well, always provided the rain stayed away!

Their destination was a farm, North Park, Pyworthy near Holsworthy, deep in the Devon countryside, where dear friends of John had set themselves up farming pigs and some sheep, and at the same time running a small B & B seasonal operation. They were Keith and Maureen Davie, Keith having been a year senior to John in the P & O Officer ranks but had decided upon farming as a preferred alternative to sea-going, and all that entailed in terms of parting from family. Factually and sadly, he would return to the P & O after losing his pigs to swine-fever but would rise swiftly to take Command of a large P & O container vessel – Maureen, or Muff more generally known, would also find her sea-legs, joining Captain Davie on occasional voyages.

Meantime, however, Pyworthy it was, and the visitors from 'Orcades' were given a royal welcome, and made to feel immediately at home, with the three children, Karen Paul and Shaun finding a visitor from the Netherlands rather intriguing, as well they should! With some sun-bathing, walks, the occasional G & T (!) and much chatter and badinage, the few days spent on the farm passed pleasantly enough. An early incident that should have involved car-washing brought amusement and, perhaps, a point of definition to the growing relationship between John and Ankie. Asked if she would mind washing the car (John seeking to deploy himself assisting Keith in a pigsty construction project) her hesitation in displaying enthusiasm was perhaps missed (she was wearing a swimsuit at the time), although the loud clang of the metal bucket onto the car's bonnet brought sharply into focus Ankie's point that car-washing was definitely not her 'part of ship'. Point taken, and swift re-deployment from pigsty project to car-wash duties for, guess who?

Brief meeting was also arranged with John's mother and stepfather who were holidaying in the County, with parental enthusiasm overflowing on meeting with Ankie (as she was introduced, not Anna) as she, with great grace, charmed with her presence. Noting that his mother was, with raised eyebrows, looking pointedly at a ring on Ankie's left hand, the now alarmed John shook his head vigorously (but discreetly), knowing as he did that the Dutch wore a dress ring on that hand, not to be confused with the British engagement ring!

As the Ethiopian Proverb would have it, "A belt fastened while running will come undone while running!" Think about it!

The Long One, Voyage 1279

With shore leave done, and Officers returned, on October 5th, 1966, 'Orcades' slipped, and proceeded to sea. Well, that was a Royal Naval description, not usually deployed within the Merchant Navy vernacular, nor indeed that of the P & O. However, in that Captain Harris, RD, RNR. was in Command, with Staff Captain Harrison RNR, (oft-times referred to as HMS Harrison) aboard, and Second Officer J. Perry RNR as Navigator, the description was almost apt. Plus, of course, fact that 'Orcades' wore the Blue Ensign rather that the Red, as was the formal entitlement and choice of the Captain.

With brief calls into Le Havre and Lisbon, courses were set toward Trinidad, some seven days in which to settle into routine Watch keeping, and indeed the dusting off of sextants unused during the cruise programme. For the Second and Fourth Officers, back too was the post-Watch (0430 hours that is) half hour of convivial conversation enjoyed with a tincture of whisky and water, prior to a brief few hours of sleep before the day's navigational noon action called for attention. Navigational laurels were not to be rested upon, however, for 'twas during this voyage that the highly detailed planning for the following voyage was to be completed, which meant that both the Second and Fourth Officers would once again be kept very busy, fortunately, and ably assisted by WAP Ankie (geregistreerd als Anna!), demonstrably raring to go. As academic interest, the voyage to be approached would be the fairly standard Mediterranean, Suez transit, Aden, Colombo, Fremantle, Melbourne, Sydney, Wellington, Sydney and thence, Whitsunday Passage, Goods Island, Darwin, Hong Kong, Inland Sea, Kobe, Yokohama, Guam, Rossel Spit, and back to Sydney, with return to the UK almost a reverse of the outward journey. Phew! Details of the planned voyage complexities attached, a standard work at the time, requiring meticulous detail, but affording a high degree of professional satisfaction once completed, and approved by the Captain.

Back too was the daily announcement of the ship's distance steamed since the previous noon, and once the Noon Position Book had been submitted to, and approved by, the Captain, the information eagerly awaited by the passengers was announced by the Second Officer over the public address system, commencing with the words, "This is the Officer of the Watch speaking," and so into the detail. At this point, he became vulnerable to mischief visited upon him by fellow-Officers (but not when the Captain was on the Bridge!), with shoes laces being tied together, and even trouser belt unfastened, issues about which he could do nothing, other than continue to address the passengers who hung on his every word, ignorant of the difficulty in maintaining an even delivery. Never a dull moment, as previously observed, and moments of high good humour that never detracted from the high professional standards that existed aboard. A happy ship, indeed, or mostly so.

Trinidad, apart from a too brief shore visit with WAP Ankie, brought back memories for the Second Officer, when serving as Third Officer aboard the P & O tanker 'Maloja'. He was taken for a Land Rover drive across the Trinidad asphalt lake, an eerie experience in the knowledge that had the vehicle broken down, the asphalt was hot, deep, and with serious quicksand qualities! Deep respect for the vehicle's owner/driver!

From Trinidad, courses were set toward Cartagena, Colombia, and thereafter to Cristobal Colon, prior to commencing transit of the Panama Canal October 19th. Cartagena, of course, held much interest for tourists, as indeed did the Panama Canal, but for some ship's Officers, only a brief chance to stretch the legs ashore, and so was it for Second Officer John and WAP Ankie, together with Fourth Officer Keith and N. Sister Jenny. They chose to dine together on the evening of arrival to Cartagena, and to a local hotel they indeed proceeded, there to spend a delightful couple of hours enjoying the local cuisine under the starlight, served at their table close to the hotel's swimming pool. (Noteworthy is fact that John's shore-going apparel had passed muster!) So, a convivial evening, and fortunately, they had finished eating when a rat, an exceptionally large rat indeed, wandered casually past their table, prompting quick intakes of breath, and lifting of feet from the ground. In the general scheme of voyage matters this was not to be logged, but in situ, that was a rat of a size not to be ignored!

Cristobal presented, a day later, a different challenge in that the question of time difference between the two ends of the Canal came into large question, the potential one-hour difference being, in itself, not insurmountable, were it not for passenger excursions and the need to re-join the ship on time in Balboa. Thus far into the voyage, the Staff Captain had been remarkably quiet in matter of questioning the Navigator's work, trousers, or working relationships, but to get any necessary clock change wrong here would be to invite a probable storm of disapprobation, criticism, et al! That an hour's difference was in effect between certain dates was a fact, but the Pilot Book gave no clues as to the dates.

Orcades - Homeward Bound from Mediterranean Cruise

Right: Orcades Bridge - Navigator and Ankie, with rarely seen uniform hat!

Wellington, New Zealand - Shore leave

Nothing loathe, the Second Officer, dressed in immaculate white tropical uniform and uniform cap, took himself along the quay to an American flagged cargo ship that was berthed further along, there to avail himself of local knowledge probably held by its Officers. Going aboard, he was met by one he judged to be the equivalent to, perhaps, a P & O cargo ship Chief Steward, in his air-conditioned office, who in turn took him to meet the ship's Chief Mate, who sat in his non-airconditioned office, dressed in shorts, flip-flops, and shirt of doubtful recent laundering.

"No idea," came the short reply to questions of time, "not my end of the Canal!"

At this point, 'Orcades' Navigator decided to take a chance, a walk back to 'Orcades', and retribution should he get it wrong, and clocks were accordingly changed by one hour. Thankfully, the guess was good, and life aboard went on as normal – almost like clockwork, one might be tempted to offer!

Passage through the Canal went ahead October 20th, and it is interesting perhaps to note that the Panama Canal is the only place in the world where Pilots have full navigational and manoeuvring control and responsibility of and for the vessel, rather than the Captain. The Law might have been varied since 1966, but certainly it was the case then.

Acapulco was the next port of call, and that became interesting too, for different reason!

Acapulco, October 22nd

Extract from P & O Regulations – Outline of Officers Duties

"Staff Commander – The Staff Commander will assume whatever duties he is requested to by the Commander from time to time. Normally, he does not bear responsibility for the navigation of the ship but is expected to devote himself primarily to the entertainment of passengers and he is to regard this in its widest sense as his particular responsibility." (N.B. The terms 'Commander' and Staff Commander' had long been superseded by 'Captain' and 'Staff Captain')

With arrival off Acapulco close to noon, the Second Officer was on the Bridge (12-4 Watch) as 'Orcades' nosed her way toward the anchorage area. It therefore came as a complete surprise when the Staff Captain approached him with the words, "You are required to take the ship to anchor, as a 'blind anchorage exercise', and to that end the position in which you will drop anchor is marked on the chart." To say the Second Officer was astonished would be a gross understatement, in that the ordered exercise was something undertaken only by the Royal Navy, and certainly not P & O. That the order came from the Staff Captain was cause for further concern, in that it appeared to herald a further phase, quiescent since departure UK, of his perceived and puzzling attempts to embarrass the Second Officer.

However, whilst undertaking RNR training as a Lieutenant some eighteen months before, John had been appointed as Navigating Officer aboard HMS Repton of the Vernon Squadron, during which time the Mine Sweeper had been deployed in extensive precision sonar experiments, requiring electronic equipment to be dropped into very precise pre-determined positions. He had also trained the Midshipman aboard to make blind anchorages, so was not totally unprepared for the sudden challenge. Having examined the chart, and surrounding topography, the Navigator took up position at the radar, and was duly curtained off. Cautiously, and with minimal helm and telegraph orders, approach to the designated position was made. In due course, he gave the order "Let go port anchor," and with a resounding splash, said anchor dropped into its marked hole in the sun-dappled waters of Acapulco bay. Job done!

Just what Captain Harris, affectionately known as 'Dumbo', thought of all this is unknown, but to be generous, one must assume that he had delegated the matter of bringing 'Orcades' to her anchorage to the Staff Captain which, to be fair, 'Staffie' had done, although his disgruntled looks begged the question as to whether the result pleased him.

The training exercise aboard HMS Repton those months before had a more amusing ending, in that it became quickly apparent that the Midshipman had picked up a wrong bearing, his resulting directions therefore bringing the vessel rather closer to the beach than required. Noticing that his navigator was about to intercede (courts martial not a pleasant prospect), the Commanding Officer quietly signalled him to wait and, picking up the Bridge address microphone, solemnly announced 'hands to paddle', followed by 'slow astern', a way of handling the situation that would surely stay with that Midshipman throughout his Naval career. Honey, rather than vinegar, as Ankie may have remarked, had she been there!

Sadly, with charts to be sorted, and northerly courses to be laid off for Los Angeles, shore leave was not an option. The Navigator's thoughts were also turning to matter of highlighting the mysteries of the International Date Line, and therefore, preparing (scribbling) yet another sheet of nautical bric-a-brac for WAP Ankie to bring into printed readable form. Never a dull moment!

For Second Officer John, the voyage along the west coast of America, with calls at both Los Angeles and San Francisco, was a reminder of the maiden voyage of 'Canberra' in 1961, when he had served aboard as the Third Officer, junior Watch Officer to Sammy Bradford, one of the four First Officers. By direct comparison, however, 'Orcades' entry to those ports went all but un-noticed, whereas 'Canberra' had invoked extraordinary scenes of greeting and celebration. Vancouver too, Canada's beautiful western city, with Honolulu to follow, scenes of rapturous excitement for 'Canberra', whilst 'Orcades' slipped apologetically in and out, un-heralded. For WAP Ankie, however, when shipboard duties allowed, visits ashore were eagerly seized, for this indeed was proving to be the voyage of a lifetime for the girl from Baarn determined, as she always was, to make the most of it. Arrival to Honolulu November 5th was, however, in pouring rain (yes, really!) that prevailed for most of the day, but resolute as ever, Anna Petronella persuaded one of the Customs Officers who was going off duty, to drive her around the city – no sun-bathing on Waikiki Beach that day!

No let-up from navigational; duties however, and with Suva and Auckland to be visited before arrival Sydney November 5th, followed by a brief 'cruise' to Wellington, Auckland, Brisbane and return to Sydney, time was pressing for work completion on the voyage plan that was to follow 'Orcades' return to London January 12th, 1967. Close liaison was therefore both necessary and enjoyed between Navigator John and WAP Ankie, in formatting plan presentation, with afternoon tea a regular rendezvous in his cabin. Fourth Officer Keith's substantial and professional contribution to the plan formation continued unabated as his First Aid knowledge continued to develop, and he, Jenny, Ankie and John continued to grow into their friendship, gathering together socially as often as duties would allow.

Clearly, the Staff Captain was indeed devoting himself 'primarily to the entertainment of passengers', which was proving a comfort to all concerned, albeit a hiatus viewed with some caution.

The matter of crossing the International Date Line did, however, require some attention in terms of keeping passengers advised as to just what it was, and why, so to that end the Navigator, aka the Second Officer John, scribbled an explanation that WAP Ankie carefully brought to typed and readable format, which was then read over the Public Address system by the Fourth Officer during passage from Vancouver toward Honolulu, the reading planned to take just three minutes, Readers may choose to time it themselves, as hereunder, should interest there be.

The International Date Line

"It is a readily apparent fact that the Sun, as it moves around the Earth, provides daylight at different times at different places on the Earth's surface. Consequently, the daily business of one country is being carried out, whilst in another country, on the other side of the World, the inhabitants are sleeping. These are the two extremes, and in places between these two extremes, a state somewhere between complete darkness and daylight will be manifested.

To simplify the matter of timekeeping, and to ensure that places in similar longitudes are maintaining the same time, the World is divided into zones, each of 15 degrees of longitude, or one hour, however you choose to name it. Hence, and as there are 360 degrees of longitude, and by the simple expedient of dividing 15 into 360, we see that there are 24 zones, each of one hours value. As a datum Point, Greenwich Mean Time is considered zero, and depending on whether a place is east or west of Greenwich, so its zone in named plus or minus.

If people were happy to stay in one place, the matter of altering clocks to adjust to the time kept in another country would not arise. However, this is not the case, and a problem therefore presents itself. Moving westwards, a traveller would have to retard clocks until reaching the 180-degree meridian, when clocks would be 12 hours behind GMT. Eastwards would require clocks to be advanced until reaching the 180-degree meridian, when clocks would be 12 hours ahead of GMT. Thus, if you imagine two persons standing one each side of the 180-degree meridian, one would be GMT plus 12 hours, and the other GMT minus 12 hours. Should each continue the journey around the World, each would have to continue changing clocks to the rules. The westward traveller, on returning to his or her start point, would find the clock now 24 hours behind GMT, whilst conversely, the eastward traveller would have gained 24 hours, on reaching the original start point.

It, therefore, is practical to correct this gain or loss at some stage of the circumnavigation of the World, and what more practical position to all concerned than the 180-degree meridian. It is therefore in the vicinity of this

180-degree meridian that an arbitrary line has been established and named the Date Line. Here, the westward traveller advances the clock a full 24 hours, thus experiencing a loss of a full day. A Wednesday arrival, for example, will bring Friday as the next day. Conversely, the eastward traveller retards the clock 24 hours, thus experiencing a gain of one day, such that a Wednesday arrival to one side of the Line will again be Wednesday on crossing the Line. The position of the Date Line is settled internationally for practical purposes, and follows a sea route, thereby ensuring that all islands in the same group remain together on one side of the Line, for the convenience of the inhabitants. Case in point is that of the Fiji Islands, all of which lie to the west of the Date Line, and keep time ahead of Greenwich, although some of them are actually situated in a westerly longitude."

Although the writing may well have warranted an ice-pack and a lie-down, the voyage proceeded apace, the now almost standard 'cruise' Sydney to Sydney of some 14 days having long since seen the demise of a week's layover in Sydney when it had been almost standard practice for the P & O Liners to stage a 'Sydney Ball', much sought-after by guests and ships' Officers, all in evening finery. Such an event was fondly remembered by the Second Officer when, as one of the Cadets aboard 'Strathaird' in 1958, he had 'played' the washboard in studied beat to fellow-Cadets Keith Davie and John Harrington playing guitar and tea-chest bass respectively, singing in extraordinary harmony as a Skiffle Group to attendees of their Sydney Ball. Happy days!

However, and all that aside, the 'Orcades' cruise this time, to New Zealand in general, and Wellington in particular, was to hold special significance, although finding New Zealand after three days of foul, overcast weather proved interesting. Balls Pyramid, some 12 miles SE of Lord Howard Island had been found by Dead Reckoning (passengers impressed) but only one wavering, misty loom of a light with which to eventually fix the ship's position on making eventual landfall during the night 12-4 Watch. However, 'Orcades' berthed successfully in Wellington, and lo and behold, the sun came out to play, bathing the city in cheerful light, and, moreover, persuading Second Officer John, and WAP Ankie that a run ashore, with a trip on Wellington's famous funicular railway, was to be embraced, and so it was.

They returned a few hours later, and repaired to John's cabin for the now customary tea and tabs, and having settled down, John posed what to him was an unusual question. "This may sound a bit strange or silly," he started, "and I don't know a better way of saying it, but will you marry me?"

Ankie, almost as if expecting the question, paused but briefly, and then calmly responded, "It doesn't sound at all strange or silly, and yes, I am very happy to accept your proposal of marriage!" Well, happy, laughing words to that general effect! Tea was abandoned for wine, and fate's nudge embraced! As was Ankie, and had the Staff Captain then entered the cabin, he would doubtless have been surprised to similarly receive a hug! Happily, he was otherwise engaged, so to speak.

The euphoric Wellington moment was clearly one for celebration, but at the same time, it sponsored much thought as to how, and when, to make the engagement public, with some seven more weeks still to complete the voyage to London. Further to this, what would be the Corporate reaction once the news became public, and in this there was absolutely no precedent that might encourage a bending of yet another Extract from P & O Regulations (Discipline), that unequivocally pronounced, 'wife not to travel on husband's ship'. This specifically related to wives as passengers, with any thought of married Officers sailing together a considered heresy save, perhaps, in Scandinavian cargo ships. After deep and thoughtful discussion, the now engaged couple came to the following conclusions, recognising the physics adage that 'every action has an equal and opposite reaction', in that Nature's nudged action, no matter how joyful, had brought about the need to acknowledge substantial reactive commitment from each of them, which only the near and medium future would, or could, judge.

- Both would have to leave 'Orcades' in order to marry.
- John would have to anticipate appointment to another vessel, post marriage.
- Ankie (her decision entirely) would resign, rather than another sea-going appointment.
- They would have to find, and establish a home, between leaving 'Orcades', getting married, and John's probable appointment post marriage, in whatever capacity.

Doubtless other concerns would arise, but that which they had identified seemed to be more than enough with which to cope, pro tem! To borrow the motto of the Royal Air Force, *'Per Ardua Ad Astra'*, but here used in the subjunctive tense!

Celebration, there was, however, as inevitably the news must get out, and invitations were sent specifically to the Captain, Staff Captain, Chief Officer, the Purser, and Deputy Purser, Chief and Second Engineers, and to those other Officers that were off-duty, or who cared to attend. Barry Collins, the ship's young Surgeon and good friend to both the Second Officer and WAP Ankie, offered the use of his large cabin for the event, which took place en route, as the voyage continued. Captain Harris attended and offered his congratulations, as did all the other senior Officers, with the notable exception of the Staff Captain which, sadly, came as no great surprise. All in all, it was the largest, and most successful, party of the entire voyage, with a wealth of congratulations to the happy couple.

In passing, it occurred during these months that 'Orcades' responded to a Mayday call from a cargo vessel, with the patient being brought aboard by one of 'Orcades' lifeboats. It transpired that he would require some drastic (a colostomy) surgery, which, for the Surgeon, was probably a first since Medical School. The Officers of the Watch kept the ship steaming slowly into the seaway whilst the operation was performed, and at 0100 hours in the morning, Barry appeared on the Bridge, his full-length white scrubs absolutely covered in blood, declaring the operation as successfully completed. "Well done," responded the Captain, "but I hope you didn't come through the passenger accommodation in those bloody clothes," and ordered the ship back on course, and required speed. Muted congratulations, which would hopefully be enlarged upon, eventually, by the patient, now being cared for by an exhausted Nursing Sister Jenny. Never a dull moment.

N.B. It is perhaps timely (some might say 'not before time') that apology is made for the applied admix of 'John', or 'the Second Officer', or 'the Navigator', as possibly leading to some confusion, if not irritation. It is merely a somewhat clumsy device to format the narrative within a 'third person' presentation, rather than the 'first person'. Stay with it!

And so 'Orcades' proceeded, now homeward bound from a voyage that to most employed aboard was just another to be seen through, but to Second Officer John, and WAP Ankie, an unexpected life-changing event induced by pure chance, a UK Seamen's' strike that achieved absolutely nothing of its intent, whilst at the same time bringing about a relationship leading to marriage, and an exciting, loving, and varied lifestyle that would sustain them throughout the next fifty three years.

There remained, quite apart from continued duties, time ashore together in Melbourne, Singapore, and Colombo, with Ankie also joining a passenger excursion that disembarked at Suez, spending the day visiting the Pyramids, and re-joining 'Orcades' that evening as the Canal transit was completed at Port Said. To say that this was the calm before the storm would, however, be another understatement. 'Orcades' arrived Tilbury January 12th, 1967, and Second Officer John was duly relieved by a good friend and past shipmate, Willy Newson. At the same time, he was advised that he was to take up appointment as Second Officer aboard 'Orsova', due to sail for Australia on or about February 15th, i.e. just a month away!

So, all that had to be achieved within that time was for Ankie to return to Holland to visit her parents and siblings, then re-join John at his parent's home in Stourbridge, followed by the need to obtain a Special Licence for marriage, find a home somewhere, get married, settle Ankie into afore-mentioned (somewhere) home, and get John to London to join 'Orsova'! Not exactly a doddle. Oh, and just to add further impetus, as they discussed the challenges that, in fairness, had been discussed and vaguely anticipated in Wellington, a smiling Ankie murmured, "Ik denk dat ik zwanger ben" – only she murmured it in English! A moment of sharp surprise followed by joyful embrace and added mutual determination to successfully achieve all that needed to be done, in the allotted time. Decision was also taken not to share this news with either set of parents just yet, and not at all with the Staff Captain!

Amazingly, it worked! Ankie (now no longer a WAP) returned from Holland with more personal possessions (which included an ironing board) and appointment was made with the appropriate cleric to meet at the Stourbridge Church Manse in pursuit of the required Special Licence. It was a dark and stormy evening and having entered the Manse door that had creaked loudly as it opened, they were led along a dark, cold passageway to the barely illuminated room where the paperwork was to be done. "What is your name please" asked the cleric of Ankie.

"I'll spell it for you," started Ankie but was interrupted.

"I can spell, I can spell," he said sharply, "Now, so what is your name?"

Ankie smiled, and replied in a clear, slow voice, "Anna Petronella Breeschoten."

The cleric sighed, looked up, and asked "Can you spell that for me please?"

Special Licence was granted, marriage date set for February 11th, and invitations sent out to Dutch and English families and friends, and services secured of John's older brother, Michael, as Best Man.

Housing was next on the agenda, and once again, fate took a hand. During 'Orcades' voyage, the two had become firm friends with Jimmy and Pat Foot from Dorchester, a couple sailing as passengers that had left open invitation to visit them as they left the ship. Coincidentally, John's father was the Entertainments Manager of Weymouth, so journey to Dorset seemed appropriate to both renew friendship, and introduce Ankie to John's father who, it must be said, was a virtual stranger, after his divorce some twenty-three years previously. Friendship was renewed with the Foot family, John's father had a close friend who rented out (furnished) part of his family home overlooking Portland and Chesil Beach Weymouth, which was inspected, found to be clean and spacious, liked, and booked – the owners, Harold, and Dot Hilton, were also to become firm friends over the months to come. Job almost done, and yet again, fate was to prove choice of this apartment as their home hugely prescient, as the near future would soon demonstrate.

Actually, the job was far from done, with such goods and chattels as currently belonging to the couple, now to include of course the recently imported ironing board, having to be transferred to Weymouth, with Ankie, thereafter, requiring to return to Holland to organise, with the undoubted help of her mother, her wedding dress. In all of this, she displayed the organisational skills that were to be the hallmark of her massive contribution to the many moves that were to be experienced in coming years, but more of that in due course.

John, meantime, temporarily released from Second Officer duties, now prepared to switch uniforms, to present himself in his RNR Lieutenant's uniform, complete with sword, for the wedding ceremony, with careful practice in matter of wearing the sword such that he would not embarrass all and sundry with, literally, a trip down the aisle! Ankie returned having successfully sourced her wedding dress, and so they advanced to the next square on the board, preparation for the big day when they were to be wedded at, to give it its full name, Old Swinford Parish Church, with the reception thereafter to be held at the home of John's mother, and stepfather. In passing, and whilst it was more usual practice for the Dutch to marry in a Registry Office rather than a church, Ankie had agreed to the wish of John's mother. Regarding the service itself, prudence and diplomacy had brought about the mutual decision to dispense with the 'and obey' bit!

On the day before the wedding, from Holland came Ankie's father, Johannes, and mother, Aleijda, her sister, Nel, favourites Uncle Theunis and Aunt Roos, and her father's sister, Aunt Truus. He, cleric of the Special Licence issuance, would have required much spelling had they been involved in the application!

John's brother, Michael, and sister-in-law, Joan, also arrived from Holland, Michael at that time being seconded to Unilever's office in Rotterdam. There, he was referred to, respectfully it must be said, as Meneer Papegaai (Mr Parrot) in recognition of his swift assimilation of the Dutch language which, in that Ankie's father and mother spoke not a word of English, would perhaps become most useful in Stourbridge, if only in support of Nel whose English was good.

He was, in the fullness of time, destined to become Chairman of Unilever UK, a Knight of the Realm, and Commander of the Nederland Order of Orange-Nassau – all this in addition to serving as John's Best Man!

February 11th, 1967

Anna Petronella Breeschoten entered the Church, on the arm of her father, Johannes, and she shone. Her attention to every dress detail, her composure, poise and bearing, all combined to illuminate the gathering of families and friends, and not to put too fine a point on it, she glowed with self-assurance. It was her day, and she captured it wholeheartedly.

John, too, aware of previous advice from Ankie as to states of attire, had taken care in preparing for the ceremony, and stood proudly, his Lieutenant's uniform, sword tight to his side in dress context, and marvelled, as the bride-to-be moved down the aisle towards him, that this was the woman that had unhesitatingly agreed to become his wife. What he knew not, at this moment, was the degree to which she would contribute to the building and continuity of his multi-faceted career that was to become their life together. Yet again, fate was delivering a perceptible nudge, yet to be recognised, however, in its full manifestation. Assuredly, life was not going to be dull or routine!

With vows and rings exchanged, blessings gratefully received, and formal signing of the Register completed, the happy couple led the way toward photographic confirmation of the event, and thereafter the Reception, so well received by all.

Ankie & John - Just married

Eventually able to get away, John and Ankie repaired to the Hotel at which he, John, had stayed the previous night, Ankie having taken up residence elsewhere for that night, as custom dictated. Changed into something less formal, they had dinner together and, as the Hotel's resident band began to play, so they danced together for the first time, and found themselves in perfect accord. The refrain 'Edelweiss' from 'The Sound of Music' was the music to which they danced, and it was requested, and played enthusiastically by the band, some six or more times as the evening progressed. It became 'their tune' accordingly. Other guests may have become less enchanted, or perhaps they all left, but who cared! It was their night.

Sadly, February 15th loomed large, and therefore, the sailing of 'Orsova' to which John had been appointed as Second Officer and yes, Navigator. Accordingly, the newly married couple had concluded that the best way forward was for John to join the ship soonest, and Ankie would stay aboard with him until the actual sailing date. So did the ludicrous situation evolve, the spending of their so-called honeymoon in Tilbury Docks which, it has to be said, rated as probably the most unromantic place on Earth, a venue that, it is recommended, should be avoided at all costs, particularly in February. However, and as Sir Winston Churchill is credited with remarking,

"Life can either be accepted or changed. If it is not accepted, it must be changed. If it cannot be changed, then it must be accepted." This maxim would be remembered in the near future, and change would come about accordingly. 'Quis Nos Separabit' Remember? Watch this space!

To Tilbury, therefore, the couple proceeded, after fond farewells to both the Dutch and English families, the plan as mentioned above to have Ankie leave the ship as late as possible before sailing, when she would then drive the now family car back to Weymouth, where Harold and Dot Hilton would help her settle in to the new home, and indeed to the job that she would shortly secure, as Secretary to a firm of Solicitors in Dorchester, namely Lock, Reed and Lock. Awaiting to help her as well were Jimmy and Pat Foot, so John was at least part-comforted by fact that she would not be alone, but rather among good and generous friends.

Ankie & John - Just married

The actual sailing date for 'Orsova' is irrelevant, indeed forgotten for the purpose of this narrative, but suffice it to say that it fell shortly after February 15th, that being the date that newly appointed Second Officer had 'signed on'.

The family car had been packed and stood close to where 'Orsova' was berthed and at the appointed time, John and Ankie walked slowly down the gangway and to the car, he worriedly conscious that the 172-mile drive to Weymouth for Ankie was a challenging enterprise, no matter her clear and proven driving ability. "As agreed, my love, you will get into the car and I will return aboard, neither of us looking back toward the other." She nodded her agreement, they embraced again, and so began their first separation that would last for three long months, with 'Orsova' scheduled to arrive back to London come May 26th. Letters between them would be many and were eagerly awaited by both. Amusingly, her first related that as she sought to drive away, she could not find the reverse gear, and had to beg help from a taxi driver parked nearby, taking great care thereafter to park such that she would not have to reverse the vehicle! Fortunately, John's younger brother, Brian, himself on leave from P & O where he served as a Cadet, was a welcome visitor for a weekend, and was able to instruct Ankie how best to select the elusive gear. Her sister, Nel, also visited from Holland, so what with work in Dorchester, family visits and the thoughtful attention of friends, Ankie was kept busy. Never once, however, did John's father make contact. Another letter advised John that she had purchased "our own three-piece suite, and coffee table". The mentioned cost of which caused the Second Officer to have a brief lie-down!

Meanwhile, and just prior to the departure of 'Orsova' from Tilbury's filthy waters, Captain S. Ayles RD, RNR, bade his newly joined Second Officer to his cabin, and opened their relationship with an astonishing, and wholly inaccurate, delivery. "I just hope," he commented, "that you will not be as much trouble here, as you were aboard 'Orcades'!" Clearly, Staff-Captain Harrison, himself newly appointed to "Himalaya", had seen fit to fire a final salvo, in the sure knowledge that it would cause harm. "Quis Nos Separabit" – who shall separate us – here phrased in the subjunctive tense. Who indeed!

Factually, it did more, for on leaving Captain Ayles cabin, his new Second Officer made a firm decision that, apart from his watch-keeping and other navigational duties (yes, preparation of the next voyage schedule for 'Orsova') he would totally exclude himself from all and any social activity aboard throughout the voyage, and so it transpired. Further, and on reaching Sydney outward bound, he submitted request to Head Office to be relieved on return to London, such that he could involve in further RNR training that was due. This request was refused on the somewhat spurious grounds that "we will not have an Officer of sufficient seniority to relieve you". In response, Second Officer John (William) Perry tendered his resignation from P & O-Orient Line, and on arrival London May 26th, he was relieved by Andrew Tinsley, possibly surprised by his sudden and unexpected promotion! Ankie had been kept up to date as to decisions made and had relayed news of his resignation to John's mother, whose response was merely, "What a naughty boy!"

In John's planning, RNR training for some three to four months would then see the end of his sea-going career, in that it seemed to him totally incompatible with a successful marriage. This would mean a business life ashore, and he recognised the unknown challenges that such a transition would bring about, and the probability that, altogether, the deeper water is ashore. As he would later learn, 'persistence and determination alone are omnipotent' and in John and Ankie, that would prove to be the case, in spades! Per Ardua Ad Astra, and never, ever, in the subjunctive tense!

So, Indentured to P & O as Apprentice (Cadet) 1 October 1955, and resigned from P & O-Orient Line as Senior Second Officer effective May 26th, 1967, to embrace a whole new life ashore, marking twelve years of satisfying and productive sea-going experience. There would be moments of sadness from time to time, with retrospective thoughts as to the camaraderie and friendships woven with fellow Officers, but overall a new sense of purpose, of adventure even, in marriage, family creation and fresh challenges. First though, there was the small matter of completing a few months of RNR training, and to this Lieutenant John now applied himself, happily "at home" in 104 Buxton Road Weymouth, overlooking Portland Harbour that was itself soon to feature substantially within the training context.

Collected from Tilbury by Ankie, now casually competent in finding reverse gear in the family car, and without a backward glance at 'Orsova' (actually, that was sad because John had put two Spanish duelling foils on a nearby packing case whilst loading the car, which were left behind, to the undoubted pleasure of a Tilbury dock worker!) the happily re-united couple had returned to Weymouth, there to enjoy as it turned out, some three weeks together before he, John, had to join HMS 'Keppel', a Blackwood Type 14 anti-submarine Frigate. The further downside was that the ship was being re-commissioned in Gibraltar, meaning a Royal Airforce flight thereto on June 14th, with the vessel's operational deployment thereafter as yet unknown, or at least, undisclosed. Undeterred, and with Ankie on holiday from her Dorchester place of work, the couple set about making the most of the three weeks, simply happy to be back together again. It should be said that John felt obliged to luxuriate as often as allowed in or on the new three-piece suite, but opportunity was largely denied by more constructive social deployment to and with friends, or just the two of them in harmonious close togetherness, to employ a broad-brush euphemism.

Ankie, of course, had confirmed her pregnancy before 'Orsova' had taken John away for some three months, and with her due date looking like sometime in September, anxious question as to where 'Keppel' was to be deployed post Gibraltar went, pro tem, unanswered. In the event, it would transpire that 'Keppel', after work-up in the Mediterranean, would first return to Rosyth for a brief few days, and thence to (loud hurrahs!) Portland, where she would be worked up to Squadron readiness. Retrospective dates remain time blurred, but indeed arrival Portland was at least a month in advance of the birth, and indeed the birth would be worked into the Navy's potential reaction should it happen whilst 'Keppel' was undergoing exercises at sea. More of that later, however.

During the three weeks now embraced, the continued friendship made with Jimmy and Pat Foot during their time aboard 'Orcades' as passengers became further enhanced, and interestingly it came out that his quiet-spoken but cheerful persona neatly cloaked a more robust period of his life. Now owning and operating a successful company as an Agricultural Merchant to the local farming community, he had at one time not only served as an Officer in the then Dorset Regiment, but also as a member of the renowned S.B.S. or Special Boat Service. Instant renewed respect! In September 1967, Pat Foot would agree to become the Godmother of Ankie's first-borne, Duncan.

Friendship also further blossomed with Harold and Dot Hilton, owners of 104 Buxton Road, with John particularly grateful for their thoughtful kindness to Ankie during his 'Orsova' débacle – Harold would also feature in Lieutenant John's return home from Plymouth at the end of his 'Keppel' appointment, introducing John to the medicinal benefits (as promised by Harold) as he proffered, nay, thrust, the dreaded glass of his concoction named as 'Prairie Oyster' to be consumed. The record does not show how he came to that name, but surely not approved by the Regulator MHRA, should such a body have then existed!

HMS 'Keppel'

With June 14th fast approaching, John prepared himself for his final sea-going appointment which, as it turned out, was to last for a full five months, ending in Plymouth on the 24th November. Happily, a good slice of that time would be spent in or around Portland Naval base, once the ship had been re-commissioned in Gibraltar, and had completed her work-up exercises in close co-operation with, as it was scheduled, the Royal Air Force. Once again though, he and Ankie would have to say their fond farewells, but this time without pre-knowledge as to the length of their separation, which made it all the more poignant. Ankie, as always, was her usual Dutch pragmatic self, and with her secretarial job in Dorchester, coupled now to having responsibility for the couple's financial affairs, would be kept reasonably busy. John too, once arrived to the Rock, would be able to gather information as to the probable time commitment in the Mediterranean, and to report the good news that 'Keppel' would then be deployed to Portland for the full Squadron work-up. That would bring about several interesting connotations, including to some substantial part, involvement with the Royal Dutch Navy. More of that later, however.

Notwithstanding, parting brought the now accustomed sweet sorrow, and whilst time again has shrouded which was the Airforce Base, or indeed how Lieutenant Perry RNR got there, he took the RAF flight to Gibraltar that June 14th, 1967. Frequent calls to the Rock had been made, always briefly, with P & O, but the rather hair-raising arrival of the flight into Gibraltar, with the Pilots clearly flying 'by the seat of their pants' as goes the expression, was distinctly different, and the landing distinctly praiseworthy!

P & O Regulations, now abandoned, were to be superseded by Q R & A I, 'Queen's Regulations and Admiralty Instructions', by far the more authoritative, indeed disciplinary tome, with Courts Martial the final arbiter, should it be needed, which overall tended to focus the minds of all ranks!

Named for Admiral of the Fleet Sir Henry Keppel (1809 – 1904), HMS 'Keppel', as a Type 14 anti-submarine Frigate, had imposing anti-submarine weaponry, known as the Mk.10, or Limbo mortar, situated on the vessel's quarterdeck, capable of directing rounds of mortars such that they fell in triangular pattern around the submerged target. They were directionally fully flexible, with a range of up to 1000 yards. She was otherwise lightly armed, with just three 40mm Bofors guns, and was capable of a cruising speed of 27 knots. To this then, came Lieutenant Perry, where he reported aboard to Lieutenant Commander Ronny Laughton RN, in Command, to be introduced thereafter to his fellow Officers already assembled on board. It quickly became clear that 'Keppel' was already a happy ship, well but sensibly disciplined, and it would soon become apparent that she would become a very efficient and effective fighting unit in her new Commission. Lieutenant Perry, already in possession of his Naval Watch-Keeping Certificate, would stand bridge Watches at sea, and was also given the responsibility as a Divisional Officer. For the rest, he would work as directed with individual Officers, particularly the TASO (Torpedo and Anti-submarine Officer) Back to the world of military acronyms! In essence, John was, in the parlance, a 'gash' Lieutenant, which would mean more gangway duties than most, when so required in Port!

The ensuing weeks would see many Mediterranean sea-days exercising anti-submarine war games with aircraft of the Royal Air Force based Gibraltar, and the tense warning 'Torpedo, Torpedo' over the Tactical voice network would prompt almost automatic and swift reaction by the Officer of the Watch to turn the fast-moving Frigate towards, but off-set from, the incoming threat which thankfully was always imaginary. The turn was made using a variation of the Williamson Turn.

Such was the case one day when, forenoon exercises having been completed, 'Keppel' was running at some twenty knots plus towards the next designated exercise area, with 'all hands' piped to lunch meantime, and Lieutenant Perry having the Bridge Watch. With at least some forty minutes to run before commencing the next planned exercise, the Tactical voice network suddenly boomed a tense warning, "Torpedo, Torpedo, Torpedo, green three zero" (n.b. thirty degrees off the starboard bow) to which came the immediate and automatic response from the OOW, (the afore-mentioned Lieutenant) turning the ship fast to port (thereby causing a substantial starboard list) through some 30 degrees, and then reversing the turn fast to starboard (thereby causing a substantial port list) through some sixty degrees, until the vessel was facing the incoming missile, but with sufficient throw-off for it to pass harmlessly past the starboard side. To accompany this came a cacophony of noise from below decks (the vessel not being secured for action stations) as plates, mugs, glasses, and people were thrown hither and thither (well, first to starboard, and then to port to be precise), and the bellowed question from the First Lieutenant as he crawled onto the Bridge deck shouting, "What the f…s going on!"

Thankfully, the Commanding Officer reassured the somewhat chastened OOW that he had taken the correct action, and late that afternoon, a cleaned-up 'Keppel' berthed back in Gibraltar, with those Officers that were off duty invited to dine at the Royal Air Force Officers Mess that evening. To their question, "Did it work?" came the laughed response, "Bloody right it did" with stories of lockers opening as the ship went one way, into which flew plates or mugs, with the locker doors slamming shut as the ship went the other way. Assurances were given that there would not be a repeat of 'out of exercise' torpedoes, and so back to work the next day. In fact, there were days when 'Keppel' did not put to sea, and free time was enjoyed at the local swimming club which, being mid-summer, meant that Mediterranean tans were indeed achieved. Letters home too to be written, or received from home, and reassurance that all was well in Buxton Road Weymouth gratefully noted.

Eventual return from the Mediterranean brought three further memorable experiences to Lieutenant Perry's service aboard 'Keppel', one of which was a visit to the Rosyth Naval Base in the Firth of Forth. The timing of the visit, or indeed the purpose, is again shrouded in the mists of time, but insofar as her sister-ship, HMS 'Palliser' was based there as a unit of the Fisheries Protection Squadron, it may well have been a portend for 'Keppel's' future deployment. Interestingly, the Commanding Officer of 'Palliser' was being Court Martialled for either hazarding his vessel in an icefield or bending a bit of bilge keel on a submerged rock, and Perry was detailed to attend for a day, as part of his exposure to Naval matters. Fortunately, common sense prevailed, the Court merely issuing a reprimand, recognising possibly that Icelandic waters in winter are not necessarily the easiest waters in which to operate a Type 14 Frigate, having no ice-strengthening to the hull. The ceremonial sword, therefore, remained undisturbed.

HMS Keppel - towards Gibraltar

There was another experience too. Faced with a long weekend doing nothing in poor weather, suggestion was floated, very briefly discussed, and then agreed, to hire a car and drive south, to the homes of three off-duty Officers, to include the 'gash' Lieutenant who, it should be emphasised, was persuaded to join post decision. The other two just had to mention 'Ankie', and he was in! Permission was granted, and a small car hired. "I'll no be charging you mileage," said the owner, "as clearly you'll no be going far in this weather." As goes the saying, an opportunity is never missed – if one does not take it, someone else will, and clearly the TASO had not seen fit to advise operational plans. Assuming an unlikely average speed of 60 mph, the journey would take some eight hours and fifteen minutes to Weymouth, with no less than five hundred miles to cover!

Gangway Officer, Gibraltar

The much put-upon car would then proceed to Portsmouth, to return at an arranged time Sunday to collect John and return to Rosyth. Sheer, absolute madness! Notwithstanding, Lieutenant Perry was able to awaken Ankie that Saturday morning at 0600 hours (she had been pre-advised) and enjoy a full day at home, being collected at circa 1400 hours Sunday for the romp home, a lot of which was done riding the slipstream of a fast-moving National coach in thick fog. They arrived back to the ship at about 0200 hours Monday morning. Retrospectively risible, irrational, irresponsible, or all those things? Perhaps, but one heck of a way to fill a bad weather weekend in Rosyth!

At 0700 hours, HMS 'Keppel' slipped, and proceeded to sea, leaving a car-hire vendor to puzzle out just how his vehicle had achieved well over a thousand miles on the clock, during a wet weekend in Scotland.

By an extraordinary coincidence, John & Ankie were, much later in their life, to become good friends with near neighbours in Woodbridge, Suffolk, namely Mike and Marian Garnett. During 'Keppel's' (1967) brief time in Rosyth, Mike had been serving aboard HMS 'Palliser', as a weapons and electronics specialist, but more of that later, with many home and geographical moves still to come for John & Ankie, indeed for Mike and Marian, before Woodbridge.

Portland Naval Base

To have chosen Weymouth, and Buxton Road overlooking Portland in particular, had indeed been a prescient choice, as 'Keppel' arrived to Portland Naval Base from her Mediterranean re-commissioning exercises. Portland base was tasked to bringing newly commissioned Naval units to Squadron readiness, in every aspect prepped for front-line action as required. Not only British units, but also those of other NATO nations as required, the training being full-on, all encompassing, and hard work for all ranks aboard over an extended period, until final 'examinations' were able to be passed with credit. Interestingly, 'Keppel' would be brought to this state of readiness by Officers that included four Dutch Naval Officers assigned to the Base, and noteworthy is fact that they were hugely professional, dedicated to their assignment and hard taskmasters, determined to achieve the only the best performance from their 'pupil' units.

Much of the time would be spent at sea, with time in Port reluctantly granted, save for those exercises involving divers trying to attach mines to ships' hulls, or otherwise interfere with operational norms to always achieve states of high readiness aboard. Surprisingly, and in view of Ankie's pregnancy, it was incorporated into the overall exercise planning for 'Keppel' that Lieutenant Perry would be air-lifted from the ship if at sea by the Fleet Air Arm and transported to Weymouth Hospital for the birth. In the event, the airlift would not be required, with 'Keppel' by chance undergoing 'diver repelling' in harbour when the time came.

Lieutenant Commander Ronny Laughton had joined the Navy as a Seaman, and through sheer hard work and application, had both achieved his Officer Commission, and Command, of which he was justly proud. That he expected the best from 'Keppel' was clear, and in this he whole-heartedly led by example. It therefore came as no surprise that, as 'Keppel' was due to proceed to sea on a particular day, he expected his Ship's Company to shew a disciplined and appropriate greeting to the newly commissioned County Class Destroyer due to arrive, as she was the senior vessel. Hands were ordered to face to port and salute as the two ships passed at the harbour's entrance, and Boatswains Calls trilled loud and clear across the narrow stretch of water separating the two vessels. Ronny stood to attention, his right hand at rigid salute, his usually florid face glowing proudly, knowing that his Officers and men were similarly honouring, as is Naval tradition, the senior vessel.

A new sound, a loud 'whump' was heard from the 'Keppel' quarterdeck, and from the Mk.10 Limbo, a mortar curled lazily into the air toward the Destroyer. Ronny's face turned sharply left, completely white, and looking uncomprehendingly horrified, he watched its slow fall trajectory. The mortar splashed harmlessly into the water some twenty feet from the Destroyer's side, and equally harmlessly, being unarmed, sank to the seabed.

Ronny left the Bridge at flank speed toward the quarterdeck, and although the subsequent discussion with the Boffin that had inadvertently caused the incident went unrecorded, it certainly evidenced Ronny's degree of angst and displeasure in time, colour, and volume! The Boffin was probably bed-wetting for months to come thereafter! In that Lt. Cmdr. Laughton was not only an avid squash player, but also a former Hampshire and Royal Navy rugby player, the guilty Boffin was probably happy to settle for a round rollocking, rather than being drop-kicked overboard, which would have rated as impolite, if deserved!

As for Ronny, signal from the Destroyer's Commanding Officer (a full Commander) thanked "Ronny for your unusual and interesting welcome", and wished him well, so that at least calmed the situation such that 'Keppel' was able to complete her day's exercises without further trauma, and Ronny's face to, eventually, return to its near florid appearance.

Ankie went into labour on the September 21st, and their first son, Duncan, was born during the early forenoon of September 22nd. Lieutenant John was given special leave to attend at the hospital and was present throughout the birth, and much involved too when, with one of Ankie's legs across his arm, he heard the mid-wife say, "Stay calm, just popping out for a cup of tea," which gave John pause for thought, whilst Ankie continued to recognise that pragmatism was not the most immediate and appropriate response to current goings-on! She was magnificent!

Walking almost unaided from the delivery room, she politely declined the offer of a fish and chips meal (a bizarre offering it must be said) and as she was put to bed, John took himself, still in full scrubs, to the nearest exit to have a cigarette. No sooner was it lit, than an order was delivered by the passing Matron. "Put that cigarette out," she hissed, "you might be mistaken for a Doctor!"

For the record, the most immediate cost attached to the birth was that of a case of Champagne (small case!) promised to the Wardroom of 'Keppel', duly delivered and accepted. It is fair to say that both Lieutenant and a recovered Mrs Perry would contribute to its despatch in due course.

Some three weeks later, on October 15th to be precise, son, Duncan, was christened aboard 'Keppel', the ceremony being carried out in the ship's Wardroom by the Naval Padre Rev. Braithwaite, the inverted ship's bell as surrogate traditional font. The small Wardroom was crowded with Officers and friends, and whilst the Western Gazette and Dorset Evening News both reported the occasion correctly as taking place on board HMS 'Keppel', presence of three Dutch Naval Officers clearly confused the local television reporter, who advised viewers of the evening news that the ceremony had taken place aboard the Dutch warship 'Keppel', much to the annoyance of Lieutenant Commander Laughton RN, justifiably proud of his Command!

Of Sidney Perry, Publicity Manager of Weymouth, and father to John as previously and briefly mentioned, there was no sign, despite fact that he had been invited. Zero. Nada. Rien, or to give it a Dutch flavour, Niets! Sad really, if predictable.

HMS 'Keppel' having successfully completed her work-up, passing with flying colours, was scheduled to depart Portland three days later, on Wednesday October 18th.

To digress briefly, it is probably fair to say that whilst the matter of leaving his sea-going career had progressed apace, it had occurred to (currently) Lieutenant Perry RNR that small issue of achieving gainful work ashore had, by default, gone completely unaddressed. Further, that with only a few short months to go, it was time to do something about it. Fortunately, this mental light bulb had glowed before recent return to UK waters, and some start had been made, and given sudden impetus by realisation that Ankie was to give birth in September. It should also be emphasised that rushing about aboard a Type 14 anti-submarine Frigate was not necessarily the best platform from which to launch a pattern of job-seeking mortars, so to speak. It therefore came about that, having read an advertisement for a Sales Representative required to work in Essex for British Drug Houses (BDH), application had been duly made to the BDH head Office in London which, to his surprise, had resulted in a job offer to commence in the New year 1968, with all necessary training to be undertaken in London. This was given much thought and discussion 'twixt John and Ankie, and on the mixed metaphor basis that a bird in the hand is better than half a loaf,' it was concluded as a way forward, and an opportunity to further evaluate the job market more associated with John's qualifications and experience, from a position of employment ashore. In prescient terms, a good decision.

At this point, it should also be mentioned that at the time of marriage proposal in Wellington, John's financial estate comprised, roughly speaking, of a car, and a tailor's bill courtesy of S.W. Silver & Co of London, suppliers of uniforms. Not a lot had changed since, save that Ankie had worked in Dorchester, (three-piece suite and coffee table, remember?), but in that a new home was soon to be on the agenda, with Ankie unable to look for paid employment, financial pressures would grow, possibly apace. Regardless, a move from Weymouth to somewhere in Essex would have to be accomplished, post release from 'Keppel' which, as it would turn out, would be in Plymouth on November 24th, 1967, just one month away from her departure from Portland September 18th.

Fate had more in store too, as the move to Essex would but foreshadow a series of further moves in the UK, Europe and further afield, to the extent that later review would confirm the establishment of twelve homes during the first twenty years of their marriage, seven in the UK, three in Europe, and two in India, all ninety nine percent arranged and organised by Ankie, to the extent that Pickford would seek to put the family in their annual budget plan. So, Essex was not to be a nudge of fate, but rather a shove, a full-on, 'stop pussy-footing about and go for it' shove! Gratefully embraced!

Meantime, however, good-byes had to be made yet again, but now to mother and child, as 'Keppel' prepared to leave Portland, prepped for whatever duties which, as planning would have it, would include 'Keppel' in a substantial RN task force responding to a simulated state of war between two Nations, somewhat ironically staged (the exercise, not the war) in the Irish Sea.

Ankie was home with baby Duncan, families were due to visit, and all seemed well on that all-important front, allowing John to re-focus on his shipboard duties, and ponder afresh as to the future which, at that stage, looked far from clear, but at the same time, a challenge to be overcome, come what may.

He was to find, shortly, that his Bridge duties were to take on aspects of Naval manoeuvres that would both challenge and amaze him and enhance his respect for the Royal Navy as it went about its business – not to mention those moments of surprise, and anxiety, now to be faced in real time, rather than under the watchful eye of a Staff Officer at Portland, British or Dutch!

Merchant vessels, save for the Royal Fleet Auxiliary (RFA) which is a hybrid organisation, tend to stay well clear of each other at sea, close quarter situations developing only if one vessel or the other has either disobeyed the all-embracing 'Rule of the Road' strictures, or somehow otherwise transgressed. This is not to say that such situations do not occur, as all seafarers well know.

It was therefore an unknown experience for him to find HMS 'Keppel' part of a close quartered squadron of warships moving, both in line and abeam, with adjacent vessels through the Irish Sea, particularly worrying during the night Bridge Watches when all vessels were completely darkened. Added to this was fact the 'Keppel', in her anti-submarine capacity, was tasked to perform sonar sweeps through the fleet, using a particular manoeuvre named, as hopeful memory recalls, 'Rum and Coke.' This entailed moving slowly through the Fleet from the rear-most to the leading vessels, and on reaching the van or forefront, turning tightly and at speed through one hundred and eighty degrees and moving at high speed back through the lines to the rear, turning again to move slowly back toward the leading vessels. This was repeated throughout the night hours, the Officer of the Watch having to know both when to make the turns and then execute them which, with a completely darkened Fleet as before mentioned, demanded total accuracy, and provided moments of acute anxiety, not to mention involuntary tightening of a certain sphincter muscle! (Apologies to Naval purists for any incorrect terminology relating to the manoeuvre as referenced) Sudden appearance of Buccaneer jets of the Fleet Air Arm (assigned to 'enemy' role) flying at just above sea-level straight at 'Keppel' as dawn broke was also unnerving, with every anticipation of being roundly stitched up had it been for real.

All went well though, and as the exercise was completed in the early, still dark, hours of the last morning, order was made for vessels to disengage independently which produced an absolute mêlée of vessels doing just that, but assuredly a skilled RN mêlée, as if choreographed to ensure negative collisions! Just another touch or two of involuntary sphincter tightening perhaps?

HMS 'Keppel' disengaged, and set courses for Plymouth, arriving thereto during the forenoon of November 24th, where Lieutenant Perry's five months of training aboard would come to a close, as would his entire sea-going career.

As the vessel approached her berth, Lieutenant Commander Laughton turned to his Officer of the Watch and addressed him thus, "John, you are relieved from Bridge duties, and required to report to the Junior Petty Officers' Mess, please." It was the beginning of a busy, and entirely memorable (well, most of it) day.

With the ship berthed, John repaired to the Junior Petty Officers' Mess as instructed, to be greeted with great good humour, and the requirement to quaff several beers as he was bade a resounding farewell, with sincere good wishes for his future. He in turn thanked his hosts for their professional support during his time aboard and wished them well for the remainder of the ship's Commission. He was then informed that their instruction was to deliver him to the Chief Petty Officers' Mess as his next port of call, and so thereto he was guided where once again good wishes were exchanged, thanks were proffered to the CPOs for their support and oft-times guidance, whilst further beers were pressed upon him as they too bade him sincere farewell. It was all totally unexpected and indeed heart-warming, although a somewhat bibulous experience!

More was to come, however as, on making his way to the Wardroom, he found that Lieutenant Commander Laughton had mustered all his Officers to a farewell send-off for their RNR Officer of five months, and whilst toasts to his time aboard and future ashore were many, and genuinely sincere, Lieutenant Perry was becoming very thankful that he would not be required to drive home to Weymouth, or anywhere else for that matter, in that a friendly offer to get him home had been received from a person with previous knowledge of RN farewell liquid generosity! The Commanding Officer was duly horrified at the news that John would be taking up employment with BDH and forecast that much better opportunities would shortly be identified and grasped, and the First Lieutenant humbly confessed that, as he set up the Wardroom for the christening of Duncan in Portland, water in the inverted ship's bell had received just a tiny drop of vodka, but before the Naval Padre had blessed the bell's liquid content. He was mollified in hearing that as no indelible cross had since appeared on the child's head, the Church and Parents would probably rest content.

Departure from 'Keppel' that afternoon was reluctant, the five months service aboard having exceeded all learning curve expectations, and the camaraderie throughout a shining example of how a well-run and sensibly disciplined unit could, and did, become a highly effective fighting unit. Oh, and not to forget the much-improved game of Squash, tutored at every opportunity by the ever-exuberant champion aboard, namely Lieutenant Commander Ronny Laughton, RN.

Return to Weymouth, to the waiting arms of Ankie was not, however, immediate as he who had kindly offered to drive John home, himself an RNR Officer, had been invited to a champagne party somewhere in Dorset, to which he, the driver, felt morally and thirstily obliged to attend, if John had no objection? Clearly no objection was expected, and courses were laid off accordingly, party bound, with the car's passenger now proclaimed as an honorary guest. To this point, it is reasonable to say that the day's alcoholic intake had been, although unusually excessive, nevertheless containable. The Devil though comes with the detail and offer of a glass or two of champagne from people that John had never seen before in his life now seemed quite reasonable, and relatively harmless, surely.

Arrival to home sweet home in Weymouth was now earlyish evening, and the waiting arms of Ankie, together with a welcoming party of Harold and Dot Hilton, found a somewhat 'worse for wear' delivered to their care, a situation over which Ankie immediately took sympathetic and (partly) understanding control, guiding husband and no longer seafarer John gently upstairs to bed, better there to sleep it off, and ready for the challenges of the next day, being yet another example of her perceiving Hubby as 'work in progress'! The main challenge would appear in the shape of Harold Hilton, bearing glass of the so-named 'Prairie Oyster,' a vile tasting concoction of his, guaranteed to dispel any hang-over, or so he repeatedly told John as he chased him around the small lounge that following morning. En passant, it did work!

Embrace they did the following day though, (Ankie and John that is) and it is true to say that her intervention of the previous day would never be required again, thereby, not distracting her in future from her focus on moving the family on to better things. Dad was also reintroduced to son Duncan, who would one day be told of the christening day confession, but much to be achieved before that, as things would turn out.

Time was fast approaching when tentative feet would have to be put into those deeper waters ashore! Onward and upward!

British Drug Houses (BDH)

Employment with BDH was due to commence in January, 1968 which, in fact, presented another family related logistical challenge, broadly defined as 'a move from Weymouth to unknown accommodation somewhere in Essex' within the space of just over a month, not forgetting the Christmas holiday meantime. This prompted a reconvening of heart-to-heart discussion between John and Ankie, not dissimilar to that held in Wellington those months ago, to further define the individual parts that would make up the whole. In this, BDH had confirmed that hotel accommodation would be provided in Chelmsford for a limited period.

First decision was that home purchase was preferable to renting, which led inevitably to question of funds sourcing (nb tailor's bill and outstanding hire purchase for the car had been settled by Ankie in her designated family accounting role – see previous references) which in turn led to regrettable decision to encash John's Merchant Navy Pension fund, as sensibly suggested by Ankie. Second conclusion was that a visit to Essex was of immediate importance to establish housing options and preferences, basing themselves meantime in Chelmsford en famille, courtesy of BDH. Son Duncan was too young to be left with grandparents, so he would travel to Essex too, his first exciting journey. Many more were to follow in due course.

Recognition was also ruefully made that their only home furniture amounted to a three-piece suite and coffee table (remember?) and nothing else, which pointed to further substantial cash purchases which, in the event, were largely accommodated by visits to shops that specialised in second-hand retail, and an old, old, washing machine contributed by John's mother. In passing, or en passant, further reference was made to necessary change of dress code, in that naval uniform would no longer be de rigueur, and that John would perforce have to upgrade his civilian wardrobe. Although this recognition came from John, the final arbiter of clothing choice fell elsewhere, within the 'work in progress' definition.

So, the one hundred and eighty-four-miles journey to Chelmsford was undertaken, and residence taken up in an hotel close to the city centre. Loins were girded in house search mode, which eventually brought them to a property in the village of Southminster which, as they later discovered, was generally viewed at that time as being on the wrong side of the tracks, compared to Burnham-on-Crouch, just a few miles down the road. No matter, it had a cheery pub, a petrol station cum repairs garage, a village shop, florists, and a Surgery. The house price of £3000 or thereabouts was within reach with a small mortgage, it boasted a garage for the car, and a small garden. It worked. Back to Weymouth for eventual fond farewells after Christmas, and employment of Pickford's Removals, and as the purchase moved with remarkable alacrity, they were enabled to move in early in January 1968, or thereabouts. This was home number two, and as it would turn out, their second in a total of twelve homes established within the first twenty years of their marriage, ninety-nine percent of which were organised by Ankie. Pickford would call occasionally to check for the next move. A slight exaggeration, but close! Some weeks after they had moved in came a knock at the front door which Ankie opened, to hear in an unmistakable accent, the following from the young woman on the doorstop. "I have been told that you are from Holland. My name is Luthie, and I am Dutch, and we also live in Southminster, close to you." Luthie, and her husband, Geoff Langfield, would become life-long friends from that day on! The village had just become that little bit friendlier!

However, another form of training had to be undertaken by the now shore-bound Master Mariner, and to London he had to go, to BDH headquarters, for a period of product enlightenment. This form of reference seemed more than appropriate, in that the main product that was to be more firmly brought to market was Nuvacon, the BDH anti-pregnancy pill, requiring a substantial product knowledge not only for its researched capability, but also potential side effects, slight or relevant as they may be. Oestrogen, progesterone, amenorrhea, the corpus luteum, et al, all now became defined and integrated into the sales exponent's ability to discuss and explain with and to the medical profession., a clear and definite departure from latitude, longitude, meridian altitudes, and Great Circles.

There were two other products also to be taken aboard (staying with nautical jargon), namely Fluoderm, a corticosteroid for relief of inflammation, and Sealegs, a sure-fire preventer of travel sickness, the latter to be brought mainly to the attention of Chemists. Fluoderm, whilst effective in its advertised purpose, had rather an unfortunate side-effect, in that it stained clothing blue or purplish as you will (sell around it was the general advice of the product tutor).

Product training completed, and then a return to Southminster and family, and indeed to receive a large company car which its previous owner had clearly neglected judging by the general mess and dog hairs that defined the interior. Additionally, information as to the names and addresses of Family Planning Clinics, GP Surgeries and Hospitals within the 'patch' defined as Essex, which information experience would shortly show as both poorly put together, and inadequately updated. Note that product training was completed, and although some play-acting had been indulged in as sales training, it was altogether cursory, and therefore 'hopeful' rather than definitive. Surprising in a way, in that BDH was a substantial Company, with Mead Johnson of America having acquired thirty five percent of BDH shares in 1961. Glaxo was to acquire those Mead Johnson shares in 1967, and indeed take over BDH in its entirety. This will become impactive in due course, but fortunately of only passing, albeit helpful, interest to John and Ankie in the event.

The vehicle was brought rapidly to a state that could be described as 'shipshape and Bristol fashion', and whilst Ankie applied herself to bringing their new home to a similar state of comfort, John navigated his way through the County, amending and updating his 'target audiences' information, having established as his personal approach that with the exception of Chemist shops, he would not make 'cold calls', but rather only with an appointment, as this to his opinion better suited the medical environment in which he found himself, and afforded respect to the Doctors and Nurses that were his potential customers, be that in GP Surgeries, Hospitals or indeed Family Planning Clinics. It also largely did away with the always possible 'cold call rejection' factor!

Representatives of rival products had, of course, their own approaches, as was demonstrated in one GP Surgery when, as he was called to the consulting room, an extremely attractive representative exited, re-adjusting her skirt as she did so. As they passed in the waiting room, she grinned and muttered, "You've got no chance, mate," and strode from the Surgery. Clearly, she had confidence in her own product, as well as her selling ability.

On the other hand, appointment granted to a previously unidentified surgery became an embarrassment as it turned out to be a Dental Surgery. Note to file: 'in any sales capacity, always clearly identify that all members of your target audience are relevant to that which you have to sell!' Lesson acquired and etched on brain. In self-defence, he would point out that all surgeries in new town Harlow were built to a standard structured appearance. No excuse, really.

Southminster turned out to be a safe and pleasant haven, the friendship with Luthie and Geoff growing apace with visits to each other's homes, there to admire the quality of each other's second-hand furniture, although that did not include Ankie's three-piece suite and coffee table (remember?). The local hostelry also provided both cheery and comfortable get-togethers, and the sampling of local ales. In this, it had been made clear to Ankie whilst aboard 'Orcades' that to ask for a G & T at a pour-out on board was OK, whereas ashore, beer would be the response to the question, "What would you like?" and that dictum had held good thus far into their life ashore, largely for the reason of near-impoverishment, relative to the costs to be considered. By sheer coincidence, yet another Dutch girl had come to light, also ex-P & O, having married a Writer from the ship in which she had served. They, however, lived in Burnham-on-Crouch, he having successfully started a Company in London dealing in Claims, although there existed the possibility that his earnings from the sale of stamps to Passengers on board ship may have helped?

John continued to develop his 'patch' so-called and became enthusiastic in matters of both the selling of his products, but also the customer interface or focus, so important he believed in market loyalty generation. Indeed, he was pleasantly surprised to learn that his efforts had exceeded expectations, which may well explain the absence of any support or guidance from his area Manager who, presumably had other rows to hoe. That said, it was that absence that prompted further thoughts that would serve the future, the 'delegation without supervision can amount to abdication' factor.

Ankie devoted her time to her gladly embraced role as a mother, and son, Duncan, grew apace in the welcoming comfort of the home that Ankie had created, helped of course by John's burgeoning DIY skills, to not always complete success.

Meanwhile, of course, plan of action as discussed prior to stepping ashore was deployed, with letters of introduction or application with CVs being generated to such Companies as deemed to offer a career structure more suited to John's qualifications and experience, short of returning to sea, all suitably typed of course by ex-WAP Ankie. One such Company was Ferrymasters, which had secured the U.K. Agency contract for SeaLand, an American new-comer to the European shipping scene, that specialised in the carriage of containers, system created by one Malcolm McLean, initially serving only U.S home-trade waters. Tentative telephone call had been made from Weymouth to the Managing Director of Ferrymasters, namely Ted Haynes, whose somewhat laconic "and what is your particular forté, Mr Perry?" had at the time seemed rather unresponsive. At any rate, nothing further had been heard, although CV and address change had been forwarded to his attention.

Some seven months into the inspiration that was working as a Salesman for BDH came a barrage of information which would prompt much discussion, analysis, and career decision, all to be evaluated and chewed over. The first was that Glaxo had completed the take-over of BDH and re-named the now subsidiary. The second wave brought news that as a function of this take-over, the Master Mariner cum Lieutenant RNR cum BDH pill Salesman in Essex was to be declared redundant!

Disaster? Not a bit of it, for while not necessarily concomitant to, but by coincidence in the next day's mail delivery, came two good job offers from Corporations in London that operated Tanker fleets (one of which was Trident Tankers, owned by P & O), together with letter from Ferrymasters-SeaLand in Felixstowe Suffolk, suggesting that subject to successful interview, the position of Marine Manager for SeaLand in the UK would be on offer. There was also tentative offer from North Sea Ferries Hull, albeit that would come forward later.

On the face of it, their home in Southminster would give relatively easy, daily rail access to London, whilst Felixstowe would mean a round-trip car journey of some three hours daily (no Orwell bridge at that time) or more, with wind and tides bringing further possible travel constraints. Further, John had served as Third Officer aboard the 'Maloja' one of P & O's tankers that would become Trident Tankers, so hands-on experience aplenty. There would be further considerations (loss of company car for one) but notwithstanding, decision was made to attend interview in Felixstowe while the BDH car was still available, and then make further evaluation. And so, it came to pass, in biblical terms, a meeting with Ted Haynes and his fellow Directors, plus the SeaLand European Marine Manager as it turned out, Dutchman Nicko van den Heuvel, in the Ferrymasters office in Felixstowe. Just prior to this meeting, BDH advised the amount of redundancy compensation that was due to be paid, which amounted to enough to pay for a reasonable second-hand car. This tipped the scale, and at further Board Meeting of 'Team Perry', it was decided that, if the Felixstowe interview was successful and offer made, then it would be accepted. It was, it was, and so onward to the next square on the board, more decisions re housing, but back to the maritime world – not going to sea, but rather helping others back to sea, which seemed to mark positive progress. Time would tell, and we all know that time and tide wait for no man!

The Essex appointment, although brief, had more than served its purpose, however, no doubt as much by luck as judgement in timing terms. Nevertheless, it had worked as a springboard into something that gave every indication of potential growth in what was, effectively, a shipping revolution in the happening, with the Company that was bringing about real change that demanded truly flexible thinking and application. No surprise that it was American! There was added benefit too that had been accrued during the seven months, the recognition of marketplace realities, importance of product knowledge, establishment of target audiences and, most importantly, customer focus. Oh, and delivery of that which was discussed and agreed with customers. Here, meetings with Family Planning Clinics had brought home the importance of clear definition of pathways to required outcomes. "No, Madam, dropping the contraceptive pills into your husband's/boyfriend's tea each morning will not, repeat not, prevent pregnancy." This was, reportedly, a commonplace and necessary rebuttal of liability! Probably happened in other Counties too!

Sealand, Felixstowe

To reflect awhile on the Port of Felixstowe in the mid-sixties, it comprised largely of the so-called Dock basin (home to the swarm of MTBs of HMS Beehive during the Second World War) and re-developed for small merchant ships most of which were involved in the home trade. The Dock was equipped with a Scotch Derrick built in 1966, with a lifting capacity of 32 tons at a 90 ft. radius. There were, of course, other cargo support facilities, but no state-of-the-art container handling capabilities, only the Scotch Derrick.

In essence therefore, it was a small, privately owned Company that had not therefore been included among the 150 Firms that comprised those governed by the National Docks Labour Board (NDLB) introduced by the then Labour Government in 1947 and supported by local Scheme Boards made up by equal numbers of Dockers, and Owners' personnel. Any registered Docker laid off by any one of the 150 Firms associated with the Scheme was guaranteed either full employment elsewhere, or a £25,000 pay off! Felixstowe had been too insignificant in 1947 for enforced membership, and insofar as the Scheme was not abolished until 1989 by Margaret Thatcher, Felixstowe was free from labour demarcation tribulations that beset and held back other Port enterprises, and free to grow as a modern and efficient Port, which clearly it did, with a dedicated and disciplined work force, augmented by ex-RAF personnel from the many Suffolk bases, that had completed their National Service.

Clearly, fact that Felixstowe was not part of the NDLB Scheme had attracted the attention of SeaLand, as well as other Lines, and indeed small beginnings were made in the late sixties with a feeder vessel named the ADA, with a capacity of some 30 x 35 ft. container units (SeaLand's standard size at that time) worked under the Scotch derrick, using a Port-constructed spreader bar. Equally as clearly, no deep-sea vessels would call until such time as custom-built facilities were made available, a situation not lost to Felixstowe's Management in terms of business opportunity. Factually, the first 500 feet of what was known then as New South Quay became operational in July 1967 with one Vickers Paceco container crane, with a further 800 feet being completed in March 1968, together with a further Vickers Paceco crane. Expansion of holding land also took place, and in 1973 a further 700 feet of berth was added, and a third Vickers Paceco crane. The facility would be renamed Landguard terminal in due course.

Noteworthy at this point is fact that despite the growth opportunities being grasped by the Port, highway infrastructure improvements were lagging, building of the Orwell Bridge, part of the Ipswich by-pass scheme, not being commenced until October 1979, completed in April 1982, and formally opened in December 1982.

In 1976, the Port was taken over by European Ferries Ltd., and in 1987, it was acquired by the P & O Group. In 1991, seventy five percent of the Port was acquired by the Hutchison Whampoa Group of Hong Kong, the balance of twenty five percent (by then Walton Terminal) by Orient Overseas Holdings Ltd., or OOCL. In 1994, Hutchison Whampoa acquired one hundred percent ownership.

De facto, size really did matter back in 1947, enabling development of what is today one of Europe's top container handling Ports, handling some forty percent of the UK's container traffic, together with substantial volumes of so-called Ro-Ro traffic moving to and from Europe via Holland. Such is the power and benefits of private enterprise unfettered by Government bureaucracy, or ofttimes misguided Union interference.

To this then, came John, released (nay, made redundant) from BDH employ, and as SeaLand's first direct employee in the UK, hoping that nautical knowledge gained and attained of his Masters Certificate and practical experience would not have deserted him, come the testing. He was warmly welcomed by Ted Haynes, and indeed his Operations Manager George Spraggett who, surprisingly, would often turn up to the Office wearing carpet slippers. That in no way detracted from his professional work application, with shoes always ready to hand (feet?) when necessary. He was a character, and whilst a character is often described as 'an idiot with personality' George was no idiot! Ted Haynes, as it transpired, was of the Management ilk that if he suggested a jump into the Dock water would solve a problem, his Staff would readily comply. Note to file: Work with your Staff, do not patronise them. Roy Mettam was also introduced as the Ferrymasters lead Salesman for SeaLand and would become a valued colleague as events moved on.

Introduction was also made to Tony Cross who, it transpired, had been employed by Ferrymasters to bring some sea-going experience to the handling of SeaLand's containers, and by extension, ships, the tentative arrival of feeder vessels from Rotterdam. The ADA, working in the Dock had been the first, and with New South Quay's emerging availability, further small feeders were being introduced, the Ragna and Stadt Aschendorf, with deep-sea vessel calls an increasing possibility. His sea-going experience had been as a Quartermaster aboard a cross channel or North Sea ferry, and it quickly became apparent that he was completely out of his nautical knowledge depth, his initial reason for employment therefore overtaken by the fast events that would define this new maritime operation. He would last but a few short weeks, whilst the newly appointed Marine Manager scoped SeaLand's operational intentions, and the staffing needs to facilitate them.

It became quickly apparent that the workload resultant from SeaLand's operational intentions meant that Southminster as home and hearth was no longer a viable option, and to this end Ankie set about putting the house on the market and was rewarded with an early enquiry that looked positive – so much so, that search for accommodation in Felixstowe was also set in motion, with decision taken that until the future became clearer, rented accommodation would suffice. Pause for thought. "As for the future, you have not to foresee it but to make it possible." (translation from Antoine de Saint-Exupéry)

With the house sale looking good, and after a brief visit to Felixstowe en famille, commitment was made to rent an apartment in Hamilton Road, adjacent to the Orwell Hotel and opposite the rail station and, at that time, above a wine shop. Pickfords was commissioned again, fond farewells made, and circa July 1968, the Felixstowe apartment became home number the third. At this point, it became disappointingly clear (to split an infinitive) that the then Prime Minister, Harold Wilson, and his "Kitchen Cabinet", was unacquainted with the writings of one Saint-Exupéry, in that his government imposed draconian restrictions on the granting of mortgages, to the extent that the potential buyer of the Southminster property was unable to obtain a mortgage, and the sale fell through. It would mean that for several months, 'Team Perry' would have to continue paying for two homes, not within original planning, or budget.

This brought about two lines of defence. Firstly, Ankie had to convince certain furnishing shops that the family credit was good for the curtains and carpets, (she succeeded, with great charm and aplomb) and John, who had been approached to teach coastal navigation to yacht masters once a week, thus far unenthused, felt pleased (obliged!) to accept, as means to further cash. Actually, he enjoyed the challenge once started, and having frantically revised!

In matter of workload, (now to include some navigation teaching) SeaLand's operational requirements were to place a weekly deep-sea vessel to Felixstowe, and feed to/from it with small vessels from/to such as Le Havre, Hamburg, and Rotterdam, or as necessary. The deep-sea vessel would also bunker at Felixstowe during the call, with the contracted bunker-barge coming round from the Thames. Fresh water would also be taken aboard, as necessary. All of this would require substantial cargo planning, both for the vessels' individual planning, and when working two vessels simultaneously, not to mention the production of final cargo plans. It would also require the deep-sea vessel to be brought to an even keel before sailing, with the required GM (stability factor), all of which would entail applied knowledge of stability and trim calculations for which, as reality would prove, the American Masters depended totally upon the Marine Manager. It is noted that all of this had to be achieved without the use of computers as none existed, although a calculator did come in handy at times. Equally as clearly, the Marine Manager would require qualified marine experience to assist, and to this end he received permission to employ an Assistant Marine Manager, bringing in John Peat, who became an immediate asset. Thankfully, the Dock Foremen and their teams proved themselves to be totally committed and thankfully without, at that time, so-called health, and safety constraints to interfere with the initiatives and innovative thinking that became so necessary, so needed at that time, as precursors to building reputation, and therefore business.

Introductions had earlier been made to George Blackhall the Dock manager, and Les Simpson who ran the day-to-day Port operations, both very focussed professionally, and clear asset to Ian Trelawny the Chief Executive, and here one quotes, "Who had been a much-loved and decorated MTB Commander based at HMS Beehive in the Dock basin during the War," brought into the Port's Management structure by Gordon Parker, owner of the Port.

Two other clear indications of commitment to Felixstowe were, firstly, SeaLand's appointment of an American Manager to their team at the Port, Jim Ward, who was to arrive together with his charming wife, and a 35-foot container in which, featuring large within their household goods, were a very substantial number of toilet rolls, and cans of baked beans, drawing a neat picture of just how rural their new posting had been described or painted! The rationale behind his appointment was unclear, as the Ferrymasters-Sealand team was perfectly capable of handling the increased operational business, and Jim Ward had no nautical knowledge or experience, but it probably made the European Vice-President Kalafatides (or Kal for short) based in Rotterdam feel more in control. In fact, it did bring better access to Rotterdam, increasingly and expensively staffed in management positions by American expats, as time went on. The Wards were a delightful couple, in due course introducing Ankie and John to a wonderful Thanksgiving dinner at their large, rented home in Felixstowe town.

The second was a surprise instruction from the Rotterdam office to Marine Manager John to implement an independent sweep and survey of the navigable channel to the new container berth, to verify the advertised depth of water at Mean Low Water Springs (MLWS) at circa nine to ten metres. To this end, a specialist company (Kelvyn Hughes?) was chartered in, and the appropriate sweep and survey achieved, John's presence aboard the specialist launch made even more interesting by taking horizontal sextant angles for position fixing, a function that stood him in further good stead on commencing his weekly navigation lessons to yachtsmen, not having held a sextant for at least a year! (N.B. There were no yachtswomen in attendance) So, it began. An expression used at sea to indicate pressure of work now took relevance, 'Watch on – Stop on' becoming oft-times a reality with the implementation of SeaLand's service over Felixstowe, with some five or six vessels per week (mothership plus feeders) to be worked. The Port had little of today's sophisticated means of handling containers to and from vessels, but fortunately the system devised by Malcolm McLean prevailed. Simply put, SeaLand provided its own road chassis, so the Port only needed to provide the so-called 'fifth wheel' facility, i.e., the means of towing the loaded or empty chassis to/from the vessel, but even that required some tractors, supplementary to the Port's tugs, to be hired in, reportedly from a few local farms! From small acorns do mighty oaks grow, and readers today will be hard-pressed to imagine those early days, seeing the Port leviathan that is Felixstowe today.

Preparation of the discharge and load sequence for each involved vessel, all done manually, had to be formulated and then passed to the berth Foreman, relatively straight forward when doing a discharge and load operation to one vessel, although the Foreman himself would have to produce written chits for the tug drivers to locate export containers. Great care had to be taken to ensure that the loading plan for each vessel was strictly adhered to, all of which required constant supervision which, coupled with the need to complete (manually) the final cargo plan(s) ensured that either the Marine Manager of his Assistant, or both, would spend most of the work shift, day, or night, in and out of the work caravan thoughtfully provided by Ferrymasters. At times, an expression learned on the Australian coast would be vocalised, the "Don't know any more if I'm punched, bored, or eaten out by white ants!" Very profound.

Another surprising factor for Marine Manager John was that the ships' Masters would have little or no say in their vessel's load profile, other than a cursory glance at the intended profile, which was fairly understandable with the small German feeders carrying maxim sixty-five units, as example. Less so for the Masters of the American flag vessels of the T2 or C4X class on the service, in that with bunkering and freshwater replenishment and considerable change in the container load factor, stability, trim and draft required careful calculation, all of which they happily left to the Marine Manager, accepting his reassurance that all was well to sail, on completion. Clearly, they must have been keeping their own calculations to themselves!

The feeder vessels, by definition of size, were easier to handle, and as with the Sealand vessels, a very good rapport was maintained with the Captains – save on one occasion where a relief Captain had brought the 'Stadt Ashendorf' to Felixstowe, and on completion of loading stated that he wanted two containers to be moved from their loaded position to different positions, thereby requiring an additional eight crane lifts, the vessel being fully loaded. "If we do that, you will leave Port with a six-to-eight-degree port list," came the response.

"Nonsense," rejoined the Captain, "just do as I instruct." The port list warning was repeated, again germanically rejected, and the containers re-handled to the Captain's insistence, the vessel duly sailing for Rotterdam with a six-to-eight-degree port list! "Vertrau mir, ich weis was ich tue," or "Trust me, I know what I'm doing," and the winner was? No one, really.

On one occasion, and due to poor weather conditions, the bunker barge was unable to get to Felixstowe, and John had arranged appropriate pilotage to take the C4X vessel to the Thames refinery to bunker. This the Captain point-blank refused to do unless he, John, embarked and accompanied the vessel as well.

This came at the end of a forty-five-hour, non-stop, sleepless operation during which he, the afore-mentioned John, had been "Watch on-Stop on" so was somewhat bushed! (probably white ants!) However, a call home to Ankie to advise he was going boating, to the local taxi company with request to collect him from the Thames refinery, and the s.s. 'Mobile' slipped and proceeded to sea, Thames bound, and eventually a successful bunkering. Some fifty-six hours after leaving home for work, John staggered up the stairs to their apartment home, to be eased to bed by Ankie, to sleep, perchance to dream!

The evening classes in coastal navigation continued relatively smoothly, the yachtsmen there assembled being both keen to learn, and highly intelligent, so proper preparation an absolute must. One evening, as the session was drawing toward an end, one Skipper posed a question relating to the magnetic compass, a question to which John had no immediate answer, but did not want that to become obvious. He paused in thought for a moment, and then responded, "That is indeed an important question, but in that I have scheduled next week to cover all aspects of the magnetic compass, variation, deviation, compass error and so forth, can we cover that at the same time?" Agreement reached, session ended, and a full week's grace (vessel operations allowing) in which to research response to the 'important question.' Note to file. "If unable to answer a question, do not resort to bullshit, as the person asking may already have the answer, and may be seeking to trip you up. Live to fight another day, with polite evasion." A bit like sitting Masters' oral exams really, although polite evasion was never really an option thereat!

Meanwhile, and with the summer months fast disappearing, as if in a blur of shipping activity, Ankie Perry (née Breeschoten, as further pronunciation exercise) continued to ensure that family matters were well supported, making frequent visits to the beach with growing son Duncan (and husband John where calls of duty allowed) as well as exerting constant pressure on the Southminster house Agent, to indeed finally achieve sale of the property, and therefore relief to those shops that she had convinced the family credit as sound. As usual, she kept the ship steady, so to speak, not forgetting the occasional prompt to husband John that some home decorating needed doing in his spare time. Social life was sparse, save for the friendships with the Ward and Mettam families, although occasional visits to the Orwell Hotel and Barman Shaun (or was it Sean?) were accomplished, at least once the Southminster home had been sold! Notwithstanding, they were content, with John employed in a world in which he had regained professional satisfaction, and recognition as it would transpire.

November Thanksgiving came, and with it their introduction to the American culinary mystics that accompanied it, hugely enjoyed with the Wards, and then the Christmas month, within which a certain operational decision had to be made. As Christmas approached, Vice-President Kalafatides had contacted the Port's Management, stating that he expected the vessel that would arrive then be worked and despatched on Christmas Day, something that had never been done at Felixstowe before. Perhaps strangely, George Blackhall sought opinion from SeaLand's resident Marine Manager, who concluded that rather than polite evasion, the response should be framed as a polite but decisive negative, on the grounds that it would require a voluntary workforce, impossible to achieve in sufficient numbers and skills, at such short notice. This advice accepted, and conveyed to the attention of Kalafatides, who accepted it with great reluctance, but reasonably good grace. Well, almost! Doubtless, future such requirement would be vocalised well in advance.

The year 1968 drew to a close, and it was with a good degree of well-earned satisfaction that Felixstowe was able to claim a very substantial success in SeaLand's full-service start-up in the UK.

Come mid-February 1969 or thereabouts, and during a temporary break from the Port's activity for John, discussion was entered into in their apartment as to the possibility of a visit to Ankie's parents in Amsterdam, and at her suggestion, a tentative date was set for April. After a thoughtful pause, Ankie changed the subject, focussing on how she saw the medium future. "I think that we should have a second child," she started, to receive immediate and enthusiastic support, and as John started to frame his first question, "Have you…," she interrupted with the confirmative "Yes, I've already stopped taking them," which suggested that she had already anticipated whole-hearted support to her proposal, and indeed the obvious first question. John's BDH training had not been totally in vain, nor its memory erased by countless containers! Sadly, and as a function of SeaLand's traffic flow, John would be unable to accompany Ankie to Holland in April, but before she left with son, Duncan, she once again uttered the immortal words, "Ik denk dat ik zwanger ben," and an English translation is not required. It did eventually cross John's mind that it was too much of a coincidence that Ankie had first suggested April as the month to visit her parents, enabled as she now was to tell them of their upcoming increase in grandparenthood. Family planning with a determined edge! Little did she know though, and nor did John, that sometime after her short visit to the Netherlands, another re-location move was afoot, not altogether welcomed at the time, nor seen as a further stepping-stone in their helter-skelter career development, as it would prove to be.

More of that in due course.

With Ankie and young Duncan safely returned from April's Amsterdam trip, the logistics of which remain stubbornly vague, and with Spring in the air, thoughts turned to possible further outings to Felixstowe's beaches come the warmer weather, or newly exploring the surrounding Suffolk countryside, workload allowing. The vessel service pattern continued apace, almost settled now into a routine established by experience, and assisted by gradual introduction of further Port handling equipment and expertise borne of said experience. With Ankie's pregnancy firmly established, thoughts also turned to a probable December birth, although still months away, so no need for any hurry/worry in that regard, with the apartment home well established.

There was no room, however, for operational complacency, but knowledge gained in the hectic first weeks enabled better and earlier preparation for vessels' working, which in turn reduced the pressure on the Marine Manager and his assistant, John Peat. Still no computers, and Port personnel doing vessel planning still a long way off, but 'punched, bored or eaten out by white ants' was no longer a ruminative interruption to the work process. Well, not too often.

Interestingly, or annoyingly if one was a resident in certain parts of Felixstowe, access to and exit from the Port was not to be diverted away from the town by completion of the Southern by-pass until 1973, so the increased over-road container traffic was by no means totally appreciated, the first of the Port's rail terminal also not being completed until November of the same year. However, development to be anticipated that May of 1969, with local constraints managed meantime.

Rumours were also starting to circulate that SeaLand was planning to open service over the Port of Liverpool, a somewhat bizarre decision under the Union circumstances that there then prevailed, or so went the thoughts in Felixstowe. John Perry and Roy Mettam, during one of their short and occasional pub visits, together pondered the perceived stupidity of such a decision, if indeed decision had been made, and jointly expressed genuine pity for the 'poor sods' that would be appointed to run the operation there, even if they were accustomed to the Liverpool maritime world, infamous as it was.

A very few short weeks later, Marine Manager John Perry was advised by Rotterdam that he was to be appointed as Marine and Land Operations Manager for SeaLand's new Liverpool operation, responsible for vessel operations, and thence operational control of land operations, equipment control, and loss prevention activity, whilst Roy Mettam was also thereto appointed to oversee and manage the Sales activity for the region and assist with the land operation as required. They also learned that an American had been appointed as Terminal Manager, re-locating from the southern State of Georgia, named Eddie Cawthorne. They were to proceed as soon as feasible to Liverpool to 'set up shop', establish accommodation (both office and home), and hire-in as soon as practically possible. John Peat would assume responsibility for SeaLand's Felixstowe marine activity having been adequately trained (and blooded!). All in all, a change in circumstances that readily conjured up the adjective 'unbelievable', or as Ankie so succinctly mouthed it in Dutch, 'ongelooflijk'!

As our friend, Antoine de Saint-Exupéry, has before pointed out, "As for the future, you have not to foresee it, but to make it possible." American comedian, Steven Wright, would perhaps have had it another way, suggesting that "if you want the rainbow, you gotta put up with the rain!" There was every chance that it could start to bucket it down, and without too much forewarning, fore arming was a scarce indulgence!

Team Perry convened, and perhaps surprisingly after all the work in making the apartment their home, Ankie accepted the situation with her usual pragmatism – what was to be, was to be. With son Duncan now approaching the ripening age of ten months however, she felt it better that John took the initiative in finding them a new home, in knowledge that decision had been taken to seek rental accommodation rather than to purchase property, both for reasons of cash availability, and Ankie's portends which seemed to border on the momentous, rather than calamitous. In essence, only seven months in Essex, and now just short of twelve months in Suffolk, with a rapidly expanding Company suggested movement rather than stagnation, with the imperative noun 'application' defined in terms of applied and sustained effort!

Meantime back in the office, something stirred. "A visitor for you, John," advised Ferrymasters, "from Liverpool, a Mister Smith." Puzzled, John greeted and seated the visitor, who then introduced himself as Reg Smith, owner of a Company that supplied the services of linesmen for berthing vessels in Liverpool, such service employment being mandatory in the maritime ethos of Liverpool. Quietly spoken and polite, he explained that on hearing of SeaLand's intention to call Liverpool, he had concluded that a visit in person to Felixstowe might be appreciated, and in absence of any guidance whatsoever from Rotterdam, the wealth of information that he was prepared and able to share was indeed hugely welcome. Now recognising business initiative when he saw it, John made the decision to contract Smith & Son there and then, a decision that was justified in the event in both the Company's competitiveness, and dependability always. Reg and his wife were to become good friends of the Perry family, although he came close to losing the business when, within the first month of operations, he posed a question to John. "What car would you like?" Sensing an embarrassing situation, he was asked to explain the intent and meaning of the question, to receive the response that it was (sadly?) customary in Liverpool to offer a gratis car to the Marine manager of whatever shipping Company was contracted. John's response was decisive. "Reg, the answer is a definitive no, and the subject is not to be raised again, in that we do not work that way. Understood?" Handshake with a relieved Reg, and subject never re-visited.

Preliminary visit to Liverpool was made in accommodation seeking mode, Southport being the defined search area, as being a mere 21 odd miles from the nascent Seaforth Container Terminal. Chosen was a ground floor apartment, one of four apartments in what was, in past years, the extensive home of a so-called 'cotton baron'. Situated in Park Avenue, it was conveniently close to the beautiful Hesketh Gardens or Park, which would provide ample walking and recreational facilities for the family, was within walking distance of local shops, and the centre of Southport with its famous shopping facilities in Lord Street. Altogether, the locality was to prove an excellent choice, but the apartment with its high-ceilinged rooms, storage heater heating, and dark corridors was a disappointment in the event, particularly during the cold winter months, when electric blankets became de rigeur! This would be John and Ankie's fourth home, and it is noteworthy that it was also the first and last time that John would be entrusted to home-hunt without Ankie, as she would later proclaim! In the nicest possible way! Something to do with the required length of curtains that she had to make, inadequate heating, and dark corridors!

Meantime, farewells to Felixstowe, to the enthusiastic and professional standards of the Port's Management and workforce, colleagues at Ferrymasters, and of course Jim Ward who would, presumably, return to the USA at some stage as yet undefined. Best wishes to John Peat for his continued success, and once again Ankie would contract with Pickfords to move the, by now, much travelled three-piece suite and coffee table (remember?) and assorted other furniture since acquired (and paid for), to Park Avenue Southport. July 1969 was proving to be a busy month!

Sealand, Liverpool

Who, within the SeaLand organisation, had made the decision to start service over Liverpool would remain unknown, or indeed with whom in the Mersey Docks and Harbour Board (MDHB) management structure? Its success, if it could be called that, would prove to be short-lived, and meantime, briefing from Rotterdam, SeaLand's European HQ, was non-existent, which suggested a lack of any operational research. De facto, the small team inducted from Felixstowe was very much having to make it up as it went along, which made life interesting. Remarkably interesting!

There was one source of information, additional to Reg Smith, available to John, namely David Campbell, MD of Scruttons, a Liverpool firm very involved in the provision of dockside and ship equipment. David and John had both been part of the three-month RNR P.38 Training Course at RNB Portsmouth, Whale Island, and so forth in 1959, both were Master Mariners, and David was known as a straight-talking, no-nonsense professional from Northern Island with little time for unwarranted Union interference. Friendship was re-invigorated, and Ankie became firm friends with Joy, David's wife. David and John would meet regularly after close of business for a pint and a chat, and much was brought to John's attention as to the state of Union play, which so often be-devilled Liverpool.

That aside momentarily, matters of office accommodation had to be addressed, with the MDHB's temporary allocation of a small disused Customs office having to suffice, whilst a purpose-built prefabricated building was put together. Furniture was required, and so John, together with Eddie Cawthorne newly arrived from Georgia, USA, took themselves to a second-hand furniture emporium in town, at the centre of which sat, spider-like, a substantially overweight Liverpudlian manager. He listened as Eddie Cawthorne listed the sought-after items, and clearly a student of accents but short of diplomacy addressed himself thus: "You're a Yank, ain't yer?" Eddie drew himself up to his full five feet six inches and responded, with deliberate emphasis on his southern drawl, "Where I come from, you could be hung for saying less than that!" leaving little doubt as to his sincerity.

Came then the matter of recruitment, and in this was considerable achievement in attracting good talent, with such notables as Mike Smethurst, Malcolm Grocott and Calum Begg, the last-mentioned of whom would eventually take over as Terminal Manager on the eventual departure of Eddie Cawthorne, and indeed progress into Felixstowe's Management structure in due course. More of that later though. The old Customs Office was becoming crowded meantime, and with the only power point behind Eddie Cawthorne's chosen position, his favoured expression of 'Hotdamn' would be heard as the morning coffee kettle boiled, and steam rose again from between his legs! Clearly, extension leads had yet to reach that neck of the woods.

With the approach of SeaLand's first vessel call (which vessel yet unknown) matters took a more serious turn. In his marine functionary role, John was telephoned by a Union Shop Steward requesting an urgent, but totally secretive, meeting after office hours, reasons to be explained at such a meeting. So unusual was the request, that cautious curiosity overcame a not unnatural suspicion, and meeting was agreed for that very evening for 1900 hours start, in the newly erected SeaLand office. Two young Shop Stewards attended and explained their mission which, in a nutshell, was to confound the aims of the Chairman of the Shop Stewards Committee who, as a card-carrying member of the Communist Party, had publicly declared his intent to close the new Seaforth Container Terminal. That done, to close the Port of Liverpool in its entirety. To this end, SeaLand's first vessel call would be targeted, and it was the fervent hope of the main body of Shop Stewards that the inaugural call was not cancelled. In turn, they would guarantee that the vessel would be worked using the Sealand chassis method, and any call for strike action would be totally ignored. This request must have been one of the finest examples of the expression 'trust me' ever expounded, particularly with the 'Mostangen' now declared and en route from Rotterdam, being due within the next twenty-four hours or so.

As the saying goes, 'experience is the name everyone gives to his or her mistakes', or to quote Steven Wright yet again, "Experience is something you don't get until just after you need it!" So, deep breath, a crossing of the fingers, and decision taken to support the promised confounding of the Senior Shop Steward, confirmed by the age-old custom of shaking hands. With fingers still crossed.

"Mostangen", a Norwegian break-bulk vessel chartered in by SeaLand, duly arrived to the Mersey, and 'locked-in' to the Seaforth Terminal. Factually, SeaLand could not have chosen a worse vessel for this, the inaugural call, although by sheer chance, and the earlier handshake, she was guaranteed. The absolute profusion of part-greased wire lashings for the container stacks in itself could well have caused a strike under normal Liverpool conditions, but apart from the occasional expletive as heads came into contact with wires, or clothing picked up grease, the agreement held, and the vessel was worked to completion, and sailed. John, however, had felt it necessary to stay with it throughout the long, cold night, and Ankie had been warned of his probable twenty-four hours absence from their (new) home. From his point of view, and indeed for Ankie too, the victory for Union democracy was of a slight Pyrrhic nature, as for the next ten days John was severely 'hors de combat', struck down and bedridden with the 'flu. Ever resourceful, Ankie now turned her hand to wider aspects of nursing not heretofore needed with child rearing, with the couple eventually sharing rueful laughter when it was all over. Actually, the day before it was all over, as she had inadvertently driven their much put-upon car onto a very low brick wall type hazard at the back of the house, forcing John to leave his sick bed to free the vehicle. Laughter, nevertheless, because that was their way.

Note to file: anyone who claims to be off work for a 'couple of days with flu' is either misguided or seeking to misguide! Proper flu don't work that way.

Ankie had by now firmly established Flat 3, 2 Park Avenue Southport as their new home, turning a challenging first aspect into a welcoming and comfortable (as far as the storage heaters would allow) living environment, and with a sandpit established by John in the back garden for Duncan and, please note, a breakfast bar designed and erected against one of the kitchen walls also by John, reacting to Ankie's thoughtful suggestion, it began to feel like a home. Hesketh Park provided excellent walking, with children's swings available for distraction, and life settled into the new routine. On Friday evenings, work allowing, John and Ankie would share a bottle of wine, or a glass or so of sherry, and Ankie turned her thoughts to entertaining friends occasionally,

David and Joy Campbell mainly, with John's mother and stepfather, Alex as occasional welcome visitors.

Although her pregnancy was proceeding without concerns, Ankie nevertheless paced herself, as the passing weeks took the year towards December, anticipated month of birth. She looked, throughout, wonderful, and certainly John never ceased to count his blessings, enabled by her thoughtfulness as he was to devote his attentions to the challenges that Liverpool continued to throw up. If Felixstowe could be rated as chalk, then Liverpool by definition became the cheese.

The differences manifested themselves in many ways, not least of all in the management/labour infrastructure where, in Felixstowe, it was demonstrably a team effort, whereas in Liverpool the perception was one of 'us' and 'them', each out to score points over the other. In Felixstowe, there would be almost daily discussion between Les Simpson and SeaLand as to where, if possible, operations could somehow be streamlined. In Liverpool, sightings of the Seaforth Terminal Manager were largely confined to his morning arrival to the Terminal in his large car. Achieving smoother methods of working in the warehouse, or in the Terminal itself also proved to be difficult, with what were reasonable requests being ofttimes declined with much tooth-sucking, or 'against the rules'. This coming within the province of the now Marine and Land Operations Manager John, meeting was arranged with more senior management within the MDHB, he who had overall responsibility for the Seaforth Terminal who, it was said, had come to this position from a West African Port, his former employment. Mists of time hide his name unfortunately, but his attitude and approach during the brief meeting was indeed evocative of such a former appointment, prompting an exasperated question for him toward meetings end. "Would it not be more beneficial for the MDHB overall if you were to recognise that you are in Liverpool in the year 1969, rather than Port Harcourt or Lagos in 1869?"

His blustered response, "You can't talk to me like that," brought the measured reply that "I already have, but equally it would appear you have no intention of taking note," which brought the meeting to a close. Ankie may well have advocated more honey and less vinegar, but somehow plain speaking seemed germane. Shortly after the meeting however, it became increasingly obvious that requests for simple working improvements were both better acknowledged and acted upon, possibly in recognition that the immigrants from Felixstowe and Georgia did know the container business, and their experience could be beneficial to nascent Seaforth. Small but important gains, in everyone's interests!

Frustrations however came not only from Port sources, but also occasionally 'in house', so to speak. Ferrymasters had an established Sales office in Liverpool, with the obvious task of generating export containerised cargo. In Mike Smethurst, Sealand had an excellent container control operative, responsible not only for the delivery of imports and collection of export containers by selected hauliers, but also careful requests for special equipment which, unsurprisingly, was often in short supply. Refrigerated containers were a prime example and Ferrymasters had been specifically informed that there were none available in Liverpool, and none were expected to be positioned in, for at least a week, hopefully from Rotterdam. It therefore came as a surprise to receive booking from sales colleague David Tyler for six 'reefers' so-called, to be positioned immediately to Cadbury, for loading. His retort on being reminded that there were no reefers available was both foolish, and unhelpful. "It's my job to book containers, and your job to provide the necessary equipment." Quite banal, bearing in mind that Cadbury was a prime customer target.

This extraordinary lack of customer focus dwelt heavily on Land Operations Manager John's mind, and there began his first interest in discovering more about the concept and application of 'Marketing' within an organisation, rather than the individual aspect of 'Sales'. A light-bulb moment one might say, and it was to lead to deeper study of the marketing concept, and eventually close involvement in its practical application. Deeper water indeed, ashore! As the Captain of HMS 'Repton' once announced 'Hands to paddle'!

Operationally, lesson had also been learned, namely, to order in special equipment such as reefers as empty stock, thus enabling pressure on Sales to 'go look for business' as Eddie Cawthorne may have phrased it. As the saying still goes, "A bird in hand is better than no bread!" Doesn't it?

With the working of 'Mostangen' it was perhaps the case that Rotterdam had learned a lesson in how best to service Liverpool, as a weekly 'feeder' call now became the norm, with such as 'Stadt Aschendorf', and a fresh addition to the scene, the 'Mar Tierra' which, as language students will immediately recognise, translated as 'Sea Land' – Liverpool dockers, less renowned for their language skills, immediately dubbed the vessel 'Hairy Martyr', which kept them amused. Vessels came and went, but there was a constant undercurrent of question as to whether, or when, the next strike would occur, for whatever reason. This sense of vulnerability was encapsulated in the music hall style of story relating to the docker who, on walking past a cargo ship on which one of his friends was working, shouted greeting, "Lovely day, mate, the daffodils are out," to receive the response, "If they're out, we're all out," and the working gang walked off the ship. Silly, but as humour is often a reflection of human behaviour, it was indeed illustrative of the tinder-box reality of Liverpool Docks. A 'Mar Tierra' arrival to the locks one week brought this home to the team inducted from Felixstowe, in that the line-handlers of Reg Smith & Son went on strike (reason unknown) such that Marine Manager John, ably assisted by Reg Smith himself and his son, plus other stalwarts from the SeaLand team, themselves handled the vessel's lines through the lock and to the berth, and again for her eventual departure. Fortunately, this did not prompt the dockers to strike in sympathy, but it could well have happened.

The weeks were passing quickly, with Christmas just a few weeks away, and the thoughts of Ankie and John naturally became more focussed on the birth of their second child. Any suggestion from friends as to a possible home birth were rejected out of hand, with Southport's Maternity Hospital very much in the frame. Arrangements were also agreed with Ankie's mother that she would travel to Liverpool from Amsterdam as soon as the birth was confirmed, a most welcome addition to the nursing team, and her chance to see grandson Duncan again, his second birthday having been royally celebrated with friends in Southport in September. Whether he was to have a sister, or a brother would soon, if December was the time, be revealed.

Meantime though, another challenge for Husband John, totally unexpected and out of the blue. Well, out of the black, being a Sunday night, and as midnight heralded in another day, so came a telephone call from Anglesey Radio, patching through a link call from the Captain of 'Stadt Aschendorf', due to arrive in Liverpool sometime early Monday morning. "I have about seven hours steaming to Liverpool," he began, "but have only sufficient fuel for about two hours steaming. What shall I do?" As a Master Mariner, John's first thought was how on earth could such a situation have been allowed to develop, but as that solved nothing, more productive thinking was required which, on questioning the Captain briefly, established the vessel's position as north of Land's End, on course for the St Georges Channel. "Captain, I want you to make course for Milford Haven, and meantime, guard this channel, and I will revert shortly with details and instructions." Anglesey Radio very thoughtfully offered to put John through to Milford Haven, and with arrangements put in place for the authorities there to bunker the vessel, the Captain was given his final instructions, and told to telephone when bunkering completed. By now, it was well past 0100 hours, but call was put through to Nicko van den Heuvel, European Marine Manager in Rotterdam, to advise status. "You must get down to Milford Haven straight away," came his response, and despite John's reassurance that all was in hand, and his protests that it was close to a three-hundred-mile drive, Nicko insisted. Ankie, hearing the way the conversation was going, and ever thoughtful, prepared a cup of tea, and a pack of sandwiches for the journey. At about 0600 hours, still with many miles to go, John found a red telephone box and 'phoned Milford Haven. "Bunkering completed an hour ago," came the welcome news, "and can we sail the vessel?" Too many hours later, Ankie once again helped husband to bed for a few short hours, before back to the office, and Stadt Aschendorf's arrival bearing embarrassed Captain. No explanation was ever received and, moreover, John's mileage claim was questioned, with the query, "Who on earth would have a reason to drive all that distance on a Sunday night?" Under the circumstances, would that warrant a vinegar, or a honey response? Honey, through gritted teeth!

December turned out to be a blur of activity, with Christmas to celebrate, and with anxious thoughts of pending childbirth increasingly occupying minds. Fortunately, no question of vessels working over Christmas, this being Liverpool, and none scheduled, so John was enabled to focus entirely to matter of watchful attendance on Ankie and, as it transpired, transport to the Maternity Hospital late in the day of December 29th. Ankie, prescient as always, had called her mother forward from Amsterdam a few days before so she had arrived per Dan Air to Liverpool Airport in good time to care for Duncan, come the event. Ankie, of course, was cool, calm, and collected throughout, and during the late morning of December 30th, in the year 1969, gave birth to a healthy son, who weighed in at 8lbs and 4 oz. John, as before in full attendance for, and assisting in, the birth marvelled yet again at her calm concentration (with just her occasional admission to some pain!) as they locked eyes and exchanged smiles at final delivery. She was, as always, wonderful, and source of immense pride to John.

Thankfully, there was no offer of fish and chips from this hospital post the birth, and no Wardroom prize of a (small) box of champagne to afford, but champagne there was on Ankie's return home with newly named son Darren, their so-called 'nuclear' family now joyfully complete, a celebratory finale to a challenging and eventful year. Per ardua ad astra, and never (remember?) in the subjunctive tense!

The New Year of 1970 crept in quietly, in the sense that there were no obvious signs of alarums or unnecessary excursions, and Dutch became almost the language of Flat 3, 2 Park Avenue as Ankie, and her mother, Aleijda, happily combined in matter of child-care, to include the introduction of Duncan to his new brother which, it was noted with relief, went well.

Sadly, Ankie's mother had to return to Amsterdam after a couple of weeks, but Tante (Aunt) Roos and her cheerful husband, Theunis, came over to stay, and of course, John's mother and stepfather, Alex, made as regular as possible appearances, at which times the English language prevailed.

There was, of course, the matter of having Darren christened, and this was achieved at the local Church, with Joy Campbell gladly accepting the role of godmother. The presiding Cleric alarmed somewhat by partially dipping the head of the child in the font's blessed water (no vodka additive this time), but all went well, although no one actually asked Darren how he had felt about it!

As the weather further improved, visits to Southport's seaside became routine, albeit that at low water, the sea could scarcely be seen, so far had it receded from the shore, a well-known Southport phenomenon. Duncan started at Kindergarten, or Fröbelschool in Dutch, although as Ankie and John agreed, his having to wear a tie at the tender age of just over two years seemed just 'too, too English'. The unpopular dark corridor at home became, as Darren gathered strength, their racetrack as Duncan pushed a laughing Darren at speed up and down in a wheeled baby chair, the sand pit now held two, and all was well on the home front. As a sign of increasing domesticity, some items of 'G-Plan' furniture were purchased, and low-key entertainment of friends and relations taken more seriously. Nothing too abrupt though, as broken biscuits were still purchased, as opposed to packets!

1970 turned out to be a year of consolidation, in the business and family contexts, as well as in friendships forged with colleagues or associated enterprises. In the family sense, visitors from both the Dutch and English families were made as welcome as budgets would allow (no broken biscuits or

British sherry – yes, it did exist) for them, and Ankie quickly developed into a hostess, with occasional dinners for guests, of consummate grace and good humour, an ability that she would develop and expand upon as geographical and business interests changed in later years.

As Duncan moved toward his third birthday, and Darren his first, there was much to teach them for both Ankie and John, and every advantage was taken to explore and experience the seaside and countryside or walk and besport within the pleasant and peaceful surrounds of Hesketh Park, their adjacent neighbour. Duncan, of course, continued to wear his tie to the Kindergarten.

In business terms, the year would pass without any strike action in the Port, or at least none that would affect SeaLand., and the feeder vessels continued to move between Rotterdam and Liverpool more or less on a regular schedule. Notably, the 864 nautical miles between the two Ports would occasionally experience weather that lengthened the minimum of 7.5 days round-trip (glossing over the occasional fuel shortage factor!), assuming a 12-knot vessel speed, and 1.5 days combined Port time per voyage. Marine and Ops Manager John would ponder just how long the service could be reasonably sustained, although without definitive information as to vessel costs, or indeed Terminal costs (surprisingly, Terminal costs and budgets were not part of his remit, being that of the Terminal Manager, nor was he invited to be involved) it was impossible to evaluate. Lines' secretive Conference agreements may also have had influence. Road infrastructure also, whilst being developed fast, brought little comfortable or cost-effective connection between what was the Liverpool sales coverage area and Felixstowe, were the sea connection to be discontinued. Nevertheless, he was pessimistic as to the service longevity, which brought him consequent concerns as to the future. Notwithstanding, the service as was had to be managed, and in that he remained convinced 'that the only alternative to perseverance is – failure!', and that could not be allowed to happen.

With memories of the refrigerated container debacle still fresh in his mind, he also came to the studied conclusion that he agreed an offered definition that 'selling concentrates on the need of the producer (in this case Ferrymasters as booking Agent) whilst marketing on the needs of the consumer, or customer'. In essence, it posed the question as to whether dependency on a Sales Agent was potentially detrimental to the Principal's best interests, although beneficial to the booking Agent. Not his 'part of ship' as it happened, but a clear start to a learning curve that was, in due course, to try to fully embrace the philosophy of Marketing. Not all roads lead to Damascus, but the one from Liverpool certainly did, metaphorically speaking! These ruminations he would share with Ankie, and was encouraged so to do, she contributing where possible, agreeing particularly with the undesirable consequence of a failure in perseverance. Work in progress!

In many ways, it was also a dull year, in marked contrast to the heady challenge of Felixstowe's growth and success, or indeed the challenge of getting to grips with the perceived anachronisms seen in Liverpool and means to confront the Port with modern reality, during the previous year. The last-mentioned would continue as appropriate, with hope as always springing eternal.

Being driven into, one dark winters morning at 0600 hours, on a roundabout close to home, came as an unwelcome surprise, driver of the offending vehicle busily talking to his female companion as he barrelled onto the roundabout. "Don't you dare call me at home," he fumed. "Contact my Insurance Company," this in response to a telephone call the following day seeking payment for damage of some £200. "Actually," John responded, "my claim is against you, although it is your prerogative to claim against your Insurance Company, although your wife (heavily emphasised) with you at the time could scarcely support your claim." There was a pause of some moments, followed by, in angry tone, his agreement to put a cheque in the post, which he indeed did. A little knowledge, as it turned out, is not always a dangerous thing, depending on which end of the stick one is holding!

A September third birthday for Duncan, Christmas, and a first birthday for Darren at the close of December. Three noisy, joyful events to bring the year to a close, with the New Year ushered in by John and Ankie quietly toasting each other and pondering together just what 1971 would bring in terms of fresh challenges or opportunities.

The first quarter, as always marred by January and February's darkness and dismal weather, otherwise passed quietly enough, with Spring in the offing waiting to be greeted. However, on or about Monday April 14th, John was summoned to Rotterdam, there to meet with Kalafatides for reasons unexplained. Ominous? Perhaps, and with some trepidation, he arrived there on Wednesday, as required. Kal, as he preferred to be addressed, explained that Rotterdam was also the centre at which management of the so-called 'Loss

Prevention and Claims' activity for SeaLand's North European operations was situated, and he was dissatisfied as to its current management and therefore performance. In essence, he had concluded that someone with sound operational experience was best suited to head up this activity, and with John's considerable marine and operations aptitude, expected him to accept the offered position. He would be responsible for setting up/auditing loss prevention systems throughout the region, with particular focus on all high value goods such as refrigerated (chill and frozen) cargo, wines and spirits, tobacco, as well as anti-theft procedures pertaining to such as container seal records. Damage control systems for containers and chassis, and management of the Claims and Costs Recovery team. His remit would cover France, Holland, Belgium, Germany, Scandinavia, and the UK.

The unexpected surprise was complete, and with offered salary and some other benefits to ponder briefly, the matter was deemed by Kal to be finalised, and bade John to spend a day meeting with and chatting to other Rotterdam management. This included introduction to Rupe Hickler, who appeared to be in overall control of North Europe operations, and welcoming greetings from Nicko van den Heuvel, European Marine Manager, and close recent colleague. Further, a Dutch American brought in from the States as a temporary stopgap who clearly thought highly of himself, and disparagingly of his country of origin and its indigenous population, referring to them as 'these Dutchies' and in so doing endearing himself to nobody. Return to Liverpool was made Thursday April 15th, to discover that Eddie Cawthorne was already aware of the probable loss of his marine and land Manager, and had appropriate promotion and re-organisation plans to hand. That left the weekend of April 17th and 18th for Team Perry to reconvene for deep discussions and conclusions, with John due back in Rotterdam for a week commencing Monday April 19th, for acclimatisation and further meetings, during which Kal would be in meetings with his immediate superior Gene Black, in the United States Head Office, Menlo Park. Surprisingly, news of what appeared to be a 'fait accompli' was received by Ankie with less than full enthusiasm, but during the weekend discussions, she had clearly accepted and welcomed the imperative, focussing clearly on the upcoming logistical upheaval, with a start date of June 1st. having been required by Kalafatides. There was, however, a brief but worrying 'hiccup' to be overcome, with John's return to Rotterdam Monday April 19th, and planned working week there. The water was about to get deeper!

Back in Rotterdam as required, and with time now to address details, came evaluation and knowledge of the cost of living in Holland compared with the UK (higher), and having obtained from the then Personnel Manager Wim Kok an unexpurgated copy of SeaLand's expatriate benefits policy, message was addressed to Kalafatides in the United States, visiting Menlo Park.

"Am now in a better position to research living costs, and costs associated with setting up home in Holland, and in that almost none of the housing benefits offered to my American fellow expatriates have been offered to me, have been forced to the unexpected and regrettable conclusion that to accept the position as offered would bring a net salary well below that currently enjoyed in the UK, and therefore cannot reasonably accept, and returning to Liverpool accordingly." By Thursday, April 24th, John was back in Liverpool, essentially in employment limbo. On Friday 25th, brief response from Kalafatides – "You will be in my office in Rotterdam 9 a.m. Monday." Ankie's parting words as John left in the early hours of Monday, April 26th for the airport were clear, and lovingly put, "Remember, Darling, honey rather than vinegar." Work in progress, indeed.

Atmosphere in Rotterdam office that morning was distinctly tense, and the meeting with Kal equally so from John's point of view. Kal started, repeatedly hitting his forehead with his stiffened forefinger, as he forcefully addressed his would-be appointee. "You got me right between the f…ing eyes," he exploded, and continued in similar vein, laced with expletives, as he outlined the embarrassment the message of Wednesday, April 20th had caused him. Diplomacy now being the watchword, John responded with deep apology and obvious contrition, confirming that the position as offered was clearly a result of strategic thinking, but with wife and now two children to support, he had been alarmed by the financial implications, possibly misunderstood? The office walls ceased to reverberate, and a renewed offer was presented for the to-be expatriate UK employee, for the function of European Loss Prevention and Claims Manager, and gratefully accepted. De facto, and as the first 'European' to be re-located to an expatriated appointment, benefits as afforded to American expats would now be offered to European and UK expats too. Theoretically anyway. It was a beginning. Alternatively, it could turn out to be self-inflicted wound, as in shooting oneself in the foot! Only time would tell.

April 17th, and once more back to Southport, with a successful Rotterdam visit to report to Ankie (hugs and kisses), but also realisation that there remained but a month to organise the closing of their Southport home, the finding of a home in Holland, despatch of household goods thereto, not to mention the family relocation. In matter of the home location in Holland, it had been learned when in Rotterdam that although almost all of the American expats lived in Wassenaar, close to Scheveningen (which they couldn't pronounce!), some 35 km from the Rotterdam office, two senior Managers in the Finance Section Mike Morris (American) and Wayne Edworthy (Canadian) and their families had located to the very pleasant village of Oud Beijerland, some 24 km from the office, and had recommended it highly. Interestingly, Wassenaar was a tiny village until the railway connecting Rotterdam and The Hague was completed in 1907, at which time it developed into 'an attractive residential area for wealthy people from Rotterdam' as it was described, and possibly still remains attractively pleasant for the wealthy. It was also learned that Wassenaar was referred to by SeaLand's Dutch employees, somewhat disparagingly, as the 'American Ghetto'. Ankie agreed that Oud Beijerland appeared to be their best target area, with appropriate emphasis on suggestion that she would like the final approval to be hers! Shades of long dark corridors and fourteen-foot curtains! It was also agreed that a rental property would be sought, being usually more readily available than houses to buy, in the Dutch housing environment.

To achieve some of this, physical assistance was sought from both the Dutch and English grandparents to look after offspring, to enable Ankie and John to visit Oud Beijerland alone, to the excellent conclusion that they were able to rent a new-built house with both the Morris and Edworthy families as close neighbours. It proved to be a haven of friendship, camaraderie, laughter, and entertainment, as their Dutch neighbours were also to make the Perry family most welcome, Ankie's nationality and personality clearly making that easier. All that remained, with just a couple of weeks left, was to pack up the furniture, say their farewells to colleagues and friends, and take the North Sea ferry from Hull to Holland. Goodbye to Park Avenue Southport, and hello to Jeroen Bosch Straat, Oud Beijerland.

With more or less a week to ten days to spare, John finalised his leaving from the Liverpool Office, and the family departed Southport, to arrive Oud Beijerland just before the last week in May 1971.

Whilst unknown to John at that time, SeaLand was to roll up its tent and leave Liverpool some four or five months later and move to the small Port of

Preston, that move too lasting for a relatively short time. Obviously timing of this departure must have been known to SeaLand's hierarchy in Rotterdam at time of John's promotion offer. Coincidental, or part of strategic planning? Notwithstanding, in the matter of leaving Liverpool, some sense had prevailed, be that common, practical, or financial, or combination of all three.

With but a week to go before starting work, John assisted where possible as Ankie set to the task of turning the house into their home in her usual, and by now accomplished, fashion, rejoicing as she did so in fact that for the first time in their married life, they now had gas central heating which, after the jaded storage heaters so recently relinquished, was seen and felt as unparalleled luxury! A sandpit was constructed for the offspring in the small back garden, and grass seed put down on the very small patch of earth in the front of the house, noticing the while that the Morris family on the other side of the square and put down turf. Cheerful curtains appeared in the (standard size) windows, purchase assisted by recent illumination of re-location allowances! It was, in so many ways, a new beginning, as life in the European Head Office would also prove to be, come June 1st.

As soon as age permitted, both Duncan and Darren would start attending the local Fröbelschool or Kindergarten, and whilst it became the rule that English would be the language of the home, both boys would quickly become competent in the Dutch language far quicker that their father John who would, in his turn, attend weekly evening classes as he sought to master the language, in part at least. Amusingly, one of the first things that he asked his secretary Miriam Tiebout, having attended a few such classes, was that they spoke in Dutch for a short period each day, to which she replied that she did not think there was sufficient time to accommodate to that! Naturally, her English was perfect.

Bicycle was acquired for Ankie, and the boys in time as befitted their age and size, in knowledge that cycling was a national pastime in Holland, cyclists seemingly having right of way over everything, albeit that Duncan was to find that to not always be the case, being knocked off his bike by a car on one occasion when venturing briefly on to the road adjacent to their home, thankfully an ultra-slow incident with no injuries or damage. Unsurprisingly, their home had a purpose-built bicycle shed! Come the winter months, they would also acquire ice-skates, being thus enabled to join in the skating that also appeared to be part of the Dutch way of life. It could not have been a better start to their time in Holland, such that John could get to grips with his new appointment, in the safe knowledge that all was well with family and home.

Sealand Rotterdam, European Head Office, Striendwaalseweg

The office, situated close-by the village of Pernis, was also home to those processing SeaLand's Dutch export and import containers, as well as containers transhipped from other Terminals, such as Liverpool. Those involved in vessel activities were, naturally, situated on the container Terminal, their activity being led by the Marine Manager, Wim de Boer who, by coincidence also lived in Oud Beijerland, or nearby. Operations Manager Wim van Laar also spent most of his time on the Terminal, famously on one occasion taking over the controls of a container crane, attempting to forcibly dislodge a container jammed in the guide rails of a vessel, using brute force of craneage! Unconfirmed rumour had it that a recent intake of Jenever, or Dutch gin, had inspired and driven this display of, should it be said, Dutch Courage, but suffice it to say that it worked, without operational hiccup!

It was, though, to the Head Office building that the newly appointed LP&C Manager came that June morning, there to meet again his small team that handled cargo claims, (Jan Keizer), equipment claims, (Bert Eelsing) and Secretary Miriam Tiebout. Further, to be more formally introduced to Rupe Hickler, overall responsible for North European operations, Sales Manager for the US Gulf/N. Europe trade-lane Jack Sutherland, and Sales Manager for the Atlantic Division Richie Parks. Strangely, it was never defined as to whom he, John, should directly report in Europe, although he was to learn that the US Vice-President for LP&C was one Gene Spitz, who he would meet but once, during a future visit to the US head Office in Menlo Park, New Jersey. Once again, it seemed to be a 'make it up as you go along' assignment, not unlike Liverpool, or indeed Felixstowe. That said, Hickler did promulgate throughout the N. European area that each operational Terminal would be visited by the new LP&C Manager, to audit/assess all 'Loss Prevention' functions and systems to ensure uniform conformity throughout. Air travel was about to become almost second nature.

Other notable American expats were Ron Gabbert, Don Hamm, and W Thurber the 2nd (or was it the 3rd) each with Sales responsibilities in assigned areas of Europe, and with all the Sales oriented Americans bar one, good social and working relationships would be established, the latter in particular respect of customer focus should claims, as example, potentially impact on customer relations. Regarding the former, on occasions such as American Independence Day (Independence granted by the UK as moved by John or wrestled from the UK as believed by the Americans!) much banter and badinage would ensue, occasionally helped by a beer with a small glass of Jenever as chaser, taken together at a cheery bar in the nearby village of Pernis. After work, of course.

Where to begin though, on that first day? It was noticeable that the team morale was very low, probably not helped at all by the Dutch American sent as temporary stand-in as LP&C Manager, he who chose to refer to the indigenous of his country of origin as 'stupid Dutchies'. Eelsing seemed to be in fear of imminent dismissal, whilst Keizer was quiet and withdrawn, with only Tiebout displaying any cheerfulness. This prompted heart to heart discussions, with reassurances that their work was both necessary and important to overall Corporate aspirations, and that as a team, daily review of concerns or difficulties would become the norm. This in turn brought to light files that had been neglected for want of decisions and need to establish a running inventory of both active and completed files, open for review by other Departments as and when necessary. It was a start, and there came an early indication, within the first couple of weeks, as to why that boost to morale was both necessary, and appropriate.

It came in the shape of salesman WT2nd., who stalked into John's office unannounced, throwing as he did a file onto the desk, stating in a loud and aggressive voice that all in the vicinity could hear, "Cancel this claim, it involves one of my customers," and so saying left the room to return to his own office. Expectant silence from team desks outside of goldfish bowl office, and clear 'how will he handle this one' looks of expectancy from team members. There was no choice. Retrieving thrown file from his desk, slow walk was taken to the office of WT2nd. where, having first carefully closed the door, John gave his response. In essence, it berated both the manner, and manners of WT2nd, directed that such an arrogant display should, nor would, ever be repeated, and established that should there be need to discuss a claim, there must be pre-advised reason, at which meeting would be convened to so discuss. Further, that the claim in reference would be processed in the normal way. Finally, he enquired as to whether he had made himself perfectly clear, and as there was no response, back to work. No further discussion was sought then, or thereafter, so matter closed. As the Naval expression has it 'brass rags had been parted', finally as it turned out. The winner? No one really, but within the context of marketing versus sales, a failure of marketing purpose, which is not to resolve every issue in favour of the customer regardless of cost, but rather to help other Management to see that customers are the foundation of the company's business. Perception was therefore that WT2nd was a salesman, not a marketeer. In the event, the file was routinely reviewed, with compromise made to the customer's satisfaction. At the same time, John explained that it was a clear indicator to the claims team that their work played an important part in matter of customer focus, so necessary within the marketing umbrella of associated activities.

Meanwhile, and back in Oud Beijerland, the twenty-four km car ride between home and office now an easy routine, Ankie and John were making firm friends with the Morris and Edworthy families, with exchanges of invitations to barbecues, or otherwise dining at each other's homes. Barbecues and sun-bathing turned out to be other examples of the Dutch way of life, and oh, so easy to adopt. Sadly, purchase of a barbecue was not part of the re-location package, but undeterred, one was purchased.

Final part of the route home from the office also proved to be entertaining, as approach to Jeroen Boschstraat was along a dyke, part way along of which was a very cheery, old fashioned skittles alley, contained within a cheery, old-fashioned bar with a welcoming host, and it was not unknown for John, Mike, and Wayne to meet there, just for thirty minutes or so, before home going. Invitations from Dutch neighbours were also received, although the first one accepted by John and Ankie started off with coffee and cakes for the first hour, leading them to believe that their hosts were teetotal at least. None of it! It was the Dutch way, and once the coffee and cakes hour were done, the party developed to the point that they were glad that they only had a few feet (sorry, metres) to walk home at 0100 in the morning. Wonderful people. On another occasion, the hosts were celebrating the birth of their first child, a son, and this too became bibulous, with Hans the father repeatedly expressing himself astonished at his son's size, or so John assumed, as Ankie smiled broadly. "Welke een zak," he repeated, "welke een zak!" Ankie would later translate, as John had yet to start his Dutch language evening classes.

The village main street was also quite breath-taking, the old-fashioned Stadhuis, or Townhall, with the river flowing beneath, beautifully captured by

Anton Pieck in painting bought by Ankie. So too the village inn, the Oude Hoorn, another example of old Dutch architecture, the owner gracious in his grumpy, old-fashioned way once he had accepted a stranger's patronage. Contentment reigned!

An interesting request, and therefore opportunity, was received, asking if, in his capacity as LP&C Manager, John would address a group of London underwriters as to the mysteries of containerisation, and the invitation was readily accepted. A visit to London would also bring about meeting with the insurance agent for SeaLand equipment, be that containers or chassis, with concerns raised by Eelsing relative to their tardy responses to legitimate damage claims. Review of the files enabled a measured suggestion at the meeting that reasons for declining the claims could well bring about a perception of 'sharp practice' on their part which, whilst denied, brought about their review, and eventual payment of the claims.

The underwriters gathering was well attended, and clearly there was a lack of operational knowledge relative to containerisation, which John was professionally qualified to address. Questions came as to marine activity and loading/discharging to draft and stability requirements were discussed, as were the means of lashing or securing deck containers, stowage of open-top and refrigerated containers, and preparation/presentation of stowage plans. Also, explanation regarding seal records, careful noting of reefer containers temperature records, occasional need to use probe thermometers for particular reefer cargos, and container/chassis condition checks on receipt and despatch at SeaLand Terminals. The session was well received, and hopefully brought some clarity to an audience that had been more accustomed to the carriage by sea of break-bulk cargoes. Closing suggestion to the group that subjects of possible claim were neatly housed in a container, therefore making their involvement more easily defined, brought only rueful smiles!

Visits to all operational Terminals were indeed initiated, with appropriate systems audit, and these brought about meeting with several delightful characters, clearly dedicated to ensuring SeaLand's operational success. None more so than Dieter Schroer in Germany, and Jacques Poussier in France, both of whom would reap high benefits from their professional reputations. Schroer, sadly, had a total fear of flying, aerophobia (which neatly translates as aerophobie in German, Dutch, and French), which particular phobia (phobie) he would confess to overcome pre-flight by drinking a substantial slug of whisky, about a quarter of a bottle. Fortunately, his phobie was stronger than his liking for whisky, so flights were avoided wherever possible. Jacques, as a true Frenchman, harboured a horror of anyone that would continue to drink wine once coffee had been served, as John found to his embarrassment during a dinner together in Le Havre. Zut alors, John!

These visits aside, and after the full-on marine activity of Felixstowe, or marine and land operations, and oft-times frustrations, of Liverpool, the pace and substance relative to the Rotterdam appointment seemed to be positively pedestrian, which in turn brought self-doubt as to whether the function of European LP&C Manager, once systems and routines were firmly established, could be seen, or judged as a sinecure. Supervision of delegated responsibilities, as in all functions, was in place, so no challenge of responsibility abdication could be made, but that involved no overtime! In this, some comfort was found in the words of Calvin Coolidge, President of the United States, 1923–1929.

"Nothing in this world can take the place of persistence. Talent will not; nothing is more common than unsuccessful men with talent. Genius will not; unrewarded genius is almost a proverb. Education will not; the world is full of educated derelicts. Persistence and determination alone are omnipotent. The slogan 'Press On' has solved and always will solve the problems of the human race." Worth a try!

So, onward, and hopefully upward, as Ankie was again to agree, on John's return home to Jeroen Boschstraat from London, to this their fifth home in just over four years since their marriage, and certainly the best home to date. Something worth working for, even at a pedestrian pace! Duncan coming up to the first birthday he will enjoy in Holland in September, his fourth, and much to be seen and enjoyed at weekends and holiday times. Ankie's brother, Jan, and sisters, Nel, Thea, and Joke, together with their husbands, Hille, Paul and Ron, all to visit or be visited, with Darren's second birthday in December, his first in Holland. Much to look forward to, not to forget Fröbelschool for the two boys, and Dutch language lessons for Dad, the first of which having been somewhat disconcerting. From his booth, he could see the tutor, and having no idea what he was supposed to do, attracted the tutor's attention by waving his arms at him. "Ya, meneer?" questioned the tutor, to receive the response, "This is my first evening here, so what am I supposed to do?" The answer was clear and precise. "This is the only time I shall speak English," stated the tutor, "so you must speak Dutch. Look at your books!" And that was that. Total immersion, or some such.

Eventually, first meeting with Gene Spitz, Vice-President LP&C, was to be achieved, with gathering of all regional LP&C Managers called for in Menlo Park, New Jersey, with the requirement that each be ready to make a short presentation to enlighten all present as to that individual's geographical area of coverage and responsibility. Flight from Schiphol Airport booked, and with fond farewells to family, first visit to the United States in a business capacity embarked upon. It would prove to be the first of many, as time would tell. Factually, anticipation generated by the meeting invitation was disappointed in the event, with little to make the trip useful, or indeed memorable, save possibly the presentation by the Japanese attendee who, perhaps predictably, had made a photo slide presentation, which he proudly commenced to click through. Somehow though, someone (probably his American Line Manager judging by his consequent behaviour) had slipped a rogue slide into the set, with LP&C San (name lost in time mists) loudly protesting his innocence as the very naked female appeared on screen. It was not a clever diversion however, as the 'loss of face' factor quickly evidenced. The second contribution to less than positive memories was advice from Gene Spitz that the European LP&C Manager's hotel room had been elected for a session of card playing, with the consequent press of attendees emptying the mini-bar and ordering fresh stocks as thirsts demanded. Consequent payment of his Hotel Bill was eventually expensed back in Rotterdam, thus completing Europe's contribution to that particular evening's entertainment. The Perry conclusion as to the overall benefits that accrued from the visit to Menlo Park was not requested, which was probably fortunate, as it would have been derogatory! Or, to borrow yet again from Steven Wright, "A conclusion is the place when you get tired of thinking." Quite so! Party pooper? Perhaps.

Back home in Oud Beijerland Holland, a weekend of relaxation with the family and friends, although sometimes weekends offered other entertainment, in the form of the Schiedam Hockey Club. No, not playing hockey, but rather cricket, as many Dutch Hockey Clubs would turn to playing cricket during the summer months. Indeed, each year, a Dutch team would play against the MCC in England. Ankie, learning that John had captained the Schiedam Second Eleven to a recent victory, chose to attend the next home game, and indeed quickly acquainted herself with the score book's intricacies during the innings of the opposing team, preparing herself to faithfully record John's batting score in due course. He strode to the wicket as due course arrived, watched carefully by Ankie as she sat, pencil in hand, for his promised attack on the bowling. Puzzled, she watched further as, after the first ball, John strode back from the wicket having faced, and missed said first ball, to be out for the proverbial 'duck'! "What happens now, darling?" she asked quietly, to receive the response, "I shall probably sulk for the rest of the day," followed by a rueful grin. Happy, sunlit days with laughter.

Daily office attendance became too routine, with just the occasional minor triumph for the claims team to celebrate, if only to prove that systems now in place were both necessary and working. It took but a few weeks to pick up the claimant seeking redress against water damage to his container of rice, in that he was moving the container, albeit as a paper exercise, between European locations, and lodging claim at each 'arrival' point. Sad, but true. In matter of 'special equipment' however, namely refrigerated or reefer containers, business was brisk with much to occupy the mind. The importation of containerised horsemeat into both Holland and Belgium from the United States was flourishing, as were mounting claims against 'damage due failure to maintain correct temperature'. All came via Rotterdam. As in the carriage of many refrigerated foodstuffs, a chilled product would achieve a higher selling price than it would if frozen, and this was certainly the case with horsemeat, all of which was shipped chilled. Claim investigation would invariably tell a clear story that the container had maintained the correct temperature throughout voyage from Texas, prompting the exasperated but unlikely equine observation by John that, "They must be driving the bloody horses into the containers on the hoof." This observation was subsequently offered in humoured question form to a group of Texan horsemeat shippers, all of whom boasted large cowboy hats in that Dutch winter, who failed to understand the humour, and consequently strongly denied the 'on the hoof' reference. The situation also begged the question as to whether the receiving Terminal in the States had taken receipt temperatures of product with a probe thermometer, which should have been standard practice, but came there no definitive response overall. Some yes, some no, and some maybe. Notwithstanding, there came some improvement, so at least something was achieved.

Evening classes in the Dutch language continued weekly, and whilst Miss Tiebout had ruled out practice in the office, added to which all the Dutch employees spoke immaculate English, John's improved grasp of the language would serve him well in the, then, unforeseen future. Both sons however were gaining fluency, to the degree that children of that age have fluency in any language, as a function of exposure to Dutch children of their own age, and their 'Dutch mother', as they would increasingly, and lovingly, refer to Ankie.

As time moved on, retrospective analysis came to show that between John's arrival to Rotterdam from Liverpool, and Christmas of 1971, the SeaLand operation in Liverpool would cease, and move to the little-known Port of Preston, where it would survive for a relatively short time before total abandonment of service to the west coast of the UK. Retrospectively speaking, it also showed that this Service closure would pass totally unremarked in the Rotterdam office, with no general promulgation of the change. This spoke poorly for Corporate communication skills, or lack of them (perhaps deliberately in this case) possibly due in part to the churn of Management change that deadened communication, the word 'churn' being well applicable to SeaLand in matter of personnel. This perceived Corporate fault would continue to manifest itself with further Service start-ups to the Middle East, and thereafter India, throughout those regions where Rotterdam, or acolyte regional offices of Genoa or Dubai, had operational control. Management churn would only intensify, and in any marketing environment, regardless of product, good communication is, or should be, paramount! It was not!

As Christmas approached, unexpected gesture of 'Good Will' arrived, in reefers from the States, containing sufficient large and frozen butter-ball turkeys for all Rotterdam staff, but sadly it had not been recognised that very few Dutch homes had ovens of a size to cook such an offering which, if nothing else, suggested a lack of market research. Or, perhaps, poor communication? Fortunately, John and Ankie had brought their cooker from the UK, which served them well.

With 1971 birthdays for off-spring, and Christmas all enjoyed en famille, social life in 1972 Oud Beijerland progressed apace, with friendships there formed further cemented and enjoyed, with just the occasional dramas. Some came with the winter's ice skating, yet another pastime eagerly embraced by the Dutch as their canals froze over. It was not unusual to see someone, usually male, at speed on Oud Beijerland's narrow canals with hands clasped behind the back, to suddenly pitch head-first through the ice that was not quite thick enough. Dramatic for the skater, and cause for relieved laughter by the observer as the dampened skater resumed his exercise. As a Nation however, the big one was the Elfstadentocht (eleven towns expedition or journey), the 200 km canal race through eleven towns in Friesland over natural, and thick, ice. Not unnaturally, that required extremely low temperatures, not achieved since 1963 with minus 7.7°C, and would not occur again until 1985. However, as an ever resilient and 'can-do' Nation, the Dutch introduced the Fietselfstadentocht (bicycle eleven towns expedition) held every year on Whit Sunday since 1947, a bicycle race through virtually the same Friesian towns, but staying strictly on the roads! Entries limited to 15,000 cyclists! Students of the Dutch language will note that for ease of learning, the name given to the race is compressed into just one, easily pronounced, word.

Daily attendance to the office in Striendwaalseweg was only occasionally diluted by journeys to London or operational Terminals, but in itself was a cheerful enough environment with its admix of nationalities comprising mostly Dutch, several Americans depending on the churn factor, one British, and Rudi Baumkotter the one German, an ever-cheerful Engineer. It was seen as surprising that so few other Europeans were brought into the Head Office, or rather that Operational and Sales Management functions were not distributed to a greater extent to SeaLand employed Europeans within their own regions, rather than bringing over American expats to Europe at great expense in both salary and relocation cost terms. As much as anything, it was probably like the adage of engineers reluctant to engage in routine maintenance, on the basis that 'if it ain't broke, don't fix it'. Scarcely a formula for progressive innovation, and certainly not in terms of overall marketing.

1972 would, therefore, pass without major incident or upset within the confines of the European LP&C Manager's function, although he became increasingly concerned as to the pedestrian pace of work with consequent concerns as to whether he was missing something. On the other hand, and as son Duncan approached his fifth birthday in September, John and Ankie had to address the matter of further schooling for him, be that a Dutch or English education, the latter only fully available at the English School in The Hague. Experience to date with SeaLand deemed it wiser to focus on the English School, with little historical evidence to suggest that John's future was to remain in Holland, however, overall attractive that may have seemed. In turn, that posed the question of, wait for it, a possible home move to be closer to the school, and in time for the start of School Term in early January 1973. Again,

Ankie's pragmatism switched in, pointing out that within the Dutch housing system this would only entail finalising the current rental, and finding another property of similar size to rent close to the school. With the combination of maps, local advice, Dutch family input and several weekend car journeys, Rijswijk became the area of choice, being finally narrowed down to almost the clone of the Oud Beijerland home, in Doctor H.J. van Mooklaan 101, and in late 1972, move was made into family home number six, and no prizes given for guessing who made the re-location move arrangements! Indeed, none other than Ankie, by now well-seasoned in such things. Farewells were made with their Dutch friends in Oud Beijerland with appropriate refreshments taken, and sad farewells to their home there, and the village that had so many attractions, not forgetting the old-fashioned Bar on the homeward dyke, with its cheery welcoming host!

Curtains and pictures to re-hang, and in matter of pictures or anything that had to be attached to a wall, many Dutch homes were erected using prefabricated concrete walls, so purchase of an electric hammer-drill was mandatory, or no picture hanging. Further reference to this important purchase will be made later. Curtains too seemed but a decorative item in the Dutch home ethos, as they were invariably left open at night, being not a function of laziness, but rather pride in their homes. Christmas would be celebrated here, and son Darren's third birthday, so a cheerful beginning in their latest home, yet again with central heating!

Both Duncan and Darren would attend the, then, English School in The Hague, obviously at different scholastic levels, with the School accepting pupils between the ages of three and 18 years old, and it would not be until 1976 that it was renamed The British School. Interestingly, all Dutch children must attend primary school from the age of five, notably earlier than in the UK, but clearly the English School found market in the lower age of three years. Observation by Darren's Head Mistress was that 'clearly his mother tongue is Dutch' which came somewhat as a surprise, but both boys were to settle in well to the school's busy environment. Ankie meanwhile, ever one to spot an opportunity, managed to obtain some part-time clerical work, where doubtless her language skills, spoken, written and shorthand in Dutch, English and German, enhanced her value.

Doctor H.J. van Mooklaan boasted a few local shops, including one that sold only cheeses, even to the degree that on one visit by John, he was to observe a maggot crawling from one such cheese which he chose to avoid in terms of purchase. The cheese, not the maggot. Happily, and in the absence of cheddar, the purchase of Dutch cheeses became the obvious, and pleasurable, choice. A supermarket was also situated reasonably close-by, and Ankie would cycle there, sometimes with Darren in the child seat, although on one such visit, her bicycle was stolen as she shopped, something that somehow shocked more having happened in Holland, rather than the UK. Clearly, ungodliness as a social impediment flourished here too, goddeloosheid (pronounced as written) in a (Dutch) word.

Adjacence to Den Haag, Scheveningen, and sandy beaches such as Kijkduin brought much opportunity to explore with the family at weekends, with the Dutch propensity to take the sun at every possible opportunity a fine example to follow. Interesting too, to learn that people suspected of being German fifth columnists during the war were challenged to pronounce the name Scheveningen, as the correct Dutch pronunciation was very difficult for a German national. It was also found that whilst the Dutch motorways were excellent for swift travel, to venture from them was to discover a treasure-trove of small villages and towns, enchanting in their classic building style, and clever integration with and around canals, and countryside. Amsterdam too, home to Ankie's parents was a fun place to visit, and en famille to wonder at and enjoy the canal tours, John and Ankie being particularly interested to hear the City's history, and to sight the home of Anne Frank in the city centre. Maduradam, an obvious tourist attraction for families with children, was also in the Scheveningen district of Den Haag, a miniature model 'park' with its extraordinary display of famous Dutch landmarks on the scale 1.25 through which one could wander. Opened in 1952, it was named after George Maduro, a Law student from Curaçao who fought as a Lieutenant in the Dutch Army against the invading Germans, and then in the Resistance movement. He died in the infamous concentration camp Dachau in 1945 and was awarded the highest and oldest decoration in the Kingdom of the Netherlands, the Military Cross of William. All this and more besides, and not to forget the barbecue which, even when it rained, could be positioned in the bike shed positioned conveniently adjacent to the kitchen door, particularly as there was now a bike short in the family.

Ankie and sons Duncan (age 6) and Darren (age 4) at Kijkduin beach, Holland

1973 progressed and with 'home leave' now an option, a two-week holiday was taken in the UK, visiting John's parents for the added benefit of both grandparents and grandchildren, but also Pat Foot, Duncan's godmother, and her husband, Jimmy in Dorchester. It would become noticeable that, over the next few years as visitors to the UK, John and Ankie would visit more friends and relations than ever they would in a full year of residence there, which meant much rushing around with adequate changes of clothing, and Ankie demonstrating as always, her admirable skill at point-to-point navigation, and map reading. Well, almost 'as always', as that skill had deserted her briefly during her second pregnancy when, en route back to Southport from Cumbria, an important turn was missed, her excuse being that she had been distracted – by wishful thinking of tomato soup!

In the business sense, the pedestrian pace continued, with little to excite or challenge the mind in matters of Loss Prevention or Claims, and the occasional visit to the Pernis Bar at the end of the 'work' day for a friendly glass with a few American and Dutch colleagues. Corporate information as to personnel movements in Europe came there none, although attendance to the equally occasional Management meetings brought sightings of various visiting Vice-Presidents or, in nautical terminology 'Senior Hands' as titles were not always bandied about. One such, on his early return to the Hotel in dishevelled clothing, heard cheerful greeting from an indiscrete fellow-American salesman, "Just back from a jog, sir?" to which he growled the pointed response, "Some people could kid themselves out of a job." Was that 1973, or 1974? It matters not, in the general scheme of things, and he who posed the indiscrete question lived to kid another day!

That aside, and pedestrian or not, functions of the LP & C mission continued to address and support the overall aims of maximising loss prevention in terms of both cargo and equipment and minimising any adverse effects that claims against loss or damage, again to either cargo or equipment, might have on customer relations. In effect, an important role within the overall context of 'Customer Focus' falling neatly into that section of the marketing umbrella called 'Public Relations', itself adjacent to the section 'Sales'. This broad definition, in absence of any defined Corporate statement was that as devised and advised by John Perry, in both his Management role, and expectations. He would muse, from time to time, whether all, or just some, of the Sales presence, no matter their nationality, were aware of the eight-panel composition of the marketing umbrella, other than one, namely Sales. However, enjoying as he did both the friendship and occasional convivial glass in the Pernis Bar with several of the Rotterdam contingent, discretion proved to be the better part of valour. Plus, of course, it was none of his part of ship or, as doubtless he would have been told, none of his bloody business! The near future, although unseen or anticipated in the last gasps of 1973, would, nonetheless, make it his business or, at least, part of it. Not here though, not here!

Complaints came there none, nor concerns as to the efficacy of the LP&C overall function, so some comfort in the thought that absence of alarums and unwanted excursions, hopefully brought about by applied cause and effect, had justified John's appointment, despite his initial attempt to shoot himself in the foot in meetings with Kalafatides. However, in total absence of anything resembling a formal, or informal, performance appraisal within the SeaLand system, and adapting the Calvin Coolidge word 'persistence' to a preferred word 'perseverance', there comes the suggestion that 'the only alternative to perseverance is…failure'. With that in mind, he had no alternative but to persevere, at whatever the pace demanded, a conclusion with which Ankie was, yet again, to agree whole-heartedly.

So, into the last knockings of the year 1973, but with more than Christmas to anticipate in the Netherlands, and indeed to enjoy with the children. Traditionally, the Dutch celebration was the birthday of Sinterklaas (St Nicholas) the Patron Saint of Children, which falls on the December 6th, although his 'arrival' to the Netherlands from Spain (don't ask!) is staged in mid-November, the first Saturday after November 11th. With Duncan and Darren now both of an age to appreciate the event, it became part of their Dutch experience (one could say inheritance) and that year in particular, special effort was made to join and involve them in the festivities in one of the smaller villages. The Sinterklaas arrival was by 'steamboat' to a pre-designated Port, but in the event each village and town had its own arrival parade, with the imposing figure of Sinterklaas in his red robe astride his white horse, and accompanied on foot by his assistant, a diminutive Moor from Spain (don't ask!) called Zwarte Piet (Black Peter). They would lead the parade through the village, throwing handfuls of sweets and the like to the accompanying crowds of cheering children. The village event was an exciting eye-opener occasion for the boys, bringing further and vicarious pleasure to John and Ankie, helped even further by some draft beer with ham and cheese roll later, in small café. Trying to explain to the children why he arrived from Spain in a steamboat with his white horse and Moor assistant was best not attempted, and therefore was not!

Come bedtime, and as Sinterklaas would be riding his horse across the rooftops delivering small gifts to each home, the children put their shoes next to the fireplace (or radiator in a modern house) together with a carrot, or a small bunch of hay, and a saucer of water all for the horse, to find the following morning that in place of the horse provender, their shoes would hold a little gift. Come December 5th evening, Dutch families would exchange gifts, or in the morning of the 6th acknowledging his birthday, with Christmas much less of a celebration for most, although commercial enterprise would change that slowly over the years. However, for 'de famille Perry', Christmas could not be ignored, and Santa Claus was afforded his traditional slot come December 25th. His sleighride across the rooftops, drawn by eight reindeer, en route from Lapland with gifts for all was also best not rationalised with the children, and so it was not! Neither that, nor the large glass of brandy set aside for Santa, and a smaller one for Mrs Santa, in case she had come along for the ride!

The New Year was enjoyably seen in at their pleasant new home in Rijswijk, and with Duncan and Darren settled comfortably into their new school in Den Haag, Dutch language classes bearing fruit (Nederlandse taallessen werpen hun vruchten af!), 1974 loomed comfortably ahead with thirty months in Holland, give or take a few weeks, navigated with reasonable success. This glosses over the poor showing at one cricket match, and Ankie's bicycle being stolen, and recognises that a clear conscience can be sign of a poor, or selective, memory!

Thoughts turned to possible summer holiday venues, made more accessible being on the Continental side of the English Channel and North Sea, and Ankie spoke favourably of her youthful holidays in Italy with her best friend, Hanni Potts, so all that remained was to decide later which part of Italy should they target. For the rest, just what would the New Year bring, and as everything seemed to be going passably well, just what had they missed? Experienced now in not trying to guess the future, they settled on the intention that, whatever it was, they would together make it possible. Perseverance to the fore!

With workload in the LP&C Europe group increasing concomitant with SeaLand's success in business growth, decision had been made to increase the group's headcount, and by happy coincidence, meeting was joined in late 1973 with representative from Insurance Company of North America (INA) in matter of claim against SeaLand. His name was Jaap Verbeek and impressed by his obvious grasp of the claim at issue, together with background, experience, and flawless use of colloquial English, offer to join SeaLand was extended to him, and in due course, accepted. It was also learned that he was married to Anca, the highly regarded Secretary to the Sales Manager(s) assigned to Europe who clearly benefited from her enduring and balanced reliability. It was also information for John, in that having enjoyed conversation with Anca on many an occasion, he had never asked her surname!

Her husband took up his appointment with SeaLand February 1st, 1974, valuable addition to the team, further enhanced by realisation that he also spoke excellent French.

Group working harmony was, however, to be disturbed shortly thereafter in that, for reason or reasons unexplained, Jan Keizer chose to abandon his usual quietly taciturn persona. In loud and petulant tone, and very publicly, he proclaimed to John that he, John, fell well short of the outstanding example set by the previous LP&C European Manager. The Law of Physics states that every action generates an equal and opposite reaction, and in this case, it was clear that war does not determine who is right, but rather who is left, and Keizer was immediately removed from the LP&C Corporate team to work for the Terminal Manager. His position was taken up by one Claudio Osti, an Italian as the name might suggest, known to John in a previous setting. Breaking from that which appeared to be increasingly the SeaLand norm, advice as to the changes was sent out to all the operational Terminals.

1974 was showing early signs of becoming a busy year to come, and so it would transpire. New faces continued to appear in the Rotterdam office from America, their names, and functions largely unannounced, and their presence usually becoming known by their appearance and possible introduction in the canteen. Such was the arrival of Chuck Raymond, purportedly working for and with Kalafatides in an operational capacity. Interestingly, and as a Master Mariner, he had served aboard the SeaLand vessel 'Afoundria', firstly as Second and then Chief Mate, when the vessel called in to Grangemouth in 1966, as SeaLand opened its first N. Atlantic Service call to the UK, some two years before full commitment to Felixstowe. He would feature later in the year in matter of Management change in Grangemouth, currently still the responsibility of one Bill Mack, described by the few that knew of his presence in Grangemouth as 'a crusty Scot, with an outsize thirst', with an autocratic modus operandi!

Ankie and John also turned their attention to the choice of venue for their Italian summer vacation, a pleasant way to eke out the weekends during the awful months of January and February, finally deciding upon a small resort in the high Adriatic, only a short drive from Venice, thereby allowing for both sunshine and culture. It was the town of Lignano Sabbiadoro, and booking was made for late May for two weeks in a bungalow with immediate access to a swimming pool, ideal for the children. All that remained was to get there, and

Ankie set to with road maps to plot their route, a car journey of some 1350 kms. through Germany, with an overnight stop scheduled for Oberamagau, some 890 km from Den Hague or about nine hours driving at an average speed of ninety-five kms/hour. Thence through the Brenner Pass into Italy. No mean undertaking with two young children, although the driving would be shared in a two hour on/two hours off basis. This mode of transport was a function of cost comparison to flying and car hire, and in true Dutch style, allowed for stock of food to be carried, thereby justifying the portable barbecue, also to be packed.

The few months leading up to the planned vacation passed quickly enough and brought forth no business developments to change holiday plans with Messrs. Verbeek and Osti comfortably settled in with Eelsing to guard the shop, ably assisted by cheerful Tiebout, and all parts apparently bearing an equal strain, to use yet again some nautical terminology.

With baggage, children and barbecue all packed into their Audi 80, it was off to Italy for John and Ankie. En route, and having stopped somewhere off-road for a picnic snack, their sandwiches drew the unwelcome attention of a cohort of large, aggressive wasps, to the extent that Ankie and the boys made a dash to the car and jumped in, only to realise that sufficient numbers of said wasps had joined them, prompting an equally swift evacuation from the vehicle to John's huge and temporary amusement, as Ankie was not particularly amused! Less amusing was arrival to Oberamagau, only to find that the hotel chosen for their overnight stay declined to accept children, which seemed somewhat contradictory to the town's religious festival reputation. Clearly, the 'suffer little children to come unto me' reference had been omitted from their marketing plan, possibly as a function of translation into German of the word 'suffer', failing to recognise that in old English, the word meant 'tolerate'! Fortunately, an alternative was located, and weary heads rested.

Arrival to Lignano Sabbiadoro was achieved safely, and although many marks on the inside walls of their bungalow evidenced substantial and recent battles against mosquitos, its siting right next to the swimming pool was much approved, and the pool much enjoyed. Constant sunshine (one night however of a massive thunderstorm), daily barbecues, pool activity and laughter became the norm. One day for a drive to Venice, as a welcome diversion for everyone, free to wander through the almost empty streets and over quaint little bridges, as John recounted his experiences there as a young Cadet back in 1956, serving aboard the P&O Liner 'Iberia', then assigned to her summer cruising season. As break from the daily barbecue, visit to a real Italian Pizzeria, there to discover that the owner was an Italian submarine Commander during the war, that he harboured great affection for the British (smart Salesman!), and made a first-class pizza! All in all, the holiday was a great success, and Ankie took on her usual rich tan that further convinced that in a past life, she had been borne in a Mediterranean country, and that anything less than 25°C rated as 'cold'! Decision was taken to return to Holland via Switzerland, and the family therefore had the interesting experience of over-nighting in a typical Swiss country Hotel that welcomed children, served a stunning supper, and kept cows in stalls beneath the Hotel building, to the delight of the children. They slept away the night, and the parents, resigned to the noise of cattle beneath their room, slept less soundly.

Another thing that impressed was the number of Dutch cars that were seen during the holiday, and in mind of the oft repeated suggestion that the Dutch always brought their food with them from home, rather than purchase locally (surely untrue?) the open boot of a Dutch registered car would prompt the amused remark 'there's another one looking for the Hagelslag'! (Hagelslag translates as 'hail stones', as the brightly coloured sweet tasting spread, often eaten on bread, so resembled).

Safely back in Holland, there was the Dutch summer now to enjoy at weekends, with June already commenced, school to be resumed for the boys, and for John a review of activity during his absence, and of any need for changes or adjustments necessary to meet required Corporate outcomes, or rather perceived Corporate outcomes, in usual absence of anything so formal. The 'make it up as you go along' still prevailed, so a 'steady as she goes' epithet appeared to fit the bill.

With the arrival of late Autumn however, 'steady as she goes' became impossible to maintain, as John was called to meeting with Chuck Raymond acting in his capacity of Operations Assistant to Kalafatides. Apparently, and as offered, the Terminal Manager at Grangemouth Scotland, David Bell, had suffered some form of 'mental breakdown', being no longer able to run the Scottish operation, and would be 'retiring'. As a stopgap form of coverage, one Jan Albinson would be positioned from Sweden until such time as a replacement Terminal Manager could be announced and installed. By this point in the meeting, and noting the direction of travel, it was becoming increasingly obvious to John that a defined and required Corporate outcome was about to be divulged and he was not to be disappointed in his anticipation. "It has been decided," went on Raymond, "that you are the best qualified person to take over what is an important operation involving considerable volumes of product requiring special equipment and specialised attention, and we would want you to take over as Terminal Manager." He went on to say that it would be necessary for the Perry family to make their way covertly to Edinburgh as soon as possible, there to spend a week incognito establishing living accommodation, returning thereafter to Rotterdam such that a formal announcement could be made, allowing sufficient time for the family to prepare for relocation to Scotland. All very 'cloak and dagger', and with rationale unexplained for this very surreptitious 'mode d'emploi' of personnel management, suggestion that someone, somewhere, had something to hide. That said, and in that the decision seemed to be 'fait accompli', it remained only for John to acquaint Ankie of this wind of change, and to convene yet another Team Perry pow-wow to test the degree of retained Dutch pragmatism, and thereafter, their plan of action such as the defined circumstances allowed at that point. Journey home to Rijswijk was nevertheless taken with a degree of apprehension, garnished with a multiplicity of thoughts relating to the required re-deployment, and possible effects on the family.

It can be categorically stated that the Dutch pragmatism factor remained alive and well in Ankie as she quietly absorbed the general implications of the move, ending with a rueful smile as she glanced around the lounge of their present home. "We'll be sorry to leave this," she offered, "but we'll make really sure that wherever we end up, it will have central heating!" Discussion brought forth the obvious fact that it would interrupt the boys' schooling at the English School as they would, it had been decided, go to Edinburgh en famille. Further to that, nothing more could be done to expedite the finding and funding of their seventh home, until they arrived in Scotland. Perseverance was once again the watchword, and whilst enthusiasm had yet to be expressed by either John or Ankie, tacit acceptance of the new challenge was sufficient. The boys would be told they were going on a short holiday, to maybe see a big Castle! Their peripatetic lifestyle was about to resume, the adjective appropriately resonating with the family name!

Edinburgh was a town that would become familiar to them with its imposing castle, but arrival there to an hotel was merely to establish a base camp for home research and funding if appropriate, their focus being on areas as close to Grangemouth as dictated secrecy would allow, as John was known to the Terminal Staff. Two potentials were found as priced within their affordable range, rental having been ruled out, one property in Linlithgow, and the other in Polmont, the latter having the obvious advantage of being a new build in a small estate just off the main road to either Grangemouth or Falkirk. This advantage was sealed by knowledge that the Linlithgow property was sited in 'Jocks Hill', probable invitation to ribaldry or worse, and noting that Polmont Primary School was but a short walk from the estate clinched the matter, and obtaining mortgage became the next adventure, back in Edinburgh. Half a week gone, and still no offers of pantomime. That would come, the stage being set in the office of the potential lender for, well, grounds for subsequent laughter!

Discussion of a potential mortgage in whichever office it was held was only occasionally disturbed by Darren, who clearly felt that objects on the potential lender's desk required to be repositioned, each attempt neatly intercepted by Ankie. Eventually, agreement as to the mortgage amount was reached, leaving only the question as to when it would be made available. "Within four to five weeks," intoned the lender on enquiry, and no doubt surprised by the 'it has to be quicker than that' concerns expressed as to availability, put down his pen (and then the applicants) with the measured words "Perhaps it is time to remind ourselves, Mr and Mrs Perry, just who is lending money to who," which rather settled the matter. To all intents and purposes, No. 6, Breadalbane Place, Gilston Park, Polmont was to be home the seventh. Notably, it had central heating – or centraal verwarming as Ankie would put it. Mission accomplished, and within the stipulated week, leaving just enough time for a brief visit with the boys to the promised Castle before heading back to Holland. The beautifully phrased 'put-down', delivered in his soft Edinburgh accent by the mortgage provider, would be ruefully but laughingly referred to at many a dinner party in the future!

Return to Rotterdam brought about a maelstrom of activity, with Ankie calmly resuming her well-practiced house closure functions and sourcing a reliable Removals company that was ready to Remove at short notice. John meantime, once his appointment had been made public, returned to Grangemouth for a long weekend to briefly introduce himself to the Staff, and to meet with Jan Albinson who by now was eager to return to his native

Sweden, put off his stride by fact that the Terminal had been paralysed for some time by the wide-spread strike action of Hauliers. He was, it seemed, less than enchanted by his sojourn in Scotland. Alone in his new office on the Sunday, John found the desk drawers to be stuffed with old correspondence going back months, some invoices, and general bric-a-brac, taking the considered decision to consign the lot to bin bags for disposal, on the grounds that if anything was important, someone would eventually raise a query. He would also ensure for the future that correspondence and invoices would be dealt with by empowered Staff members, as clearly the practice to date had been 'delegation upwards' rather than down! He also learned that despite the prolonged Hauliers strike, consignees of containers landed during the strike had all been charged demurrage, the penalty usually associated with the tardy removal of their containers for delivery. Not without cause, involved importers were up in arms, probable further cause for Albinson's haste to return to Sweden! Clearly, decisive action was needed, and without further ado, John ordered that all such outstanding, unpaid invoices issued during the strike period be credited, returning then to Rotterdam, where he 'forgot' to advise anyone of his decision, using the Naval 'need to know' factor as self-justification. Unsurprisingly, it went unnoticed in the event, except in Scotland where peace returned to the importer fraternity's valley, many of whom were involved also in the export of whisky, prime 'raison d'être' for SeaLand's presence in Grangemouth. It is likely that Albinson's briefing, pre his arrival into Grangemouth, had indeed been 'brief'! At best!

By the second week of November 1974, all was ready for the move from Holland to Scotland, and ownership of No.6 Breadalbane Place Polmont secured. With Ankie satisfied that that the Removal company had satisfactorily cleared their Rijswijk home and was en route to Scotland, the family Perry bade reluctant farewell to Holland, and themselves took journey to their new home, their seventh, arrival of household goods to coincide with their arrival thereto, and so it happened. Driver of the Removals van, a young Dutchman, sought permission to look over the house before commencing delivery, and having done so, addressed himself to Ankie thus: "Het is een klein huis, hè?" he reflected (it's a small house, eh?) which was slightly worrying, but suffice it to say, large enough for their furniture, which included their barbecue, object of some amazement to the local populace come the early Spring! Also, John's kloppen (clogs) further cause for intrigued enquiry!

John had also made his farewells to Jaap Verbeek, Bert Eelsing, Claudio Osti, and Miriam Tiebout, with sincere thanks to them for their work, loyalty, forbearance, guidance and so forth, in knowledge that his relief was to be Hans van Wouw, well steeped in matters associated with LP&C, and with operational experience gained as Terminal Manager in Trieste. He was also well known to, and a friend of, Jaap Verbeek, so it all seemed satisfactory, save for fact that there had been no chance for a personal handover, such were the demands of time and tide.

On a personal note, John was presented, by the Team, with a small, engraved metal plaque mounted on polished wood, inscribed with a SeaLand motif, and bearing the words as hereunder:

PRESS ON!
PERSISTENCE AND DETERMINATION
ALONE ARE OMNIPOTENT

Rotterdam, November 1974
To: JOHN W. PERRY

It was to hold pride of place thereafter, not only for the giving, but also the important philosophy.

Duncan's seventh birthday had been celebrated in Rijswijk, with Darren's fifth to be marked come December-end in Polmont, with Christmas also looming. Importantly though, invitation had been received to attend the December 14th, wedding of John's younger brother, Brian, to fiancé, Lesley, in Rochester, Kent, and with the very recent move from Holland, Ankie had wisely concluded it best that she should consolidate the move into their new home with the children, whilst John made a quick dash to Kent to attend the great day, particularly as it had been some considerable time since the brothers had met, Brian still pursuing his sea-going career having also reached the dizzy heights of Master Mariner. The dash was therefore made, the wedding enjoyed, and back to Scotland by December 16th in time to prepare for Christmas, meagrely celebrated at the office (work to be done there!) and well celebrated with wife and sons in their latest home, almost ending the year with Darren's birthday.

New Year's Eve, however, was an experience yet to be faced, as the Scots celebrated Hogmanay, as is the Scottish word for it, interestingly, a derivation from old Norman French. With some pre-warning from neighbours, John and Ankie had stayed up for the event, and done some homework, so were not completely surprised by their initiation to the tradition of so-called 'first footing' (pronounced fust footing). This involved, certainly in the Perry's case, complete strangers calling once midnight had passed, bearing a lump of coal, and expecting to be invited in for a dram or five, their numbers generated by an interest to find out who these strangers to Breadalbane Place were, and from whence. Some two hours and at least one bottle of Scotch and a few beers later, peace descended, and John and Ankie were able to get some sleep, having first cleaned up the toilet where someone had been rather sick.

All in all, an interesting, tiring, but satisfactory arrival into their new surrounds, although the business of SeaLand's Grangemouth Terminal had been largely shelved, with promise of a bright new start come the New Year of 1975. First New Year's question, however, came from Duncan and Darren, asking just what was all the noise that had kept them awake last night!

Grangemouth, Scotland

Brief visit to the Terminal prior to re-location from Holland did not count for much in terms of getting to know the Staff, so there was the clear need for John to re-introduce himself more formally as January opened for business, and to evaluate the Team bequeathed to him. It was immediately apparent that (a) morale was low with consequent lack of forward commitment or sense of purpose and (b) questions abounded as to who or what was this new Terminal Manager going to change, as an Englishman arriving from Holland! This question had also engaged John's mind, so first and foremost, one on one interviews were initiated to allow mutual gathering of first impressions, being fully aware as he was that 'one can rarely have a second chance to make a first impression'. Initial soundings, from his point of view anyway, went well, with a depth of experience found in the Operations Manager Ian Bell, Marine Manager Alan Webster, and Office Manager Ron Fraser, not to forget Charlie Wilson, Manager responsible for the maintenance team and tank cleaning facilities, and George Hutton for Terminal accounts. For his part, John was able to outline his hands-on experience in matters of marine and land operations in both Felixstowe and Liverpool, together with accrued knowledge in matters of loss prevention and special equipment required for high value cargoes. He also made the point that he would value time spent with each Manager to understand local concerns, and in the case of Charlie Wilson, to learn about the tank cleaning facilities, and cleaning methodology. It was a beginning, with clear lines of communication and delegated responsibilities re-defined. Assurance was also given that John would always be available for problem discussion and solving, but with the rider that anyone bringing a problem should also come furnished with his or her suggestion for potential remedy, rather than seeking to put the monkey on someone else's back! More informal chats were held with individual Staff members in all departments, and overall, there was the initial indication of a perceptible lifting of spirits, so a base on which to build.

With no prior briefing as to the general state of the Terminal, it was back to the 'make it up as you go along' situation, so tour of the facility was next on the list, to include firstly the maintenance garage through which all containers, loaded or empty, had to pass as part of the delivery to road function. It was noted that the current approach to the facility required a tight right-hand turn to gain access to the garage, too often bringing damage to the entrance structure, and consequent time wasting, expensive repairs, as John was informed. The simple solution it seemed to him, was to alter the approach line for truck and container, and within a couple of days, that was achieved by small adjustment to the container parking lines. It was also observed that the processing of units through the garage was unacceptably slow due to the many minor, but still important, repairs to either container or chassis. Question was asked of the Maintenance Manager if it was practical to deploy mechanics with appropriate tools on a roving repair commission within the container storage lines (at that time, all SeaLand boxes were chassis-borne) and with answer in the affirmative, he was tasked to locate a suitable vehicle which, again if practical, could be fitted with portable generator, and appropriate power tools. Review in due course.

At home, John found himself tasked to hang pictures, and having located his prized electric BOSCH hammer drill purchased in Oud Beijerland, set about what should have been a simple, quick job. Quick it certainly was in that although the walls of Dutch homes were made of pre-cast concrete, walls of homes in Gilston Park turned out to be almost, by odious comparison, cardboard thin. As he would later describe, he was through about two houses before he could stop the drill! An exaggeration, of course, but cause of much laughter within the family, and just a little repair work.

Ankie, of course, had quickly and efficiently turned the house into a home, pointing out, in the meantime to John, that a small terrace in the back garden would be very acceptable, and grass for the small front garden would require only some digging and levelling before seeding, and best done before the advent of Spring! Hint taken, and on first available weekend, front garden digging, and levelling was commenced, having first donned his bright yellow Dutch Klompen (clogs). News of this seemed to spread quickly, with near neighbours apparently eager to see this unusual sight, and question both the choice of footwear, and sanity of the wearer! The terrace would come a little later but come it would.

Duncan and Darren too both seemed to have settled into the new home well, even taking to ledger the absence of a sandpit, and come January 6th in this year of 1975, Ankie took them on the short walk to Polmont Primary School where they were kindly received. Quite by chance, Ankie got talking to a nearby neighbour as it transpired, Esther Dougan, also dropping her two children to school. The boys would adapt well to their new school, each quickly developing a Scottish accent, no doubt as a sub-conscious means to better merge with their fellow pupils. This reminded John of travels along the Australian Coast when with the P & O Company where, and probably for not dis-similar reasons, the Aussie accent was adopted. Well, it just got tiring to be picked out as a 'Pom', or 'Pommie bastard', then having to explain that the pejorative word (that fooled them!) derived from the initials stamped across English deportation orders (POME) standing for 'Prisoner of Mother England'! Advised with conviction, so to speak.

That chance meeting with Esther would develop into a life-long friendship with the Dougans, a regular game of squash for John with Esther's husband Eric, not a few tipples all together, and Esther joining the SeaLand team in the Grangemouth Terminal come June, working as Assistant to the Accounts Manager. In time, she would become Manager of the William Martin (major Freight Forwarder in Glasgow) Grangemouth office. They had, not long since, returned from Kenya where Eric taught for some years, his current appointment being as Head of the Maths Dept at Bathgate Academy. Good people.

With the boys safely enrolled at school, and never one to let grass grow beneath her feet, Ankie sought to balance, yet again, her current lifestyle and with that in mind, found temporary work as a shorthand typist within reasonable distance of home and school. Her skills in both German and Dutch were predictably unemployed, albeit offered.

Back at the Terminal, the Maintenance Manager had located a retired British Rail minibus/van, and decision was made to both purchase and equip it with the proposed generator and tools, ready to be pressed into service undertaking repair work in the container yard, on pre-identified import and empty containers. As hoped, this proved to considerably speed up the despatch of units to road, although an unfortunate incident a few months later could be bracketed under 'The Law of Unintended Consequences', to be addressed in due course.

John also learned that any metal 'spoil' generated during maintenance was, as per a previously established edict, sold as scrap, with monies generated taken to a revenue ledger. This prompted much thought, the results of which would realise something that could be embraced within the unwritten 'Law of Intended Consequences', in that the Terminal Budget found by John failed to provide for that which he had in mind. In this, SeaLand sought to adhere to the mantra that 'once a budget has been agreed, budgeted items automatically define all that are needed'. Some flexibility needed to be generated, and no one knew from whence came the edict as above mentioned!

Discussion with Marine Manager Alan Webster and his Assistant, Bill Douglas, each with maritime qualifications, brought reassuring comfort that their 'part of ship' was in good shape, their cheerful and lively approach to handling the seven-to-ten-day (dependent upon wind and tide) feeder service to Rotterdam being well organised and executed, their working relationship with the Port authorities and work force sustaining the operation well. Office Manager Ron Fraser also seemed in control of both the import and export documentation desks. It was perhaps to him that John should have posed the question later asked of the imports clerk Robert Stevenson, enquiring if the badge he proudly sported on his jacket was that of a local bus company or club. The pained response was that said badge was in fact that of the SNP, or Scottish National Party, apparently a local political movement seeking recognition, then a potential acorn in the field of Scottish politics!

Overall, indeed, there was an air of renewed enthusiasm, which encouraged John to allocate as much time and attention as was needed in meeting with all major exporters, mostly producers of whisky, and Freight Forwarders largely involved in the whisky trade. This, as it would transpire, would require a high degree of self-discipline bearing in mind the driving required, and the importance of one's liver in the general scheme of things, in that many meetings to come would involve receiving hospitality in the form of, believe it or not, whisky or as Jim Smith Director of the large Freight Forwarder in Glasgow William Martin preferred to call it over lunches, 'wine of the country'. It was he, in passing, that would introduce John to one of Scotland's favoured meals, namely 'Haggis, served with Neaps and Tatties', to use the vernacular. In order to meet one particular Export Manager of a large whisky Brand better not named, was to get to his office before midday, as post meridian he would be intoxicatingly unavailable. That was a rare exception, to be both fair, and indeed thankful.

As these meetings progressed, the 'Law of Unintended Consequences' required to be addressed in-house, as one of SeaLand's mechanics assigned to the roving repairs minibus had conspired with two drivers from a particular Haulier to use the repairs equipment to gain access to, and pilfer from, whisky export container or containers which, fortunately, was quickly detected and actioned. No formal charges were raised, but dismissal of the mechanic was immediate, as was the banning of the two drivers from all SeaLand business. Roving repairs were continued, but lessons had been learned, mainly that which suggested such an incident should have been anticipated, humankind being involved.

Meetings with the Trade also illuminated fact the North Atlantic Shipping Conference (read Cartel!) had imposed the rule in Scotland that no one Shipping Line could position empty containers to the premises of Exporters other that when a firm export booking was made, and then only containers sufficient to cover the actual booking. This was a cause of frustration to many of those exporters with whom John met, in terms of inevitable loading delays, and this him gave pause for thought. Firstly, the rule only applied to bookings to the United States, and secondly, SeaLand had become successfully involved in the so-called 'short-sea trade', such bookings destined for European delivery. The pause for thought quickly translated into decision to position a few empty units into the premises of those shipping to both the United States and to Europe, ostensibly to cover European bookings, albeit that if one or two were used for the US, no apology would be required, and the 'pool' would be brought up to strength, ostensibly to cover US bookings made! The Trade, where involved, recognised Customer focus when they saw it, and SeaLand's overall export bookings improved accordingly. It otherwise went unnoticed, or certainly unremarked, by the Cartel (sorry, Conference) which of course afforded it legitimacy. In due course, the Conference system would be seen as legitimising cartels, and was accordingly abandoned as being illegal.

The summer months were welcomed, with the terrace in the back garden surprisingly completed, although sunshine in this part of the United Kingdom seemed rare. However, quick advantage was taken in the first weekend that it did warm the scene, despite the fact that the sacred level of 25°C for Ankie was certainly not available. Nothing loathe, and in the true Dutch style, out came the garden furniture and the barbecue, together with incredulous neighbours still sporting their winter weeds, and wondering what madness drove those at No. 6 Breadalbane Place.

Further madness would prevail, however, in that, with the stresses involved in move from Holland, new home, new school, new work challenges, and all during the dark days of winter, a holiday in the sun was deemed necessary, and a chalet bungalow in a Swiss resort on the Spanish Costa del Sol was booked for July which soon arrived. Once again, the car was packed and the long drive undertaken, briefly assisted by ferry crossing to Holland from Hull. It was to prove a fabulous two weeks of glorious sunshine, swimming in the large pool, where unusually everyone had to wear swim hats, and Darren being taught to swim by an attentive staff member. If not the pool, then into the sea from the Resort's private sands only minutes from the pool. That the Perrys were unable to afford to use the poolside restaurant was a downside, but contents of the car's boot and some local shop purchases saw them comfortably through the holiday, which was rounded off by visit to a Flamenco show, and for Ankie and John, their first taste of Sangria. They would return to Scotland relaxed, well-tanned (particularly Ankie as always!) and ready for whatever challenges presented themselves. As with the Italian holiday the previous year, many Dutch registered cars had been observed in Spain, their occupants often roadside engaged in 'looking for the Hagelslag!' Amused question was also raised as to whether the size of Holland required that a certain percentage of the population spent time away to allow others some space, as if this might explain the sheer volume of holidaymakers from the Netherlands.

Two business-social matters required attention, the first relating to news that U.S. Lines, a competitor not known for strictly ethical sales practices, was to entertain customers to a Golf Day at one of the better-known Golf Clubs, and discussion with a Haulier very loyal to SeaLand would confirm that it would be perfectly legal to park a truck closely adjacent to the short road leading to the Club. It therefore came to pass, purely by chance, that a freshly laundered, chassis borne SeaLand container was to be found there early that morning, the Haulier having unfortunately suffered minor engine fault that would be rectified 'as soon as humanly possible'.

The second issue was something that John had thought about for some time, determined as he was that this year the Grangemouth Staff would enjoy a private Christmas dinner-dance at a Falkirk Hotel, which SeaLand would underwrite. Clearly there was no budget for this so monies from the sale of metal scrap (as previously mentioned) were diverted into that which one could refer to as a 'slush fund', not to be confused with funds similarly named in occasional reference to American politicians and elsewhere. To the uninitiated, the name originated way back in the days of Nelson's Navy, where fat or grease was skimmed from cauldrons of boiling salt pork, put into empty barrels, and sold as means to fund purchases not normally available to ships' crew or employees in dockyards. This Grangemouth 'metal slush' would not necessarily cover the cost but would assist thereto. The Cladhan Hotel in Falkirk was accordingly booked for an evening in mid-December, and Staff advised to prepare themselves. It would not, however, be a free bar, as it had been noticed that Scots were not against the occasional tipple, or more.

On a more serious note, exposure to the tank cleaning plant for John was carried on apace, involving much crawling through the SeaLand 35 ft. tanks under the expert eye of the Maintenance Manager. All such tanks were of 'food-grade' construction, and as the export of bulk whisky in these tanks contributed a substantial percentage of SeaLand's business, cleaning was of massive importance, to the point that even a residual smell of any previous cargo would prompt rejection by the distilleries. There were those that recommended use of coffee grains to dispel residual smells, but that was deemed unacceptable – a residual smell meant residual product, no matter how small the amount.

At the same time, extremely strict regulations governed the pH value (measure of acidity) of wastewater returned to the Firth of Forth, requiring constant attention as failure to comply would lead to closure of the cleaning operation. This was to become critical, in that some bright spark of a salesman in the States had booked a considerable number of these tanks to carry Piperazine to Europe, a noxious product used in the production of plastics, resins and pesticides, both difficult and expensive to clean, with a strong residual odour eventually traced to the first such tank's discharge valve assembly as minute specs of residual product.

Interestingly, reports of US Customs fines against product 'lost in transit' from these tanks prompted further tank crawling for John, noticing as he did that the in-tank section of the PV valve (pressure reduction valve) was of a length for him to conclude that both product expansion due to increase in atmospheric temperature, or sufficient 'free surface effect' as vessels rolled at sea, could cause the PV valve to immerse in whisky and become, or act as, a pump, causing product loss to the ship's deck. Accordingly, had the Maintenance Manager crop the in-tank section of the valve some six inches, which thankfully solved the problem.

Socially, and in discussion between Ankie and John, it was voiced that compared to previous experience in both England and Holland, business related social events were mainly 'men only' in Scotland, to which Ankie added that on the few occasions couples were invited, she observed that many of the male invitees seemed more intent on tanking than talking which caused her some concern, indeed irritation. This would manifest itself again in an invitation received shortly thereafter for John to attend an amateur boxing evening at the Inchyra Hotel (a brief walk from their home) not only sans wife, but also a 'Black Tie' event, to watch Scottish and Irish amateurs slogging it out. As the invite came from an important source of business for SeaLand, it was reluctantly accepted, with warning from Ankie to 'take care' duly noted. Walk to the hotel took some twenty minutes, to find that he had been placed to a small ringside table for four persons, upon which stood three full bottles of Scotch! It was going to be a wet evening to all appearances, requiring once again some self-discipline and liver protection, not only for those in the Boxing Ring! It proved so, and despite frequently declining top-ups, the walk home seemed to take longer that the walk there, due to the perceived slight increase in distance to be walked. Bow tie was still in place, and thankfully, home relations happily maintained, as discretion had been the better part of valour. Who won the boxing? No idea as table vacated (discretely!) before the final bouts had been completed.

Budgets

As the winter months approached, rumour had it that Kalafatides had left Rotterdam, to be replaced by Tom Yost, and word came that he was particularly focussed on budget presentations for 1976, reviews to be held in Rotterdam. In absence of any further guidance, John concluded to develop a zero-based budget, rather than seek to build on, or around, anything previously submitted, and discussions with Heads of Departments were duly implemented to bring this about, even down to costing out annual purchase of food for the Terminal's Guard Dog.

Travel to Rotterdam was in due course made for the reviews, and as he sat near to Yost's office awaiting his turn to be reviewed, deeply surprised to observe an American colleague from Spain exit Yost's office at speed, followed literally by a bunch of paperwork flung after him, presumably by Yost, judging by the ill-tempered shouts that followed – 'and don't come back until you've put together something realistic', or words/expletives amounting to that general effect. John was reminded of the time when he was waiting to be called in for his 'Master's' oral examination by the Chief Examiner of Master and Mates in Southampton, only to see the candidate who had preceded him some ten minutes before being carried from the Examiner's office, followed by the examiner's shout, "Next!" – "The bloody fool fainted," observed the chief examiner, "so God knows what he would do on a ship's Bridge." Not the most encouraging introduction then, as perhaps now!

Yost, however, appeared to have calmed down when John from Scotland was called in, and with little left for chance in the Budget's preparation, was given a reluctant nod of acceptance, with the rider that in the general meeting later to be convened, he, John, should be prepared to offer some cost reductions, as would everyone else. The meeting would turn out to be that evening, and indeed one after the other, those that had brought their Budgets to Rotterdam conceded reductions, John's offer bringing general laughter, but an unamused growl from Yost, who gave the distinct impression that offer to reduce the Guard Dog's tins of meat was derisory, bearing on the disrespectful. De facto, and as 'zero-base budgeting had been carefully employed, there was no slack to be released, of which Yost was fully aware post the earlier review meeting. Nonetheless, later conversation with colleagues suggested that there could well be a degree of self-inflicted damage to be reckoned with, in light of Yost's apparent displeasure, known colloquially as 'shooting oneself in the foot', a possible perceived situation not unknown to John in visiting Rotterdam! Time would tell.

Another interesting factor that this Rotterdam meeting brought home was that Scotland, to all intents and purposes, was being treated as a completely separate area of operation to the rest of the UK. There was no defined reporting line to London, where an American Manager reigned, and since John and Family had arrived in Scotland, no Sales or Operational Management had visited or telephoned from elsewhere in the UK, or indeed Rotterdam before the Budget meeting. In effect, everything was being handled from Grangemouth, be that Operations or Sales, the latter in particular involving direct contact with the whisky trade., or so it seemed. All in all, a bizarre situation, saved only by the fact that pay cheques still materialised from somewhere each month, suggesting that this lonely outpost was doing something right at least.

Christmas 1975, together with Darren's birthday, was to be addressed and for this, the Perrys moved South, to join John's mother and stepfather in Cradley, their then home in Worcestershire, for the bright, homely, and thoroughly entertaining celebrations, with Duncan and Darren much the centre of their grandparent's attention, and gifts. In mind of their last busy Hogmanay, they also stayed over to see in the New Year of 1976, their connection to Scotland that evening probably enjoyed listening and viewing the songs and reels of Jimmy Shand and his Band. Being a family gathering there may have been some wrong footing, but 'first (pronounced fust) footing' there was none! 1976 loomed large as a blank canvas, and with the Scottish operation running smoothly, John and Ankie could look forward to a reasonably settled year, and perhaps some exploring. Couldn't they? As always, time would tell, persistence and determination meanwhile remaining paramount.

Back in Breadalbane Place Polmont, and the children back to school at Polmont Primary, John and Ankie reviewed the year's first quarter as best they could, with thoughts once again turning to what they might achieve in terms of holidays. No decision was taken, other than the obvious requirement for consistent sunshine and temperatures in excess of 25°C, which rather suggested a return to Spain or Italy. Food for thought, and for later review once the ghastly months of January and February were seen off, being colder and darker than more southerly climes to which they were accustomed and cause of some distress to Ankie.

March moved the year on, not high-lighted by an informal meeting between John and his Operations manager Ian bell which, instead of holding it at the Terminal, was convened for 8 p.m. at Ian's house, with Ankie advised that John would be 'a bit late home' that Friday evening. The discussion ranged over a variety of concerns that were bothering Ian, covering operational, budgetary and personnel subjects until it was suddenly realised to John's horror that the hour of 2 a.m. Saturday morning had arrived, and that he was totally adrift of station. Swift drive to Polmont, and with sufficient rolling impetus to quietly make it onto the driveway with engine stopped, only to be confronted by a desperately worried Ankie, devoid of any pragmatism! Her suggestion that he should sleep in the spare bedroom such that she could now get some undisturbed sleep was sensibly and diplomatically agreed his stupidity only to be exposed a couple of weeks later when his mother and stepfather arrived to look after the boys. "Dad has slept in the spare bedroom too," advised Duncan or Darren, to hear grandmother's, "Oh, really dear, and why was that?" Confession time; now thankfully accompanied with rueful laughter, and a 'never again' re-affirmation from parents.

Reason for the arrival of John's folks at that time was indeed to look after Duncan and Darren, in that completely out of the blue had come instruction from Tom Yost in Rotterdam for John and Ankie to make their way (discretely) to Genoa, there to meet with Rupe Hickler, now General Manager Mediterranean, to discuss possibility of a re-location to Italy! The children were unaware of the reason for parental travel, being told merely that they had to attend a meeting, not altogether unusual, save that Ankie could scarcely contain herself as to the possibilities inherent in the trip, to include the eclipsing of any holiday planning. The actual date of arrival to Genoa is unimportant (for that, read 'forgotten') but certainly the sun was shining as they checked into their Hotel situated to the north of the city, and from which they would daily take taxi to the SeaLand office.

Hickler had changed little since John's time with him in Rotterdam, quietly spoken but authoritative, and now clearly looking for someone to take on a Staff function reporting to him, based in Genoa. It was also apparent to John and Ankie that their arrival to Genoa was seen as tacit acceptance by John that the position was his. Effectively, they were on that which SeaLand termed a 'pre-trip', usually granted for house hunting and introduction to other team members, the assumption being that John's re-location to Italy was a done deal.

Equally clearly, Yost had been less than up front in his advice, bordering on the disingenuous, as John and Ankie would discuss back at the Hotel. To make matters worse, the following day they were collected from the Hotel and taken to view an apartment for rent, underlining that which they had discussed the previous evening, followed by a discourse relating to school facilities, being an American school with currently some 8 to 10 pupils. The water was getting deeper, with John increasingly reluctant to put his feet in! Hickler did not require a John Perry, he needed a bean counter, and moreover after three years in Rotterdam in a Staff position, John recognised that this was not for him. Unsurprisingly, Ankie was upset by the 'so near, yet so far' status, but recognised and agreed John's analysis of his doubts and concerns.

On the third day, it fell to John to outline to Hickler these doubts and concerns, and also to highlight just how lacking had been the explanation for their visit to Genoa. "With regret, Rupe," he added, "I do not think that I am the right one for the position, and schooling facilities for our sons would seem total inadequate. On that basis, we will best return to Scotland tomorrow," and flight bookings were made accordingly. Dinner that night was a solemn affair, with John apprehensive that he had perhaps shot himself in the foot again, and Ankie despairing of her chance to move to the sunshine from a gloomy Scotland. At the Airport the following day, Ankie came very close to tears, something that John had never witnessed before, nor would he again in the remaining years of their fifty-three-year marriage.

Two days after their return to Grangemouth, came there telephone call from Yost in Rotterdam, asking for what reason had the offered position in Genoa been turned down. As John sought to explain, starting with the schooling facilities, Yost interrupted. "Don't give me that bullshit John," he started, "but did Rupe mention Greece?" Surprised, John gave a definitive no, and Yost resumed in authoritative tone. "Within the next two days," he stated, "you will receive call from Hickler, offering you the position of Country Manager Eastern Mediterranean, based in Athens. You will accept the offer, understand, after which we will discuss timing and re-location – is that clear?" Stuttered agreement from John, end of telephone call, and swift dash to the nearest shop that sold champagne, followed by equally swift dash home to Ankie in sure knowledge that this unexpected and abrupt return home would not this time bring suggestion for John to repair to the spare bedroom! (Honi soit qui mal y pense!)

Ankie was ecstatically over the moon (an odd expression, but universally understood to indicate happiness) and as they celebrated this extraordinary turn of events with the champagne, they also told the boys of the good fortune, with their next adventure taking them to live in Greece, a land of constant sunshine (not quite as it turned out), and temperatures almost always 25°C or more, emphasised their mother. Whilst telephone call from Genoa was still to confirm that from Rotterdam, holiday planning was nevertheless off the 'to do' list, but with much to replace that item, as past experience indicated.

Call from Hickler did come as promised, confirming John's appointment as set out by Yost, and it would later transpire that one Eef de Weerd, a meticulous Dutchman from Rotterdam that John knew well, had taken the Genoa job, and whilst some would say that he was too meticulous (which probable meant he did his job properly) he fitted precisely that which Hickler had sought, a meticulous bean counter!

Once again though, and in absence of any direction from either Rotterdam or London, it fell to John to break the news of his departure (date still to be fixed) to the Grangemouth team, with no knowledge as to who would replace him. It seems no one else knew either, but as it eventually turned-out post John's' departure, the mysterious Bill Mack, the 'legendary crusty Scot with an outsize thirst' who had originally run the Terminal at start-up in his own autocratic way, unreceptive to any new ideas or procedures, was somehow reappointed by someone, somewhere. Clearly a lot of thought had gone into that!

With initial euphoria set aside, it quickly became apparent that this move, now defined as late May into June 1976, was more complex than any undertaken heretofore, starting with need to put No. 6 Breadalbane Place on the market, and that was done. Once more, Team Perry convened to size up all that would otherwise be necessary to achieve, not least of all packing of their house-hold goods and two cars to containers for shipment to Piraeus, whilst for John there remained matter of continuing to run the Terminal – thankfully, past delegation of responsibilities to Heads of Department had been gratefully received, and all was running smoothly.

Fortunately, the house sale proceeded apace, and whilst it was not a profitable sell, price obtained at least achieved a break-even result, after nearly two years of ownership. Need for John to attend meeting in Rotterdam in matter of confirming terms brought obvious decision to include Holland en route to Athens, which would also allow an all too rare get-together with the boys' grandparents in Amsterdam. Weeks moved quickly along, and on May 13th, John and Ankie were bid to attend a full Staff meeting in the Terminal office where, to John's emotional surprise, an Illuminated Scroll with wax seal was presented to him, crafted by Ron Fraser the Office Manager, and styled as if worked by a Monk in his Scriptorium, inscribed to all appearance on parchment, being two feet in length, and eighteen inches wide. It was signed by every member of the team! It is reproduced in full overleaf, but the opening words almost brought tears to John's eyes, as Ankie pressed his hand in support.

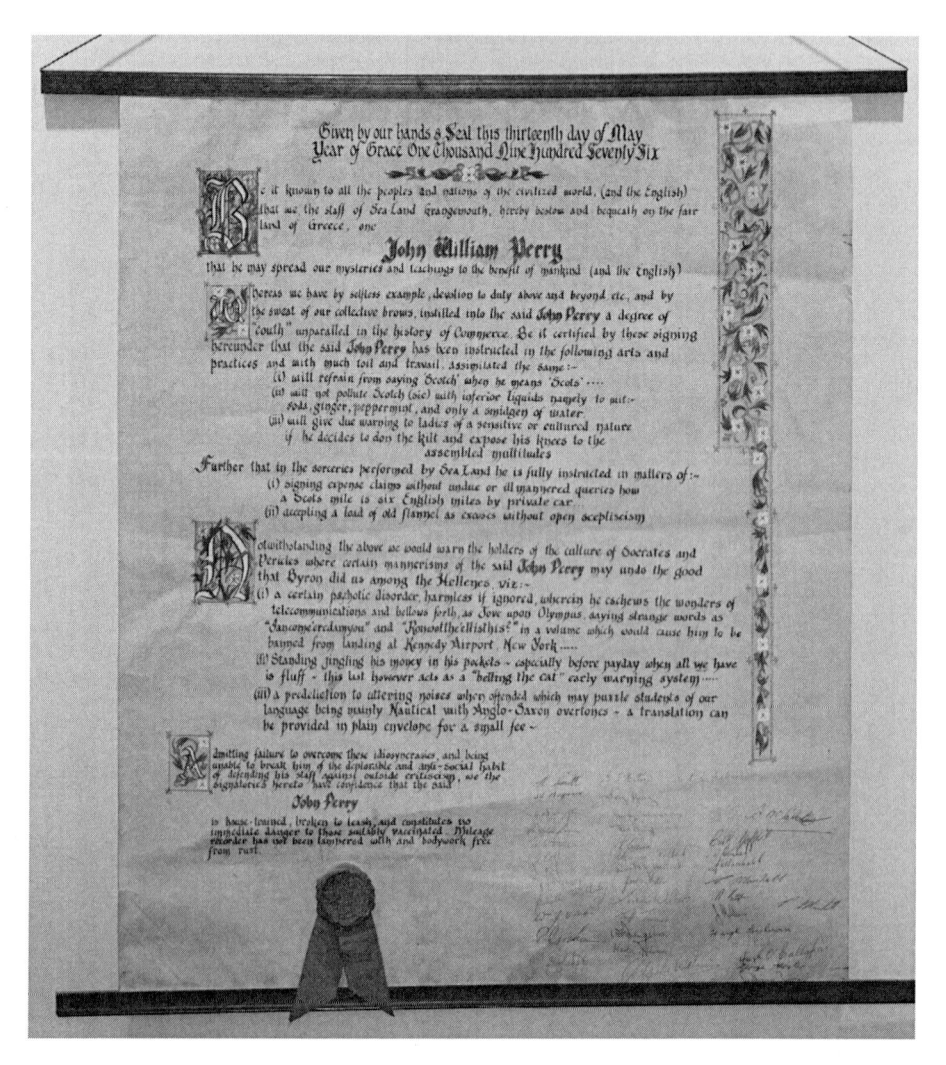

Farewell Parchment for John from Sealand Grangemouth Staff

"Be it known to all the peoples and nations of the civilised World (and the English) that we, the Staff of SeaLand Grangemouth, hereby bestow and bequeath to the fair land of Greece, one John William Perry, that he may spread our mysteries and teachings to the benefit of mankind (and the English)."

By May's end, the two 35 ft. containers had been loaded for shipment, leaving John, Ankie, Duncan and Darren to say their last farewells and make their way to Edinburgh Airport, en route to Schiphol Airport in Holland. Onward and upward, so to speak. Timing was further complicated by call from Rupe Hickler for John to attend a Med Managers' meeting, scheduled to be held in Algeciras, a substantial transhipment Terminal successfully opened by SeaLand which, it was concluded by Team Perry, could best be achieved from Holland leaving Ankie and the boys in Amsterdam. On his return, they would then leave, en famille, for Athens. Altogether a logistical nightmare, but controllable with luck, fair wind, and tide.

Now in June, Rotterdam meeting was concluded, with the interesting and somewhat surprising discovery that SeaLand considered Greece as an 'area of expatriate deprivation', with appropriate largesse added to remuneration in compensation. Additionally, John would be paid from New Jersey, where apparently a 13% tax regime applied, which was altogether encouraging.

Amsterdam proved its usual interesting self, with Duncan and Darren now better able, at ages of nine and seven years respectively, to enjoy the canal boat trips. It also gave them opportunity to air their Dutch language skills, hopefully, still in part retained, with grandparents who spoke not a word of English. John took flight to Malaga, and having joined up with Hickler, moved towards Algeciras, stopping off for lunch at the man-made Marina of Puerto Banus, some sixty kilometres south-west of Malaga Airport. There they were to pass by a large motor cruiser, moored stern-first to the quay and flying the Red Ensign of Britain where, on deck there sat two attractive young women wearing bikinis. They were separated by a wooden locker between them, on which lay a full-grown black Panther. Hickler stopped, put his hands on his hips, and proclaimed in loud voice 'goddamned ostentatious British!' before moving on. Fortunately, said Panther was chained to the locker, and the women chose to accept the compliment! Algeciras came and went, and John returned to Holland the following day, to rejoin Ankie and the boys. They were about to start another adventure! In Greece, to which they were all happy to be both bestowed and bequeathed. Bring it on!

Athens, Greece

John's appointment as Country Manager Greece that June of 1976 (it transpired that Tom Yost had been geographically over-generous in his initial description of the posting) coincided with, and was probably resultant upon, the commencement of SeaLand's Europe/Middle East Service to Dubai which would, come 1979, be extended by feeder service to India, with calls to both Bombay and Cochin. Piraeus was to be a regular Port of call both East and West-bound, also opening additional service opportunities to both the United States and Europe for Greece, as well as import traffic therefrom. Notably for John, William Martins of Glasgow would establish regular whisky traffic, using Callitsis as their Greek Agent.

Sealand's chosen Agent in Greece was of course the Callitsis Agency, situated at 56, Filonos Street Piraeus, and it was here that John would later meet the Directors Petros and Nassos Callitsis and four family members also working in the Agency. Noni and George, daughter, and son of Petros (or Peter as he was known to his American employers) together with George and Andreas, sons of Nassos, for whom no 'close' Anglicized name was apparently found. John would find that they constituted a formidable team of both experience and expertise, all completely fluent in English and, more importantly and perhaps sub-consciously, applying marketing concepts that ensured that refreshingly, all parts of the organisation were focussed on customer satisfaction, and therefore repeat sales.

Flight that brought the Perrys to Athens approached the Airport that, before the new Airport was built to the North of the city, ran parallel to the coast, necessitating an unexpected sharp bank to port or starboard (unexpected to the passengers that is) dependent on wind direction, to line up with the runway. They had arrived, to find that a car had been arranged to meet and convey them to their Hotel in central Athens, namely Hotel Caravel, with its magnificent views of the Acropolis. There they would stay until a new home had been found, and their house-hold goods and cars would arrive from Scotland. As brief reminder, that home would be their eighth since marriage in 1967, that a mere nine years ago. Peripatetic indeed!

It would prove to be the experience of a lifetime as the family embraced with open arms the Greek environment with all its shades of colour, light and sounds. Seasonal changes would unexpectedly bring anything between summer's constant heat and sunshine to winter's snows (at least where they were to live), not forgetting the unusual pleasure in eating seasonal fruit, with oranges only available in late autumn! In work terms too, John would in due course opine that to work successfully as an expatriate in Greece, one had to acknowledge and accept that whilst identifying closely with the West, some business practices in Greece had distinct Eastern shades that prevailed year-round, best recognised, and then filed! Their arrival also came very shortly after the Military Junta was deposed, and as Petros would explain, Greeks were now able to say and do things that only a brief few months before would have courted imprisonment.

Ankie, it must be said, was to remain in a constant state of unbridled enthusiasm for their Mediterranean deployment, bringing additional and vicarious pleasure to the rest of the family. She would quickly assimilate sufficient basic Greek, and indeed, ability to read the Cyrillic alphabet, to navigate the local shops, and road signs, with relative ease. She was in her element, and a year-round excellent tan would testify to her happy assimilation into this new environment, with temperatures rarely slipping below 25°C, except when it snowed, and that only lasted a few days in the winter! Most amazingly, she would also warm to summer camping under canvas!

First, however, meeting with the Callitsis family for John and Ankie was achieved, and search for a home initiated, with focus on the northern suburb of Kifissia where the St Catherine's British School was located nearby, in Lykorrissi. To the Perry's untutored eyes, rental payments to 'off-shore' Banks were not only unusual, but also discouraged by SeaLand, John having had to sign a document prior to deployment discouraging, on pain of dismissal, any form of bribery or corruption, although thought did cross his mind at the time that presumably such signings were given but grudging respect for those deployed to Middle East posts. It, therefore, became appropriate to leave all such minor discussions and agreements to one's Agent, to the extent that the viewing of a property in Politia, part of Kifissia, was offered, a detached property reportedly quite close to where President Karamanlis had his official residence, which probably hiked the rental price, but would prove helpful during the winter when the snowploughs came out to clear his way toward Athens. The family therefore travelled thereto, No. 17 Loukianou Street, to find a most attractive residence with a large balcony extending from the front to one side of the house, reached from the road up a short flight of marble steps, that section of the balcony to the side of the house being completely shaded by beautiful, massed wisteria, full-grown along supporting overhead trelliswork. With three bedrooms, a large lounge with a massive fireplace, large kitchen, and a small sitting/play/study room to boot (oh, and a dumb-waiter connection from kitchen to the bedroom floor), together with central heating (more of that later) it was deemed perfect., and would shortly become their eighth, and much-loved, home! Ankie was already visualising just where their much-travelled furniture would complement the lounge, talking of which, their two containers also arrived shortly thereafter, requiring that John present himself to the Greek Customs fraternity to effect clearance. Noting that the house had wooden floors, information was also received that Greeks would take up any carpets during the summer, and replace them during the winter months, suggesting that the new residents of 17 Loukianou might wish to purchase some form of carpeting come the Autumn. There was also a small garage, with an approach driveway so steep as to deny vehicular access, as they would later discover. So, back to central Athens, to the Caravel's pool, and much excited chatter over a glass or two of wine.

Unbeknown to John, it had been necessary for the Agents to apply for Residents/Work permits for the family, which necessarily had to be granted prior to arrival to Greece. Regrettably, and due to late advice of ETA from Rotterdam's HR Manager (no surprise there) hurried submission of Tourist visas were submitted instead, and this was cause of some confusion with the Customs Officers tasked with examination and clearance of the containers. On arrival to the Customs Hall, he found that two Officers had signed off on the clearance, but he was faced with a severe looking female Officer and her questioning. "If you are here as tourists," she started, "why are you bringing household goods, and two cars?" This was an obvious and reasonable enquiry, to which John had neither rational response nor experience in dealing with Greek Customs Officers, so sought to bring some totally irrational humour to the situation. "We British," he commenced half-heartedly, "always travel this way, and the servants follow later," which response got the reaction it so richly deserved, and John discovered that hoping the ground would open beneath his feet and swallow him brought about the same result as anywhere else in the World! A definite 'concrete zeppelin' moment. Fortunately, the Agent somehow enabled (don't ask!) appropriate clearance, and the Perrys then to move into their new home. Note to file: never try to bullshit a Customs Officer with irrational stupidity. When in a hole, stop digging!

School registration to St Catherine's School for Duncan and Darren was achieved, with the long, extended Summer holiday period about to commence, so any initial attendance was more introductory rather than of learning value, but it was a beginning. It was also learned that a school bus would collect and return the boys to a pick-up point in the nearby square, which was not only hugely convenient, but also further source of learning for the pupils as was later, much later, to come to light. The bus driver took it upon himself to teach his young wards to swear, with considerable vocabulary and fluency, in the Greek language, a gift that would remain with them for years to come!

In work terms, and as in all previous appointments, neither job description nor pre-briefing was forthcoming, so yet again it was a case of 'make it up as you go along', which brought substantial opportunity, or challenge, to both the newly appointed Country Manager, and the Callitsis organisation. More formal meeting in the Piraeus Office brought John grounds for optimism however, being introduced to both Emilious Boros (Marine operations) and Nellos Gangos (land operations), both confident and practiced in their spheres of operation. Daughter of Petros Callitsis, Noni Steriotis, was introduced as the Sales Manager, and she too impressed with her knowledge and obvious enthusiasm. George, son of Petros, worked closely with his father in organisation matters, whilst older brother to Petros, Nassos Callitsis, together with his two sons, George and Andreas, otherwise conducted business other than that of SeaLand, but were well briefed as to SeaLand's operation. He met too his to be secretarial assistant Claudia, an Argentinian married to a Greek and herself fluent in the language, not that John would know one way or the other at that stage, although mental note had registered to try and emulate Ankie in acquiring at least a basic knowledge of the language, if only in self-defence. Introduction was also made to the Sales team: Anthony Palaiologos, Dimitris Hoordakis, Alekos Politis, Alekos Kutalogiannis, and Paul Knoll, the last-mentioned being the only one that John could pronounce at that stage, Paul being a Brit, which rather reinforced the need for some language acquisition! It would come, but slowly.

It was also agreed and established that formal weekly meeting, at very least, would involve John, Petros, Noni and her brother, George, with two-way briefing as to all matters pertaining to SeaLand's operation in Greece. In

English! Further that John would also walk freely around the Office as the mood took him, engaging with Staff as deemed necessary. Whilst this was all agreed, lapses into Greek at the weekly meeting did occur from time to time, which excluded John, as was clearly the intention. However, and in time, John would listen to the brief Greek interchange, and then comment in even briefer Greek, that English was the agreed lingua franca (ironically an admix of East Mediterranean languages!) for these meetings, which worked. He would never, however, divulge the degree of his Greek fluency, reflecting as it would the degree of paucity!

During this Office meeting, which preceded the family move into 17 Loukianou Street, Ankie and the boys enjoyed the Hotel pool, and for the boys their first, delighted exposure to 'Souvlaki' or 'Pitta Gyros', as they strolled in and around the Monastiraki 'flea market' neighbourhood in the old town of Athens, a major tourist attraction, at least temporarily justifying their description as tourists! Factually, and as weekends and holidays would prove, tourists they would become, at every possible opportunity, for there was a wealth of history, travel, beaches, and friendships to be explored, and they knew not just how much time they would have in this beautiful country, as experience would constantly nag at John and Ankie. Press on. Persistence and Determination Alone are Omnipotent!

Move into 17, Loukianou went ahead with enthusiasm, and discovery of not only the central heating system down some stairs adjacent to the kitchen, but also two small rooms apparently provided for a 'live-in' servant in days gone by. The central heating system looked akin to a small engine room, and experience would prove need for an oily rag and small hammer, the latter to better coordinate the machine's purpose in moments of mechanical indecision. Ankie decided that this was her 'part of ship' and could be seen on occasion with small traces of oil on her forehead during the winter months, as she persuaded mechanical co-operation in achieving something better than 20°C for the floors above. That would also be helped by pressing the substantial fireplace in the lounge into service, lighting of an admix of pine and olive logs (John's 'part of ship') prompting brief retreat to the kitchen until the initial conflagration eased down!

However, winter months were some way off as July's heat demonstrated the veranda's shaded attractions, and alfresco meals became routinely commonplace, ably supported by the much-travelled mobile barbecue now established in the small back garden, a more obvious adjunct to Greek-style living than perhaps that of Scotland! The veranda also lent itself to ideal and occasional skateboarding for Duncan and Darren, a skill clearly not acquired by their father, as demonstrated by his brief, horizontal flight past the lounge window as skateboard clattered its swift but empty way, sans skateboarder, who shortly re-joined the veranda flat on his back, all cause of much family laughter.

Table lamps were also required and acquired, with first tentative venture into shopping closer to the centre of Athens, bringing home two excellent choices by Ankie, one in sculpted marble, the other onyx, which would grace their homes thereafter to perpetuity, much admired by visitors. Some concern as to the wiring, but no problem in the event. Plumbing would also prove, dare one say, unusual from time to time, but house-owner George Tsagris would attend, and regardless of the plumbing's problem, would always repeat, "Pas de coton, s'il vous plaît, pas de coton.", his French being more practiced than his English.

Obtaining Greek registration of their two vehicles proved to be, for reasons probably associated with cost, impractical, and in that the school bus was available, and John's transport to the Piraeus Office would normally be by Metro from Kifissia Station, need for two cars really did not exist. Obvious choice for retention was the Audi, the much older Volkswagen (once owned by Ankie's father) being dispensable, but how best to achieve that? A flash of intuition prompted John to contact Rotterdam's Dutch operations personnel to see if it could be put into service as a Terminal run-about. It could, came the response, but proof of purchase would be necessary under Dutch Law, and with the price agreed as substantially peppercorn, the vehicle was shipped to Holland, and receipt of cheque for ten Dutch Guilders ruefully displayed on the mantlepiece at Loukianou 17!

John's daily journey was indeed taken by Metro, a journey of some forty minutes which, with the heat of summer and the press of bodies, was not the most engaging or perfumed way to go, but hugely convenient, leaving Ankie with the Audi, now proudly bearing Greek registration plates which, as John was to find out, remained the property of the Greek State. This came about on one of the rare days that John drove to Piraeus when, on returning that evening and leaving the National Road, entered the large roundabout approaching Kifissia, noticing as he did that a Greek Police vehicle also entered the roundabout from a road considerably to his right. Once clear of the roundabout, John was waved down, clearly demonstrating that the Police felt a traffic violation had taken place, and unimpressed by John's protest of innocence in English, wordlessly unscrewed the Audi's registration plates, and drove off. Time for some strong Anglo-Saxon with nautical overtones!

This brought about three days without a vehicle, and an invitation to attend upon the Chief of Police in Athens to discuss retrieval of the plates, and impressed upon him by Ankie's words, 'Honey, not Vinegar, darling', meeting was joined. The Chief of Police, a cheerful exponent of excellent English, was happy to return the plates on receipt of some one hundred Drachmas, no doubt intended for a Police welfare fund or some such, but with cheerfully delivered advice that Court Proceedings would unfortunately follow, as a traffic violation had been registered. Consequent consultation with SeaLand's Lawyer prompted his question, "Do you require witnesses?", to which John replied, in his innocence, that there were no witnesses. "I understand that," came the response, "but do you want witnesses?" Having chosen not to complicate the matter further with 'rent-a-witness' assistance, the Lawyer confirmed date for the hearing, close to Kifissia, instructing John to wear a business suit, and to say absolutely nothing during the hearing, which would be conducted entirely in Greek, which indeed it was with only occasional interruption from the Public Gallery. As the Lawyer spoke at length, so the Judge began nodding approvingly, while expressions of the two attendant Police Officers became increasingly resigned. The 'not guilty' verdict came with some applause from the Public Gallery, and John was free to go. The 'what did you say' question brought forth that the Court had been advised that in Britain, the accused was lauded for his advanced driving skills, and a pillar of society, was a deep lover of Greek hospitality, and recognised Greece as the original seat of democracy. Thankfully, he did not suggest that John could bring about return of the Elgin Marbles. Note to file: avoid any future confrontation with Greek Police like the plague, as well as Customs Officers. It was a learning curve!

Back to work, and a familiarising visit to the new Container Terminal at Keratsini was organised by Emilious Boros on next arrival of an East-bound SeaLand vessel, and John's professional eye noted that the operation was going well, although somewhat bemused on sighting Straddle-carrier drivers occasionally lowering a small tin on a line. "For what?" was his question. Apparently, if certain containers required to be moved by a Straddle-carrier, the tin would be lowered in order to receive a few Drachmas, at which point the container would be moved. Clearly, there was more to it than that, but an interesting demonstration of a local 'revenue improvement programme' which hopefully would not interfere with the vessel's working. John would continue to make occasional visits to the Terminal, but saw no reason to interfere, or suggest change for anything. Back to the Engineers' mantra 'If it ain't broke, don't fix it'!

Whilst unable to retrospectively pinpoint the year between 1976 and 1980, a special visit was, however, made to the Terminal one particular year during the post-Christmas period in that, whilst the Perrys would experience some reasonably heavy snowfall each winter in Kifissia, the northern suburb of Athens, snowfall in Athens itself was unknown, and similarly in Piraeus. The winter in question, however, saw heavy snowfall in Piraeus (not Athens) to the extent that movement of Straddle-carriers were heavily compromised by this unique event, and indeed the whole operation. It had to be seen to be believed. Snow in Piraeus? Surely not, but so it was!

It was fair to say that working in Greece to date far and away presented experiences never generated within John's postings and functions in either Northern Europe or the UK, and whilst his role appeared thus far, and in the main, to be supervisory rather than hands-on, there was an excitement in anticipation of events to come which, coupled to the sheer happiness of his family in the Greek environment, boded well for the duration of their deployment in Greece, and strongly engendered that which is known as 'job satisfaction'!

With the heat of August arrived, and the population of Athens largely departed to their favoured island as was the August wont, a weekend to the islands of Egina and Poros was undertaken, aboard the converted fishing boat 'Mimika', named for the wife of Petros Callitsis, who had kindly offered the craft, together with a crew member, for that weekend. These two islands lay in the Gulf of Salonikos, within easy weekend reach of Piraeus, and was to be the first visit to Greek islands for the family.

First to Egina, through the sun-dappled smooth seas, to anchor close-to a secluded beach on the West coast of the island, whereon beckoned their first view of a beach taverna. First however, much diving and swimming from 'Mimika', and general aquatic besporting and laughter before venturing ashore for lunch in the taverna. From there, a short boat trip to Poros, where they moored in the main harbour in Mediterranean style, stern first to the quayside, before going ashore to enjoy some exploration. They would spend Saturday night on board there, giving them ample time to return to Piraeus on the Sunday, but small mishap to be attended to first. During the night, a ferry arriving to the island had passed their berth, with consequent swell causing 'Mimika's' rudder to briefly bear down hard onto the sandy seabed, such that both pintles jumped free from their holding gudgeons which, as those of the boating fraternity would recognise, is not a good thing insofar as the rudder parts company from the parent vessel. Fortunately, it had been well secured with a lashing, so did not drift off into the night. It was a simple task, that hot Sunday morning, to bring it back into service, but necessitating some considerable swimming and underwater work, at which point the seaman posted aboard (a fisherman as it would transpire) to assist during the weekend confessed his inability to swim!

Ankie looked meaningfully at John, and the boys gave their strong vocal support to her suggestion that Dad's sea-going experience made him the ideal swimming and underwater candidate to sort the job out! Plus, he was the only on aboard who knew what pintles and gudgeons were meant to do! It all brought back memories to John as to when he was serving as Lieutenant RNR and Navigator aboard HMS 'Repton', a School-class Minesweeper when, whilst on exercise in the Gibraltar Strait, a large manilla mooring rope, probably lost from a merchant ship, had wrapped itself around their propellor. A team of volunteers from the crew was mustered on the Bridge, issued with long knives, and instructed as to the task of cutting away the offending rope, the Commanding Officer adding, almost as an after-thought, "and Lieutenant Perry will be leading you", no one more surprised than the afore-mentioned Lieutenant. Plus, he was not included in the double rum issue to the volunteers on successful job completion!

That aside, and eagerly assisted by his non-swimming fisherman crew floating nearby in the 'Mimika' dinghy, plus two small boys also in the water eager to learn all about rudders, pintles and gudgeons, the rudder was reinstated, breakfast was damply taken aboard, and 'Mimika' cast off to make course back to Piraeus.

Some half-way toward their destination, a substantial 'gin-palace' of a cabin-cruiser hove in sight approaching at high speed, and as she settled down with the throttles pulled back, so shouted enquiry came from the craft's 'flying

Bridge' – "Which way to Poros, please?" a question that John found as dangerously lacking in any nautical knowledge, let alone expertise. "Follow my wake," he shouted back in sarcastic tone, and the idiot driving the cruiser gunned his engine with a cheerful wave, to seek out the fast-disappearing track of 'Mimika' through the water. All in all, a wonderful family weekend, within the heady environment that was Greece, and Ankie's tan deepened!

Athens, and probably most of Greece, was twin to Paris in that most people in August were holidaying, and business appointments of a rare opportunity. With all that had been focus of their attention since arriving to Greece, John and Ankie decided that they too needed a break, and so booked the family for a week to an Hotel on the island of Spetses, at the Southern end of the Argolikos Gulf, reached by a very brief ferry ride from mainland Kosta, itself reached after crossing the Corinth Canal, another eye-opening sighting of an amazing example of engineering. No cars were allowed on the island, but it was to be a full week of daily swimming from beaches reached by small boats operated by local fisherman, lunching at the beach taverna, and occasional ride aboard a horse-drawn carriage around town.

They were also, on one day, to sit with a cheerful group of two British families holidaying together, with not the finest outcome as John was invited/persuaded to try the local Ouzo for the first time, which next morning further persuaded him that Ouzo was not for the faint-hearted. In fairness, Ankie and John had, that same evening, tried a horse-drawn carriage ride, only to be taken by the owner-driver to a taverna frequented largely by fishermen, and offering a wide range of Ouzo, which the fishermen seemed keen to share. As before stated, not for the faint-hearted, and carefully avoided in the future. That aside, glorious sunshine throughout, Hotel breakfasts alfresco each morning, and three silly blokes showing off synchronised (well, almost) diving from a pier to a happy Ankie operating the camera, who in turn continued to add to her tan. As she and John jokingly noted, there was no difficulty in deciding which country to visit for holidays, nor much travelling to get to where they wanted to go! Notably, their many, and always welcome, visitors from more northern climes were to confirm that Loukianou 17 was a great place to start!

The holiday would have an unusual ending, but then so much of Greek experience would prove that as on offer. The daily boat service to beach and taverna operated by the fisherman scheduled the last boat of the day back to the town as leaving promptly at 4 p.m. However, an obvious entrepreneur (the French have no good translation for this word) introduced a new minibus service, with the last evening beach departure at 5 p.m. So popular was this last bus as to produce a sardine-type cramming of scantily clad people from the beach, one day to such an extent that John jokingly offered the warning that should anyone involve in sex on the bus, there would be a fine! Short thoughtful silence, and then from the back of the bus the shouted question, "How much!"

It could have happened that the fishermen would adapt their last departure from the beach, to at least match that of the minibus, but collectively decided upon a more abrupt way to disenfranchise the competition – they collectively appropriated the minibus and chucked it into the sea! Cause célèbre in the Athens Courts for months to come!

The weekly meetings with Petros aka Peter, Noni and George went well, with John's first impression as to their business qualities further enhanced as he was brought up to date with both marketing and operational aspects, and areas of his possible marketing involvement, such as the potential in exports of tobacco, and considerable movements of Military house-hold goods from the substantial US Military base close to Athens. The former would quickly develop into a visit to Thessaloniki, or Salonika as non-Greeks knew it, and a developing friendship with one Art Barfield, himself ex-US Military and settled in Athens, and much involved in the latter. Petros would also visit John's office, a floor below his own, on a frequent basis to advise or discuss issues that would arise on a day-to-day basis. It was a sound business relationship that would develop into one of easy friendship, based on mutual, albeit wary, respect!

With just a few short months into the Greek appointment, it was becoming increasingly clear to John that his position was demanding a greater business and social involvement in the shipping fraternity that had heretofore been either necessary or appropriate elsewhere. Added to this was the fact that he and Ankie would be hosting far more visitors than ever experienced in previous appointments (something to do with the weather apparently!), their growing social life within the large expatriate community and, finally, the dawning realisation that perhaps business opportunities also existed in Romania and Bulgaria, not thus far recognised by SeaLand. These would require his personal evaluation, as time would prove.

All in all, a formidable balancing act, but in happy counterpoint was a totally supportive and enthused Ankie, two sons in their absolute element, a wealth of newly developed friendships, and the proven expertise and application of the Callitsis Agency. Oh, and the strong probability that there would be no requirement to seek out holiday brochures! Deeper water? Only thus far in the sense of manageable involvement and, indeed, pleasantly warmer!

September brought but one arrival of visitors, a Dutch couple, Ger and Celia Versloot, good friends from John's time in Rotterdam, whilst Duncan's tenth birthday, his first in Greece, was duly celebrated. Acquired friendships were enjoyed as the summer weekends continued to draw many of the expats each Saturday to Skinias Beach near Marathon (site of the 490 bc defeat by Greece of Cyrus the Great and his larger invading Persian army, and consequent run with the good news) a long stretch of beautiful sands backed by trees, undiscovered by, and undeveloped for, mass tourism at that time. It boasted a small Taverna specialising in fish dishes, and the ever-present ice-cream man with his cries of 'Pagotó, Pagotó'. Never on a Sunday though, as the beach was a firm favourite with Athenians, who would arrive there in their droves each Sunday, sadly leaving their substantial litter behind them, which the St Catherines Cub Scouts together with parents, would seek to clear with organised 'litter-picks,' the local Council providing trucks (usually two) to carry away the accumulated and bagged rubbish. Sadly, probably to landfill or worse.

John's mother and stepfather, Alex, took advantage of October's continued heat in Greece to take time out from Britain's gloomy Autumn. Much of their daytime entertainment fell to Ankie, but warm, balmy evenings on the terrace, or family visits to local Tavernas always rounded off the day. They also accompanied the family to a small Hotel in Tolon, a seaside town just south of Nafplion where they stayed for two nights, they too having had their first sighting of the famous Corinth Canal over which they crossed, before turning South to the coast. Attending dinner on their final night was to be amazed, as the Waiters gave what really appeared to be an involuntary, and entirely spontaneous, exhibition of traditional Greek dancing (males only, and think 'Zorba the Greek' music) to the huge appreciation and delight of their entranced audience.

Grangemouth, Genova, Rotterdam, Algeciras, Rotterdam, Athens, Kifissia, Greek Customs Officers and Police Officers, a Court appearance, new home, new schooling, four Greek islands (to include boat repairs!) summer visitors, Tolon, and throughout need to both understand and assimilate into not only an extraordinary business and social environment but work and play within it. It had been an absorbing, lively, eventful, concerning, hectic and, dare one say it, sedulous six months, and with Christmas and Darren's eighth birthday to close the year, a family sigh of happy relief as bells announced the arrival of 1977. As a beginning to this phase of their lives, it appeared to offer potential! Press on – persistence and determination.

The weak sunshine of a February weekend 1977 brought the Perrys to Delphi, there to marvel at the amphitheatre, the acoustics, and the legends that embraced that historic place. Not to mention the rather hair-raising experience of driving Greek mountain roads, something else not for the faint-hearted. "Look over there" would breathe Ankie, pointing in wonder at a view, such suggestion resolutely declined by John, intent on avoiding the sheer drops one side or the other of the narrow, winding ascent or descent, as then prevailed.

It was also the month when they would experience their first Greek snowfall – not at Delphi, although just a good throw of a snowball from the Mount Parnassos Ski Resort could land on the ancient archaeological site that is Delphi. Well, almost. Their snowfall was back home in Politia, a good six to eight centimetres which, whilst not a lot, had similar effect to a similar fall in the UK, amounting to considerable short-lived excitement and traffic chaos! Excitement as a snowplough, in clearing the road for President Karamanlis, buried cars parked at the roadside. Further excitement as dozens of cars from central Athens, not known for their use of winter tyres, arrived to enjoy the white stuff, with each driver to build a snowman around the vehicle's whip aerial to further contribute to looming insurance claims! Duncan and Darren loved it, whilst John and Ankie threw more logs onto the already roaring fire in the lounge! The snow lasted some three days, although the temperatures stayed well below the magic 25°C level.

In anticipation of a busy summer, John flew to Bucharest early in the first quarter of the year, there to evaluate the potential for containerised goods to move from Romania to the Middle East, via the SeaLand service over Piraeus. It was to find the streets still home to dirty snow, bitterly cold weather, and the bureaucracy of Nicolae Ceausescu's totalitarian Presidency all-pervading. On the potential plus side, he was aware that in seeking to reduce the substantial National Debt, the President had ordered a massive focus on exports of machinery and other manufactured goods, added to which, John had brought a bottle of quality Scotch whisky with him, to break the ice, so to speak which, surprisingly, had not been confiscated by Customs Officers on arrival to Bucharest. On checking in to his Hotel in central Bucharest, he was to find that one could only change currency at an official centre, and to beware of anyone seeking to offer exchange in the streets, as that person could be of the Securitate, or Secret Service.

Meeting pre-arranged for the following morning was duly convened, and to John's surprise, by a severe looking woman who identified herself as the Protocol Officer, adding as she did that the whisky had to be consumed before lunch, or it would be confiscated. No one chose to argue the point with her, and as the two men conducting the meeting appeared quite happy with the instruction and the whisky, John concluded it best to crack on quickly with the detail before attention was spiritually transduced! Lunch was taken at the canteen within the office premises, with John returned to his Hotel by his hosts, and further meeting arranged for the following morning. In essence, it was to be that decision had been taken to make a trial shipment via Piraeus, to be advised at a later date, and so thankful return to Athens from an impoverished Romania.

Follow-up visits to Bucharest would be planned, the only outstanding memory being of attending, during one such visit, the Theatre in Bucharest, to an evening performance of 'Swan Lake' by the Romanian State Ballet Company, an experience of extraordinary worth, breath-taking in its setting and performance. Leaving the theatre was to find a long line of black ZIL cars, clearly allocated to State officials attending, with an enterprising driver offering ride to John's Hotel, very happily pocketing the US$10 'tip', which probably equalled his weekly wage. His family would eat that night!

Similar exploratory visit would be made to Sofia, Bulgaria, there to find much Russian influence, and a reluctance to pursue fresh thinking if that could lead to change, with decision-makers' appointments appearing to depend on a political 'flavour of the month' methodology. Nevertheless, awareness of Piraeus as a potential gateway to the Middle East was achieved, and contacts established.

With the first quarter of 1977 coming to a close, a new factor to be defined as 'different in Greece' loomed large, namely Easter, and whilst neither John nor Ankie held any strong religious views, it was obvious that the Greek Orthodox Church celebrated Easter later than that of the Catholic Church, to generalise. It followed the Julian Calendar, as designed by Julius Caesar in 45BC, compared to the Catholic leaning, the Gregorian Calendar as enacted by Pope Gregory in 1582. Reportedly, the calendars occasionally brought conjunction to the two Easters, but rarely. The factor common to both was the Vernal Equinox, in that Easter was in both cases defined as falling on the first Sunday after the full moon that follows said Equinox (please keep up!), which is to say the date upon which the centre of the Sun is directly above the Earth's equator. This had little to do with containerised shipping, but did define the date, April 10th, upon which John, Ankie, Duncan and Darren were invited to Anavissos, the summer home of Petros aka Peter Callitsis near Sounion, to celebrate Greek Easter, and to enjoy the lamb being barbecued over more than a few hours, and an open fire, the boys taking their turn in rotating the spit, and stroking with the rosemary. The event was hosted by both Nassos and Petros, with George son of Petros overseeing and timing the feast to be. There was another unusual but definitive marking of the Orthodox way, the dying of eggs red, reportedly to represent the blood of Christ's tomb. The eggs would be hard-boiled, and cracked against that of a fellow-celebrant, as they wished each other religious wellness. Irreligiously perhaps, but being ignorant of Orthodox beliefs, the Perry boys likened it to playing conkers, but more interesting! The lamb, incidentally, was not carefully sliced, but rather chopped up with a small axe, and no evidence of mint sauce! Delicious, nonetheless!

One of the major Freight Forwarders in Athens, Veinoglou, was headed up by Orphee Moschopolou, who also held membership of the BAR, or British Association of Removers, which generated considerable business for him, and by extension, SeaLand. Introduction to him for John and Ankie, and later to his wife, Annette, developed into a warm friendship, shared also with one Gordon Ball and his wife, Pauline, which resulted in frequent Taverna meals as a group, and indeed weekend visits to a so-referred Skinos beach northeast of Corinth, facing the Gulf of Corinth, where Gordon and Pauline had access to a small bungalow. All that John and Ankie were required to do on such occasions was to collect a large (very large) block of ice from a shop en route that sold, believe it or not, large blocks of ice for those that had doubtful refrigeration facilities, which covered many of the local village houses. Also, to bring the boys' tent to augment sleeping arrangements. The crystal-clear night skies would dazzle with the brilliance of stars and planets, and all would seem well in the World, with only the faint barking of village dogs to evidence the presence of other people across the valley faced by the bungalow.

Yet another interesting aspect of life in Greece was the very late hour at which people took their evening meal, with small children a common sight with their parents. To get to a taverna before 8 p.m. was to find it scarcely operative, but worth the wait as the food offerings were outstanding. This in turn defined the need for exercise, and whilst much was taken at weekends in the sea, or the American Club pool, John was astutely conscious that Ankie's perfectly retained figure bore implied suggestion that he too had a responsibility to keep himself trim (fortunately, she still saw him as 'work in progress') which prompted him to join the Ekali Club close to their residence, as it sported a single Squash Court, although somewhat different to a standard Court. The floorboards were laid from side to side of the Court rather than fore and aft, and the back wall held a coin machine for the lighting, which made for some amazing, nay frustrating, ball trajectories on the rebound. Bob Shire, the Johnson and Johnson man in Athens, first introduced as a customer, also became a good friend and Squash partner, he and his wife living but a street away from Loukianou Street.

Two issues of business concerns rankled with John; the first, the usual matter of SeaLand's communication, or lack of it. Since his arrival to Greece in June of 1966, there has been absolutely no contact from the Genoa Head Office in general, or from Rupe Hickler the Mediterranean General Manager in particular, which begged the question in John's mind whether his earlier declination of a move from Scotland to Genoa had harvested some sour grapes as a result. Indeed, it would not be until late 1978 that involved Country Managers (Spain, Italy, and Greece) would be called for a general meeting, to be held in Madrid. Meanwhile, the SeaLand 'churn' factor continued unabated through Europe and the UK, information relating to such personnel movements apparently deemed as being of no interest or benefit to other than the personnel involved. Most unbusinesslike!

The second concern related to the fact that Genoa oversaw budgetary control for the Greek operation but had neither sought budgetary input from John or advice to format a budget, nor offered any textual evidence that a formal budget existed. This in turn smacked of, at best, fiscal incompetence or, at worst, some form of potential interest conflict. Added to this was fact that expenses generated in Greece were routinely sent to Genoa by the Agency for approval, being routinely approved without question by people with neither operational experience in Greece, nor ability to read Greek, bringing imperative meaning to the French 'carte blanche'! Much food for thought, to John's conclusion that a way had to be found to at least bring more local and knowledgeable scrutiny and critique to cost reports, prior to despatch to Genoa. This in turn indicated need to appoint a SeaLand, Greek speaking, Accountant au fait with the maritime industry, or who John could train accordingly, which would require the establishment of a local Company structure which, in its turn, demanded thoughtful evaluation and research – tranquillo! Political developments and unrest over the coming months in Beirut, Lebanon would sponsor the answer as to the practical solution and wherewithal. The Turkish invasion of Cyprus in 1974 would also have a bearing!

More immediately, the establishment of a rented property in Athens had been requested/required by Middle East Management, to be utilised as a 'Rest and Recuperation' (R'n'R) facility for personnel rotating out of Saudi and Iran mainly, although clearly it was also used more casually by general Middle East Management visiting the operational area, both before and after visits to their bailiwick. The finding of a furnished property was delegated to Gordon Ball's Company, as was the provision of bed linen, towels, and general husbandry as appropriate, with costs to be borne against whichever Division had budgeted for the facility (?) and billed via the Greek Agency. All very casual. It would stay in operation until sometime in 1980/81 when SeaLand withdrew service from Iran, and expatriate life in the Middle East was more tolerable and manageable in terms of goods and services. Recollection has it that the then Belgium Country Manager for Iran had to leave the country covertly, actually hidden in the last container to be loaded aboard SeaLands final sailing from Bandar Abbas. Not to be generally recommended, but needs must, etc!

London also boasted a Company apartment close to Harrods, its use open to anyone senior enough passing through, and husbanded by the UK's then SeaLand office in London. John and Ankie would avail themselves of it one time during their Greek appointment, with Ankie concluding that purchase of a bikini from Harrods was both necessary and appropriate, with no Hotel bill to pay!

With May's sunshine becoming already persuasive, a brief week in Corfu with the family was envisaged, and an Hotel tentatively booked, only for Peter Callitsis to offer alternative free accommodation in a more luxurious Corfu Hotel, managed by an old school friend of his. Sadly, and with memories of signing the 'no acceptance of gifts above a certain value' form, his thoughtful offer had to be declined. In the event, the Hotel originally booked was so bad, with not only sewage smells pervading the grounds and surrounds, but also antagonism toward the high spirits of Duncan and Darren displayed by the Hotel Manager. After two days, Hotel vacated, ferry return to mainland, and drive to Tolon, to the small Hotel adjacent to the beach previously visited and enjoyed. It turned out to be an excellent 'Plan B', with John demonstrating to the boys how to water-ski – actually, how not to water-ski, although his coming off the skis when under fast tow was impressive! Also, a rowing boat attempt with the boys to round the (apparently) small island in the sea approaches to Tolon, known locally as the 'Breasts of Helen', only to find the island's actual size too large to handle, so to speak. Finally, in adventure terms, a day visit to Olympia, where John, Duncan and Darren raced against each other along the length of that ancient track. Ankie watched fondly the waterborne lessons from her sun-bathing position on the sands, joined in the Family swimming and cavorting in the sea, and supported the boys' assertion that they had beaten Dad in the mini-Olympics! There was also a race along Tolon's sands towards the end of the stay, but as it was after a superb supper in the Hotel, enhanced by some cheeky Greek wine for Mum and Dad, the boys' claim to a clear victory was challenged, John being sure that Duncan had caused him to trip and fall, not the Domestica wine!

With the summer months of 1977 drawing close, so did the increase of visitors to the Perry's coincidentally, and incrementally increase, but despite this the routine of business life continued unabated, with Sealand's reputation and customer support similarly expanding container liftings to and from the Middle East, the United States, and indeed the intra-Europe opportunities, despite overland truck competition to the last-mentioned. One such business development required John's personal attendance in Patras, situated in the NW corner of the Peloponnesus, to supervise the experimental filling of bulk red wine pumped into an expanding plastic 'bag' already placed into a SeaLand 35 ft, open top container, which neatly filled the container once full of wine, thereafter to be shipped to Rotterdam from Piraeus, there to be bottled and sold on. Successfully completed, evening meal was taken with the exporters at an open-air beachside Taverna, the meal sadly being disturbed by a sizeable earthquake measuring somewhere between 5.5 and 6 on the Richter Scale, judging by fact that Ankie reported that 17 Loukianou Street was shaken by the vibrations, despite being some 200 kms. from Patras. The epicentre was reported as being somewhere west of Kefalonia in the Ionian Sea. That aside, the Taverna was immediately vacated by all except John who, insofar as nothing could fall on his head as he was sitting in the open-air, there seemed little point in wasting a good meal, even if the Greek God Seilenos, God of wine-making and drunkenness, was displeased by the day's successful export to Rotterdam, perhaps believing the strong word that the robust Greek wine was to be mixed with an inferior French wine, and sold as French wine. Bacchus too would have been similarly affronted, had his patch been similarly sullied!

Back to the visitors, however, with the month of June welcoming Peter and Carolyn Parson, together with very young daughter Natalie, from Genève, Switzerland. Peter had been a year more senior contemporary of John's in the P & O, he too having left the sea at about the same time as John, finding his success with Tradax, a fiercely independent subsidiary of Cargill Inc., having risen by that time to Assistant Vice-President with all Operational responsibility for the Tradax owned Fleet. They were, indeed, long-term friends, with many reminiscences to share. Eight-year-old Darren sought to teach Natalie, well his junior, how to swim in the warm waters of the American Club pool, and much laughter and bonhomie marked their week's stay. Ankie by now had become a well-practiced host, spiriting up superb meals eaten, as always, al fresco on the terrace, in the balmy evenings.

July bought Eric and Esther Dougan, their good friends from Polmont Scotland to Loukianou Street and, indeed, Skinias Beach where, despite rather overcast skies that day, Eric managed to achieve some unwelcome Greek sunburn. As John's Squash partner in Scotland, he was most amused by the 'unusual' Squash Court of the Ekali Club, but was delighted to try the Greek brewed beer, suitably chilled. They too made enjoyable guests, and happy to embrace the Greek lifestyle for the first time, if only briefly, no doubt reminding them of their own expat days in Kenya.

September saw a second visit by John's parents, which in turn inspired another weekend aboard 'Mimika' to the islands of Egina and Poros – sadly, the beach taverna previously visited had been turned into a self-service offering which disappointed, but sea swimming and sunshine remained highly rated. No rudder problems this time, although the usual fisherman crew member had no feel for the craft in his steering through choppy seas on the way back to Piraeus, obliging John to relieve him from the helm to prevent parents from falling sea-sick! The question was pondered, but not voiced, whether he was even able to catch fish. They too enjoyed a return to Skinias Beach, with stepfather, Alex particularly keen to join Duncan and Darren, both now expert swimmers, in the sea. One jump of his, however, into a rubber dinghy on loan to John and Ankie, brought a sudden punctured end to said dinghy's further availability. Alex's obvious remorse was laughingly dispersed, his joy in joining the boys boisterous play in the sea far outweighing the now deflated dinghy.

September was also the time to greet older brother, Michael, and sister-in-law, Joan, they being en route back to Thailand where Michael held a senior role with Unilever. Joan had, pre-travel, somehow sustained a painful sprain to one ankle, and request for wheelchair support was received prior to their arrival to Greece, which the Athens Red Cross was happy to supply. The rental price, however, took Michael by surprise, accustomed as he was to the pittance that the Malvern Red Cross had charged, or he had negotiated. So much so, that he suggested Joan should stay in the wheelchair for the extent of their two-to-three-day visit, just to get their monies-worth! That joking aside, a delightful few days, with Michael sporting his Thai 'shirt of many colours', with no obvious signs of embarrassment!

Duncan's eleventh birthday was, of course, celebrated in September which, quite apart from the obvious celebrations with the boys' increasing circle of friends, also marked the beginning of his last year at St Catherine's School. This in turn would prompt discussion with Christine Tutte, the ever supportive, and much appreciated, Head Teacher. That would come later, however.

In between hosting visits, John would continue to meet with other expat businessmen, a disparate group that would gather about monthly, to discuss matters relating to doing business in Greece, employment rates, legal wrinkles and so forth. Interestingly, it was a widely held view, John was to learn, that if, as an expat, a Company kept the employee in Greece for more than five years, the Company was trying to tell that employee something not necessarily to his promotional credit. In John's mind, to hear anything from his Company, just occasionally, would be a pleasant change, but business growth alone seemed insufficient cause for contact, particularly where the American expat 'churn' through Europe kept those seemingly involved in 'empire building' focussed elsewhere. Compared to past appointments though, five years in Greece seemed a real treat to John and Ankie!

Christmas was happily spent in 17, Loukianou Street, with no disparity noted twixt the Orthodox and non-Orthodox desire to celebrate the event on December 25th, although doubtless differences existed in both theological and gastronomical customs and tastes! Surprise visit was also received during the afternoon of Christmas Eve, as Petros Callitsis arrived with many presents for Duncan and Darren, and a framed painting in oils of a rural landscape for John and Ankie which took pride of place in the lounge and would continue to so do wherever the future was to take the family. It was known that the Greeks were a strong family people, and the generosity of Petros reflected in the boys' presents confirmed that, together with his personal appearance all the way from his family home the other side of Athens. The oil painting by D. Gibbs, an American contemporary artist, was probably valued in excess of the 'no gift to be accepted above a certain value' guidance, but in the spirit of Christmas, and knowledge that none of John's American colleagues would have done otherwise, the gift was humbly accepted.

Another surprise came also, a complete tape of Christmas music compiled from vinyl records by Art Barfield at his home in Glyfada, with voice-over message offering 'a very Merry Christmas from Glyfada to my friends the Perrys in Politia', which gift would similarly travel with the family wherever the future took them.

The third surprise was that it snowed late that Christmas in Politia, which rather completed the Christmas scene of a roaring log fire, a bedecked Christmas tree, a wealth of presents to open, and a wonderfully happy family. Oh, and not to forget the substantial Flokati carpet purchased in the Autumn, to mark the date that the Greeks, traditionally, it seemed, restore their rugs and carpets ready for the winter. In a way, not dissimilar to Italian ladies who, it was rumoured, would only bring forth their winter fashion boots until a certain date. Was there turkey available? Memory falters, but assuredly the indomitable Ankie would have procured the largest chicken available, which would have passed muster. Al fresco on the terrace? With the temperature a lot less than 25°C, the Boss she say, "Certainly not."

Darren's ninth birthday, duly celebrated in style, saw out the year, whilst John and Ankie greeted 1978 also in some style, and contentment. They pondered that the New Year was as yet completely undefined and raised their glasses to each other in solemn acknowledgement that together they were ready for whatever was thrown their way! Actually, an early surprise was to discover that Maria, their regular 'baby-sitter' (a slight misnomer with sons of nine and eleven years respectively) had occasionally passed the time of night in sampling the grog locker, her preference focussing on liqueurs, samples of which she would offer Duncan and Darren, presumably to gain their silence both to her sampling, and predilections. It was quietly suggested that she was welcome to the occasional tincture, with emphasis on both 'small' and 'occasional', but not for the boys! Justice tempered with mercy or, as Ankie once again advised, honey rather than vinegar, and Maria's good services were retained.

The issue of gaining a more independent purview over operational costs continued to occupy John's mind, to the extent that he had indeed concluded that employment of a Greek-speaking Accountant was an imperative, which in turn, progressed to thoughts of establishing a Sealand office separate from that of the Agency organisation. Within Greek Law there already existed means for a Company to establish a formal presence in Greece, under the so-called Law 89, which was in fact drawn up to attract such business, offering a tax-free environment in which to operate. Traditionally, however, Beirut had in the past been favoured by Corporations seeking such a tax-free facility, but the political turmoil and factional fighting amounting to civil war, further exaggerated by the Israel/PLO fighting in Southern Lebanon had by 1978 shattered Lebanon's infrastructure, as too its reputation for cross-sectarian co-existence in the Arab Middle East. This, in turn, made Greece increasingly business attractive, and with Law 89 suitably adapted to enhance the attraction, opportunity presented itself for John to seek more formal advice as to ways and means. That in turn would lead, towards the late Summer of 1978, to the hiring of a Greek-Cypriot Accountant, he and his family being reluctant refugees from the Turkish annexation of their North Cypriot home, and now living in Athens. His name was Polis Leonida, and SeaLand's own office was opened just a block away from the Agency office in Piraeus, housing John and his Secretary Claudia, Polis, and an Assistant whose name, sadly, swirls somewhere in the mists of memory. She was extremely efficient, an asset to the professionalism of Polis, and the office almost immediately took on a business-like team spirit, leavened with good humour.

All of that, however, was to come later in the year, with much to occupy the routine business meantime, starting in February with a formal Customer reception in the Callitsis Filonos Street office, and a Dinner Dance held at the Hilton Hotel Athens in March by the Propeller Club of Piraeus Port. Attendance to guest speakers at Propeller Club gatherings were good value, if only in matter of networking within the industry, and the Hilton evening was not one to be missed, with Ankie as always resplendent in evening gown, having ensured that John's bowtie was properly tied (P & O and RN training frowned on tailor-made ties!) and his dinner jacket brushed. March too would bring a Carnival Dance to attend at the St Catherine's School, so the authorised tinctures of liqueur for Maria the 'baby-sitter' were beginning to stack up!

It was to be a year of travel too, starting with an overdue visit to the UK, home of John's parents, in Cradley near Malvern, at Easter, which that year fell on Sunday March 26th. The visit was pre-arranged by John's mother, in that all three of her sons, together with wives and families, could be present. Brian, the youngest, was on home leave from his sea-going service as Chief Officer with the Swire Group of Hong Kong, Michael as the oldest on home leave from South America, his current appointment as Chairman, Unilever Argentina, and John able to join them with his family for the unique gathering, from Greece. A 'far-flung' family indeed, happily reunited that Easter.

The Orthodox Easter followed on April 6th, and would that year be celebrated back home in Loukianou 17 by John and family, together with friends of theirs, the Smalley family. Much barbecuing of lamb chops (no space for a Callitsis style lamb roast!) and various cuts of lamb from the butcher in Kifissia, carefully selected by Ankie in her basic acquired Greek. It is here noted that there are two levels of spoken Greek, Democratikia spoken by the average person, and that spoken by such as Lawyers, a formal arrangement known as Katharevousa (pronounced as spelt) Pointing in the butcher's shop happily supported Ankie's still slim Democratikia vocabulary! Atta girl!

There were to be weekend barbecues at both the Skinias Beach with friends in April, and in May at the EMI Beach with Alan and Pat Boxer, he being the MD of EMI in Greece, with EMI boasting a small private beach. Pat Boxer was also one of the three ladies having active roles in the Cub Scouts which, although being granted use of the St Catherine's School premises for activities, was nevertheless independent of the School, providing organised leisure time activities for the boys outside of School hours. The Perry boys were both proud members of the Pack and were again to be part of the occasional 'routine' enterprise of the always substantial 'litter-picks' at Skinias Beach during the summer months. The other two ladies with active role involvement were Rosie Revel, (Pack Leader) and wife of Paul (WM E & E), and Jenny Cooper, wife of Brian (Continental Illinois Bank), the three families being totally dedicated to the well-being of their young Cubs and, it must be said, having warmly welcomed the Perrys into the expat social life that existed in such abundance. They were to remain good friends thereafter.

Summer weekends were also spent again at Skinos Beach with Orphee Moschopoulou and Annette, Gordon, and Pauline Ball (and large ice blocks) as welcome breaks from the weekly routine of travel to and from business in Piraeus. Communication from either Genoa or Rotterdam came there none, but with the Greek contribution to Sealand's liftings on the steady increase, it was hopefully assumed that both those centres of Corporate excellence were otherwise gainfully employed. The friendship and working relationship with the Callitsis family and team continued to grow with the occasional business lunch enjoyed (and sometimes joined by Ankie) at Turku Limano, or Micro Limano (small harbour) as it was to be re-named, favoured watering hole of the family Callitsis, always there warmly welcomed in the small Tavernas as long-term patrons. It is a fact that John had developed a strong aversion to that Greek culinary favourite, squid, having seen on too many occasions said aquatic catch beaten to death on rocks, before being hung up to dry. Retrospective shudder!

Unexpectedly, further travel for John was initiated by his brother, Michael, in Buenos Aires, in that their father, long retired and living in Douglas, Isle of Man, had fallen ill and with Michael so distanced, came the request for John to visit and assess the situation. It was a brief expedition over some three days and visit to the Hospital in Douglas confirmed that their father was suffering an advanced form of dementia, with the need to be transferred to a Care Home as paramount. With Power of Attorney resting with Michael, John could do no more than submit a detailed sitrep and return to Greece. The Care Home move was successfully completed, but their father was to pass away later in that year of 1978.

The summer months brought the wonderful sunshine which by now had become the norm, but this year surprisingly bereft of visitors from more northern climes. Notwithstanding, the Flokati carpet was sent for dry-cleaning, (going native!) and the shaded terrace of Loukianou 17 was brought into frequent al fresco play for family, and the entertainment of friends such as David and Elly Faulkner (he a Civil Engineer, and she his Dutch wife) among many others. In passing, it should also be mentioned that both dogs and cats of the feral variety abounded in Greece, and Politia had its share with a pack of some eight such dogs resident in an adjacent wooded area, whilst Duncan and Darren had adopted a kitten of the cat variety, allowed in the house until Ankie lost her patience, and then the kitten. They named it Kevin Keegan; the kitten having displayed adroit ball control with a ping-pong ball! That aside, domesticated dogs were rarely allowed into Greek homes, spending the hot days sleeping in the shade, resorting to communicating with other dogs in the cool of the night, and joined by those now feral. A leader of this nightly cacophony was named Brandy, owned by the Greek family directly opposite to Loukiano 17, and on one hot, humid, airless, sleepless night, at 0300 hours to be precise; this became too much for John to bear. He arrived at the neighbour's front door in his dressing gown, wellington boots (don't ask!) and clutching a golf club snatched from his golf bag, expressing a strong intention to kill their dog unless it was restrained! With cries of 'Brandy, Brandy, ellas, ellas', offending hound was bundled inside, with diplomatic relations probably severed. And so, to sleep, perchance to dream. It is a matter of record that some weeks later, another close neighbour, presumably similarly sleep-deprived, put poisoned meat into Brandy's reach, sadly a more finite solution than a brandished golf club!

As autumn approached, there came further unexpected need to travel, this time to attend a Mediterranean Management meeting to be held in Madrid, the first such gathering since John's arrival to Greece some two years before, or certainly the first to which he had been invited to join. Details of that meeting have largely faded but suffice it to say that John was introduced to Matt Quartel, the Dutch Country Manager for Spain, and Dick McGregor, the newly arrived from America Country Manager for Italy, and replacing Jerry File. Also, Marcello Arpino, the regional Pricing Manager, an Italian of great charm and ability. The first day of the meeting was concluded with some welcome refreshments, and with dinner scheduled for another part of town, John and

Dick McGregor took taxi thereto, together with the remains of a liqueur bottle, rather than letting it go to waste! At the end of the second day, during which John briefed Rupe Hickler as to the planned creation of a SeaLand office in Piraeus and its purpose, the midnight departure of Ethiopian Airways back to Athens was taken, John marvelling firstly as to the length of the Ethiopian Pilots arms as they walked to the flight deck (the irreligious and unfair word 'camels' flitted briefly through his mind), and secondly that he was the only passenger on the flight, which brought immaculate in-flight service! Return home was warmly greeted by Ankie, even at that ghastly time in the morning, and return to the office brought about the implementation of planned hiring of Accountant and move from the Agency office to the newly established SeaLand office.

One of the first visitors to the new office was the American Don Hamm who, having been moved by Tom Yost from his operational responsibilities in Rotterdam to responsibility for the intra-Europe services, saw the need to improve his knowledge of the growing Greek involvement. John's Secretary, Claudia, had also just returned from brief pregnancy leave, and was clearly having trouble in regaining her figure, so was somewhat distressed by Don's cheerful greeting, "Hi Claudia, and when is the baby doo?" (spoken phonetically!) Fortunately, Don's inherent charm and ready wit, not to mention diplomacy, saved the day, such that peace and happiness was quickly regained. Don Hamm, not unlike Dick McGregor, was one of the too few Americans sent to Europe that chose to assimilate, enjoy, and work with the culture of whatever country into which they were pitched, benefiting accordingly.

Review of monthly Agency cost reports began to show a pattern of assumptions over certain cost allocations to SeaLand that Genoa had to date accepted and approved without question which, by default brought further and continued assumptions legitimacy. In due course, and after careful cross-checking, these were discretely brought to the attention of the Mediterranean General Manager in Genoa, together with the suggestion that John could bring the matter to a close, although the quantum of past approvals would remain unaddressed. Response from Genoa came there none, with a delegation from Menlo Park subsequently arriving unannounced to Piraeus, convening meeting with the Agency from which John was excluded, and outcomes of which remained unadvised. A sad display of ignoring established norms of

Management etiquette, but life went on as if nothing had happened, save that SeaLand's East Med cash flow/margins did improve!

With Christmas, Darren's birthday, and the New year of 1979 all properly celebrated in Loukianou 17, once again John and Ankie, now into their third year in Greece, paused to re-evaluate the runes, the magic signs or hidden lore that apparently governed the SeaLand personnel 'churn'. With equally apparent exclusion from any personnel re-location information in their corner of the organisation, the 'make it up as you go along' aspect of SeaLand employment had to prevail, and that included schooling, particularly for Duncan whose time at the St Catherine's School would end in September, come his twelfth birthday. They chose to assume (always a dangerous game) that they would not be re-located during 1979, and after discussion with Christine Tutte, Head Teacher at St Catherine's, saw the Campion School in Athens as the best option to pursue.

Of significant interest was the Headmaster Jack Meyer who, at the age of sixty-eight had in 1973 taken on the Headmastership of Campion, having previously established the Millfield School in England in 1935, there remaining until 1971. Graduating from Cambridge with a double First in Classics, his scholastic reputation was high, as well as having inspired some tales as to his eccentricity! Meeting was duly arranged, and having suitably impressed the Headmaster, Duncan was accepted for entry in the September Term, subject only to potential runes, magic signs, or hidden lore!

Meantime, both Duncan and Darren involved fully in the St Catherine's sporting and cultural programmes, Duncan as Shakespeare's Mark Anthony praising and burying Caesar, and Darren as a highly active Morris Dancer in whatever cultural bracket that portrayal fell!

SeaLand's vessels came and went, but the Master of one such vessel, having slipped and fallen into a hatch of his vessel in the Middle East, arrived to Athens by air. He was being flown to the United States on a commercial flight, but the aircraft's Captain, concerned that the severe injuries sustained would bring death before arrival to the States, diverted to Athens, the Patient being disembarked and transferred to a small community Hospital. News of this fortunately came to John's attention, and he made haste to visit that Hospital, there to find the Patient, clearly in great pain and distress, virtually unattended in an open Ward where other Patients were being fed by their attendant relatives. Immediate discussion with Consultants at Athens major

Hospital Evangelismos in Kolanaki brought about an ambulance being swiftly despatched therefrom, and the SeaLand Captain being stretchered from his then Hospital bed back to Evangelismos Hospital where, post several very necessary operations, he resided in Intensive Care for several worrying weeks. The move looked and felt almost like a 'body snatch', with absolutely no medical Staff from the initial hospitalisation being in evidence during the Patient's removal, although John had to hope that some liaison had taken place between hospitals. The operations were successful, and repatriation to the States eventually achieved. Some weeks later, a letter of thanks from the Patient was received by John, but factually his life had been saved by decision of the aircraft's Captain to divert to Athens.

Otherwise, business life continued apace, and weekends were similarly pursued at pace, with social commitments unabated, almost exhaustingly so. Embarrassingly so on one occasion when John and Ankie arrived to a diary-defined dinner party to be greeted at the door by the should-be hostess, her hair in curlers and clearly dressed for gardening at best. "Next week, Darlings," she laughed, but nevertheless accepted the proffered bottle of finest Greek wine! Ever resourceful, they repaired to Papa's Pizza House in Kifissia (the finest pizzas in the world, by popular vote) a favoured venue for the Perry family, and indeed for most of the expat community, there to discuss just who had made the diary entry. To her credit, and John's relief, Ankie accepted responsibility, "And another glass of wine, please!"

Skinias Beach at Marathon as usual bore the brunt of much expat. presence each Saturday, one such day enlivened by the unexpected, and indeed unwelcome, arrival of a clutch of 4x4 vehicles of the Land Rover ilk manned by a group of middle-aged men clutching walkie-talkies (long before the advent of mobile phones) and playing at soldiers. Seemingly ignoring the many children on the sands, their attention was finally held by Ankie's Dutch friend, Elly Faulkner, who, her Dutch pragmatism sorely absent, dashed to the leading vehicle and thrust a large armful of wet seaweed onto the driver's lap, suggesting in loud tone that they should 'push off'! Later, laughing review drew the firm conclusion that it was 'push', rather than, well, something else that perhaps it should have been. Whatever, Elly's bikini-clad assault won the day, and the 'soldiers' retreat!

June 1979 marked the full three years of John's appointment to Greece as Country Manager, and not unlike his concerns mulled over during the last year of his Rotterdam appointment, he once again felt worried as to was he missing something? Operationally, the ships were being despatched promptly, container liftings were well within targeted levels, customer focus was high, and the SeaLand office was proving successful in its intended role. Relationships with the Agency remained strong and productive, but to put no finer point to it, was his appointment becoming a sinecure? This became matter of discussion between John and Ankie as Team Perry, together with John's expressed concern that at no time during his employment with SeaLand had he been subject of a performance appraisal, and his growing belief that Hickler, as the Mediterranean General Manager, had to all intents and purpose, chosen to ignore John as a team member. Conclusion? Once again, Steven Wright the American comedian and wordsmith seemed able to encapsulate the concerns. "If everything seems to be going well, you have obviously overlooked something." No great comfort, but press on, to meet whatever the future would bring.

August once again drove Athenians to their holiday islands or beaches, but to Loukianou 17, brought a most welcome visit by Karen Davie, John's goddaughter, fresh from a six-month stint of employment as an 'au pair' in, of all places, Genoa! From Greece she would go up to Oxford in the autumn to read French and Italian, but meantime and as she most succinctly put it, she loved exploring Athens, with fun bus rides in the centre, beach visits with Ankie and the boys, parties, and cold beer in the 'fridge'! Not forgetting visits to the American Club pool. As Ankie observed, she had changed from the young girl that they had met in Devon back in 1966, to a personable, self-confident, and outgoing young woman.

September, as planned, brought Duncan, at the well-celebrated age of twelve, to the Campion School, into which routine and atmosphere he appeared to blend reasonably well, remarking on one eccentricity of the Headmaster, which was to acknowledge that whilst schoolboys smoked cigarettes, in his school only when sitting in the small courtyard that opened out from the Head's Study! Unsurprisingly, it stopped a lot of smoking.

His attendance to Campion also sponsored further deep discussion within Team Perry as to his future schooling, based on assumptions (further dangerous ground) that (a) John's re-location would surely happen within the next twelve months or so, (b) that it would not be back to the UK in that the Country Manager's position there appeared to be destined for Americans only as per to date and (c) that continued education within the UK system was necessary. This inevitably pointed toward Boarding School, into which system several St Catherine's pupils had already been enrolled, but which, to both Ankie and John, was anathema! Notwithstanding, and if assumptions proved correct, it was something that would have to be defined in terms of costs and complexity in due course, with reality firmly grasped and maturely addressed.

Sometime in late 1979, news came via the Agency network that Rupe Hickler had resigned from SeaLand and joined a rival Company Trans Freight Lines (TFL), with Jack Sutherland recalled from the States as Mediterranean General Manager, but based in Madrid, where Dutchman Matt Quartel sat as Spain's Country Manager. Further, and about that time, Scott Palen was posted to Rotterdam as Vice-President Europe. Another 'churn' but more was to follow, and although the waters got no deeper, they would become less defined in terms of specific gravity, the ability to keep so many highly paid appointees afloat! 1980 would turn out to be a year when much would be revealed (via the Agency network!), albeit slowly. It was probably true to say that the Agents appointed by SeaLand in Europe, namely SCA Italy, Burgos Spain, Network of Holland and Germany, and Callitsis in Greece retained a loose alliance or association, with inter-communication fine-tuned for business survival, or indeed development to put it broadly.

Christmas 1979, therefore, and Darren's tenth birthday, passed swiftly by, the boys at that stage unaware as to the Team Perry discussions relative to potential future planning, so the passing was both celebrated and joyful, Christmas Day yet again ushered in with recorded Choral music at full blast, by now an annual treat by John, not necessarily totally appreciated by the rest of the family! A cautious, perhaps apprehensive step into 1980, as John and Ankie once more toasted each other in re-affirmation of their mutual determination to keep the subjunctive tense from 'Per Ardua Ad Astra' – never in question! Always in the affirmative!

There was, too, more snowfall to start the year, and with Ankie now having masterful control over the Loukianou 17 central heating engine room, and John in full control of the massive log fire, guests to their home over the holiday period were greeted both warmly, and with warmth. The annual showing of Athenians testing their winter driving in Kifissia/Politia on near bald tires, complete with must-have snowman on the bonnet, was again enjoyed, indeed admired, with the wintry scene never failing to both please and astonish, that Greece could regularly produce such a seasonal contrast.

There was a further contrast worth mentioning too, but sadly adverse, and nothing to do with the change of seasons. On first taking up residence in Greece in mid-1976, John and Ankie would marvel that from the balcony of their home, the lights of Piraeus, some 30 km distant, could clearly be seen as darkness fell. With the arrival of 1980, that was no longer possible due to air pollution over Athens, which was largely blamed by Government on vehicle exhausts. Within the process of some time, rule was brought in that cars with odd numbered registration plates must only drive on alternate days to those with even numbered registration plates, which was either ignored, or cause of an upsurge in purchase of second cars! Rule abandoned as unenforceable.

Although the actual timing is lost, once again in the mists of those involved, meeting in Rotterdam was called for some time in April/May of 1980, probably/possibly to coincide with a further change in the European Management structure, notably the re-location of Jack Sutherland (the Med GM) from Madrid to Rotterdam. This too would prove to be the precursor to yet further shakeouts in the aforementioned structure as realisation began, some would say belatedly, to recognise 'structure overload'. Happily, the meeting would also allow John the only opportunity to broach the potential issue of Boarding School costs/requirements to Scott Palen, the European VP, despite the obvious timing incompatibility, perhaps embraced within the suggestive phrase 'grasping the nettle'! Flash-back memories of relocation allowances 'discussion' with Kalafatides briefly prevailed, but what the heck, nothing ventured and faint heart never won fair lady, as Ankie was to remind, together with further brief reference to honey and vinegar!

General detail of the Rotterdam meeting is inconsequential, but discussion with Palen was important, and he listened carefully to the assumptions that John and Ankie had discussed, and therefore, the potential Boarding School conclusion. Surprisingly, he appeared to accept the three tenets, saying however that SeaLand had no experience in offering Boarding School costs coverage, to which John replied that via his brother Michael, he felt sure he could obtain from Unilever confirmation of how that august Company, with its considerable experience in overseas postings, approached and dealt with such matters, to which Palen agreed. Unilever did indeed proffer the required information, and before returning to Greece, John had Scott Palen's agreement that, in the event, SeaLand would indeed cover both the School costs, and up to two annual flights from/to the UK to cover holiday breaks should that become relevant. Arrangements would be concluded, again in the event, via SeaLand's London office.

Sutherland's re-location from Madrid to Rotterdam on timing terms is also shrouded in time and memory mists but suffice it to suggest that it took place circa June or July of 1980, which also marked confirmation of the re-designation of Matt Quartel to General Manager West Med, and Dick McGregor General Manager East Med, with John remaining as Country Manager Greece, although he remained completely unadvised of the re-designations as above notated.

With ignorance traditionally breeding bliss, so June offered blissful weekends in Greece, with a garden party at the Cooper's home (they boasting a pool as well as a barbecue!) to open the batting so to speak, each of the wives present extremely comfortable in their bikinis, as the six or so assorted children besporting themselves in the pool with attendant dads, whilst Brian Cooper busied himself with the barbecue which, as always, required a man's expertise!

With July came the first camping expedition for the Perrys, as evidenced by the extraordinary array of four camping chairs and a table, two tents and other assorted gear strapped to the roof rack of the much put-upon family Audi 80. They would join other good friends in Candia, close to Tolon, and although John would have to leave after the first long weekend to attend business matters in Piraeus, Ankie and the boys stayed there for that following week, with John re-joining them again come the next (early Friday!) weekend. It was a stunning location, and with separate tent for Duncan and Darren and a larger one for John and Ankie, all comfortably fitted out with barbecue, table and chairs all close to hand, as was the sea. Blissful indeed, although how they managed without John to tend the barbecue was a puzzle!

A second such expedition was later taken to a site in the Pelion area south of Volos, and within a short boat ride to the beautiful island of Skiathos which they would visit, and vow to return to which, some weeks later, they did, but to an hotel. Their pitch was established, and with news of a possible rain burst, John sought to dig a trench (having purchased an ex-Greek Army trenching tool!) around the tents, causing howls of laughter from the two boys as the trench depth achieved amounted to some three inches, or seven centimetres. if that makes it sound deeper. Thankfully, no rain came but as Ankie and John lay together on the sands enjoying the hot sunshine, there did occur an earth tremor, a slight shock wave from a distant earthquake to which John was enabled to mutter the immortal question, "And how was it for you, Darling." only to receive a sharp punch in the ribs, accompanied by laughter!

Duncan and Darren helped extinguish with sand the exploding cooking fire of two young female campers close-by, they having inadvertently spilled boiling oil from a cooking pan, whilst any feelings of camping luxury inspired by their own tents were dispelled by sight of a Danish registered Camping Van which, together with its erected canvas extension, was completely air-conditioned! A long way to travel in search of the sunshine, only to sit there thus cooled. Bliss it was, but with Palen's unquestioning acquiescence to John's Rotterdam request for (in the event) support for schooling funds, it was clear that re-location was becoming increasingly likely, and not to the UK. Emphasis was therefore placed in experiencing as much as was possible that Greece still had to offer in abundance, based on the concept of 'enjoy yourself, it's later than you think'! It was time too to acquaint Duncan with the probable schooling conclusion which, to all outward appearances, he appeared to accept, with plans, therefore, made to take some extended home leave in the UK by mid-August, to better evaluate possible options. Cheltenham would be the starting point, in knowledge that the three children of Michael and Joan Perry were already in Boarding School there, (Cheltenham College) and fact that it was within easy distance of John and Michael's mother, and stepfather Alex, in matter of College exeats. The die was, yet again, cast and no one more saddened than Ankie and John in so doing. In later years, it would horrify them to learn that Duncan had, whilst putting on a brave face, somehow concluded that his parents had stopped loving him, which could not have been further from the truth, being finally able to retrospectively reassure him.

Late July saw the avowed return to the island of Skiathos, and with Darren now of a stature sufficient to take water skiing lessons, an Australian Greek, or was it Greek Australian, was engaged to get Darren upright and waterborne, whilst Duncan too improved his skills. The tutor was superb, with John and Ankie, oft-times in the towing craft, taking great parental pride in their boys' ability to, eventually, each flip to a single ski and still stay upright, and oh so casual! The hotel was memorable, their Host and his Staff outstanding in their typical Greek hospitality and good will. Opportunity was also taken to visit Portaria and Makrinitsa, in between much sun-bathing, and swimming in the limpid seas. Much to do and see, possibly on borrowed time! Early August brought their last planned camping expedition, this time a weekend on the island of Evia, with further howls of laughter from sons (and Ankie) as John strove to drive tent pegs into what first appeared to be solid rock, to finally succeed in the hope, that there would be no strong winds to test the tents doubtful stability.

Surprising though it may appear, routine office work, and meetings, together with Customer contacts were maintained between these expeditions, but in recognition of the usual Greek propensity to vacation during August, it was the right time to visit the UK to grapple with schooling options for Duncan, and accordingly the family made their way there by mid-August, basing themselves upon the hospitality of John's parents in Cradley, some twenty-five miles from Cheltenham. It would prove to be an almost frantic chain of events, based on the early decision that Dean Close College in Cheltenham was the school of choice, need to enrol Duncan thereat after successful meetings with Messrs. Bacon and Padfield (Headmaster and Housemaster, respectively), and to spend much money in fitting him out with appropriate uniform and sporting kit. Early September would mark the start of the Michaelmas term, Duncan's first, so no time to spare. Further decision was made to purchase a 'pied-à-terre' in the town, and with great good fortune, a two bed-roomed Apartment was found in Cedar House, a brand-new building of nine apartments in Bath Road, close to the town's centre, with immediate purchase available. With the good offices of Bill Stallard, family lawyer, family member and good friend, ownership was achieved in record time, and furnishing undertaken, with just the occasional deep breath taken. With Ankie's extraordinary and loving application, it soon became a small, but cheerful, home. It would prove to be a fortuitous purchase, and once again, the good Antoine de Saint-Exupéry had it right: "As for the future, you have not to foresee it, but to make it possible." Tellement, très, très vrai!

With the experience and memory of John and Ankie's parting so painfully soon after their marriage, and brief 'honey-moon' in Tilbury Docks, so was their parting with Duncan planned. Once loving embraces, au revoirs, and 'see you in December' reassurances had been concluded, Duncan would walk into the College (his large and loaded trunk having already been delivered!) whilst John, Ankie and Darren would walk away, with everyone agreeing not to look back. In this, Ankie's Dutch pragmatism was tested again to the full, but it went as planned and as she would ruefully remark later, "At least I didn't have to ask someone how to find the car's reverse gear on this occasion!" Duncan, as photography would testify, looked very composed and grown-up in his College uniform, and that too brought some reassurance. Additionally, knowledge that SeaLand was picking up the College fees of £1190 per Term for Boarding students brought some welcome relief.

Return to Greece once their Apartment had been secured, and keys entrusted to John's parents, was achieved shortly, thereafter, and in time to get Darren back into the St Catherine's school routine, whilst John received confirmation that all had gone well in the Office in his absence, 'all parts bearing an equal strain' to bring maritime tone to bear. No contact from Rotterdam or Genoa had been received meantime, so it was not too presumptuous to believe that the Piraeus organisation was both robust and delivering to expectations.

For the first time, and with Duncan's thirteenth Birthday coming up on September 30th., came need to locate and send Birthday card and greetings to him, and with a Loukianou 17 house-party for friends and some customers to organise, September 1980 went out with a bang with both John and Ankie feeling that it had been a hectic month, but hopefully worthwhile. They would receive reports of the successful use of the Cedar Court Apartment by John's parents as they hosted Duncan during the two exeats of the term, and indeed use of the Apartment themselves as a kind of holiday retreat from time to time, which was good.

December brought a dinner party at the Hilton Supper Club for Customers, but more importantly, anticipation that Duncan was to return home for the Christmas holiday weeks, so enabled to join in Darren's eleventh Birthday celebrations, and indeed, the snow that once again arrived to mark Christmas. This year in the snow, the boys wore with pride the SeaLand 'bobble-hats' that John had purloined in Rotterdam, and at Darren's party, the P & O uniform hats of John and Ankie, and John's RN cap, were shared for photo-calls by their assembled friends. It was a cheerful, full of laughter and good cheer way to end the year, and unbeknown but possibly anticipated, it would be their last Christmas in Greece!

Darren pre-school, Dean Close, Cheltenham (age 11)

Duncan pre-school, Dean Close, Cheltenham (age 13)

1981 was to prove a year of some confusion, largely initiated by SeaLand, and by extension a degree of stress. Movement there would be aplenty, from country to country, as SeaLand's planning for Management structural change in the Middle East and India seemed to flex almost by the week. Sometime in May, or thereabouts, John was called to Rotterdam, there to be interviewed by Palen who, seemingly satisfied with the results, informed John that he would be sent to Saudi Arabia for a week's pre-trip (shades of Genoa all over again) with the planned intention that he would take over from the Australian Ian Blackman as Country Manager. Hardly the best news in the world, but with absolutely no knowledge as to the operational or social set-up in Saudi, clearly the pre-trip was designed to change that. The Saudi visit would take place in early June, or thereabouts once again, which gave John and Ankie time to muse over the implications, and indeed worry about the implications which, as they agreed, was rather pointless until more information came to hand. Flight to Dammam was taken, there to meet Ian Blackman, a down-to-earth Aussie, himself due to relocate to Dubai, although whether he knew of that at the time was open to question.

Impressions gained during the week brought little comfort, certainly in social terms, with the growing knowledge that women were largely constrained in matters of clothing, and banned from driving, whilst expat living accommodation meant residence in a compound. Additionally, and since 1952, alcohol was prohibited, expats largely resorting to the home-brewing of Siddiqui, referred to since oil exploration began as the 'life-blood of expats living in Saudi', with alcohol content of 90%, bottled in used water bottles to avoid detection. This information was gleaned in passing, together with the ironic translation from Arabic for the home-brew, which was 'my friend', although detection of alcohol by the authorities was a very real danger as house raids were known to occur if undue noise was made, as in a house-party. Finally, there were the Mutawa, or Religious Police, constantly on the look-out for disregard of religious laws. All in all, an almost complete reversal of the liberal lifestyle to which the western world was privileged to enjoy, and with two sons in Boarding College that were accustomed to coming home twice a year, what hospitality would, or could, Saudi offer?

This all pointed to a Team Perry meeting with need to seriously consider John resigning as result of turning down the proposed Saudi posting which, of course, may well have been Palen's objective as he had agreed to Sealand picking up the Boarding fees, some £9K per annum and rising, with drive on in the organisation to dramatically reduce personnel costs, the levels undoubtedly a function of too many American expats involved continuously in European deployment, and the short-terminism of their deployments bringing about in-built relocation costs as an unsustainable budget line. In effect, failure to generate adequate European employment.

Flight departure from Dammam back to Athens too brought some surprises to the uninitiated, in that the black outer garments worn by those indigenous females of the region aboard the flight would be removed in the aircraft's toilets to reveal the very modern western garb previously covered, whilst their menfolk would casually indulge themselves in the well-known beverage of Scotland, not that known as Irn-Bru! Each to his or her own, indeed!

Arrival home to Loukianou 17 was to discover that Ankie had been much alarmed by the most unusual threat to their home, with trees in adjacent woodland catching fire, and burning perilously close. The cause was never offered, but with pine and olive wood mainly comprising the area, the casual lighting of a campfire could well have been the cause. Duncan was home for the Easter holidays, and both he and Darren were away visiting friends, so she was alone with the small garden hose, and with no means of contacting John, not that he could have helped much anyway from the sands of Saudi. Undeterred, she sensibly concluded to put 'must have' items into the car in the event of having to abandon the house, although her choice of 'must haves' later caused much discussion and (relieved) laughter. Her Passport was, of course, very appropriate, but the only other designated items comprised of her mink coat purchased in Greece, and her bikini purchased at Harrods of London! Oh, and not to forget the oil painting, past Christmas present from Petros Callitsis. That she was safe was the main thing, the fire having burned itself out, and hence the relief expressed in the laughter as the tale unfolded.

Earthquake whilst John was in Patras, and fire when he was in Saudi! What next?

The Team discussion on a potential Saudi move came to the decision to wait and see, based on another call to attend meeting in Rotterdam, but resignation was acknowledged as something that John must be prepared to offer. It also recognised fact that because of the Corporate search for substantial cost reductions in personnel, John and Ankie were highly vulnerable by virtue of costs associated with placement of their sons to Boarding College, which would amount to circa £9K per year, plus the two flights per year agree for their holiday breaks from College. Timing of the Rotterdam meeting was delayed by, as would subsequently come clear, vacillations that must there have taken place, but eventually it happened, with the surprising news that rather than Saudi Arabia, latest decision was that John should take over the function of Country Manager India from the American Larry Roberts, whose expat team of three: Sales, Operations and Documentation Managers had gradually been disbanded during 1980, leaving the Bombay Agency Ranadip to now operate along the same lines as Callitsis in Greece for the northern States with the Chakiat Agency of Cochin responsible for the southern States of India. In effect, one replacement expat for the four original expats, so John's cost vulnerability as recently discussed between John and Ankie was, apparently, sufficiently reduced, whilst his experience covered marine and land operations, loss prevention, marketing in all its facets, and financial overview.

Whilst never formally disavowed, vacillation involved in resolution of the Indian Management structure was function of plan by the involved Vice-President in Europe to anoint Ranadip Bombay as overall responsible for SeaLand's Indian presence, with the Chakiat Agency reporting to the Ranadip Managing Director Dilip De. Through huge, good fortune, wiser council prevailed in Dubai, home of the area General Manager, persuading Rotterdam away from that which would have been disastrous, as events and history would in due course prove.

The revised plan for John's deployment away from Greece, albeit with no pre-trip on offer, was discussed over a phone call between John and Ankie, together with the re-affirmation of the schooling deal previously agreed but now for both sons. Also, and as part of the package, two 'rest and recuperation' (R'n'R) trips would be funded for John and Ankie additional to annual home leave, at a cost not to exceed Business Class return flights between Bombay and Singapore, but in any direction. Finally, news that position of Country Manager Greece would not be replaced. In this, there had never been any criticism by John as to the operational efficacy, customer focus, or freight generation abilities of the Callitsis organisation, and his establishment of the SeaLand office in Piraeus was seen as bringing adequate support and financial overview to allow Dick McGregor, as the newly appointed General Manager for Eastern Med, to take Greece under his competent wing, so there was sound logic in this cost-cutting plan. With Ankie's voiced support, the posting to

India was accepted (honey rather than vinegar), with a mutually agreed date for change-over in Bombay as late September 1981, this allowing for much that would have to be logistically achieved before then. The throwing of dice appeared increasingly as part of the job description, if not all of it!

Above and below: Callitsis family farewell to Perry family, Piraeus

In early July, the Callitsis family assembled their Staff and staged a farewell party for John and Ankie, together with Duncan and Darren, with

Petros Callitsis presenting them with a silver bowl, together with generous words of thanks to John for his help and guidance over the five years. He also presented John with a gold signet ring, with his initials in Greek engraved thereon. With so many of their formative years spent in Greece, John and Ankie would present both Duncan and Darren, on their 21st birthdays, with a gold signet ring similarly engraved with their initials in Greek, and in due course, their grandson, Angus, too, as family tradition. It was an emotional farewell, with John, in his turn, thanking Petros Callitsis, his family and team for their friendship and loyal support, and for the Perry family's Greek experience which had brought them such joy and happiness.

It remained for John to bid farewell to Claudia, his loyal secretary of five years, and Polis Leonida who, once John had cleared his desk, would report to Dick Mcgregor in Genoa, for as long as that arrangement stayed in place under the shifting sand of SeaLand's personnel policies.

There was, too, just enough time for one last boat trip, a final weekend offered aboard the new craft of Petros Callitsis, a motor cruiser again named for his wife, Mimika, and proudly wearing the Red Ensign denoting UK registration. This vessel was more professionally manned by a Callitsis employee, so the chosen trip to Tolon and back, with the luxury of sleeping aboard, was welcomed with open arms. Much diving and swimming from the craft took place (Ankie's Harrods bikini featuring small!) and chance to re-visit one of their favourite seaside villages for the last time, the well-remembered scene of the boys' first exposure to water skiing (well, sort of water-skiing demonstration by John), and the island famously referred to as 'The Breasts of Helen'. Eventual departure from Tolon, however, led to an incident in that a length of rope hawser was snagged around the propeller (shades of a long-ago incident aboard HMS Repton) which would have required John to go overboard with a kitchen knife, were it not for the fortuitous sighting of some Greek sponge divers who offered to do the job. Fortuitous too for them, as the payment they asked for the work well exceeded that which they would have received in the sale of their sponges. All in all, a wonderful way in which to end the Greek appointment, with even more memories to cherish. Some years later, John would receive a letter from Petros Callitsis, just prior to his passing, reiterating his pleasure gained from working with John, and the meeting with Ankie, Duncan and Darren, ending with his expressed best wishes for the future for all. It made for emotional reading, and it was hoped that John's response, couched in similar vein and sent post haste, reached him before he passed away.

Onward to the next square on the Board, which involved a rather emotional farewell to Loukianou 17, the many friends made over the five years, both expats. and Greek, and the return of household goods to the UK, there to conclude what was to go into storage for an indefinite time, and that which would go with them (containerised of course) to an unknown apartment in India that awaited them. Temporary accommodation was taken up at the American Club during this period of substantial disturbance and no small distress, but eventually, and sadly, the bullet had to be bitten, with departure from Greece finalised by flight from Athens to London. In business terms, the five years had provided invaluable exposure and experience, particularly perhaps in both marketing and politics, (read into the latter as you will!) whereas in social, historical, and geographical terms, extraordinary warmth and good-will in friendships, and depth in all else. Oh, and a bloody good place to get a deep tan, and a mink coat!

Flat 7, Cedar Court Cheltenham, its purchase the previous year now serving as another fortuity in the general scheme of things, would be their home for the next few weeks, serving as, in terms of notation, home number nine since John and Ankie's marriage in 1967, a mere fourteen years back. Peripatetic indeed, albeit with time to take a recent breath in the birthplace of democracy!

With both Duncan and now Darren, taking up residence at Dean Close College in early September, the so-called Michaelmas term, much to be done to ensure both boys adequately kitted out, and psychologically ready to go. Ankie and John also had to rationalise that both boys would be lost to them during term time, and indeed that feeling of loss would only intensify once arrived in India, there to learn just how difficult it would be to make even telephone contact. So, much emphasis placed on the Christmas holidays to come. Came there the 'back to College' parting, and as before the 'never look back' routine was deployed, with Ankie's pragmatism once again sorely tested.

However, with much to occupy her busy mind prior to departure for India, and with visits to John's parents, Bill, and June Stallard (legal eagle and lovely wife, friends, and family) the pain was somewhat dulled. Flights were booked by John which, as Business Class was obtainable within their SeaLand seniority level, life was made easier and more agreeable., In passing, it would fall to SeaLand's London Office to organise and execute the bi-annual logistics exercise of moving Duncan and Darren forth and back between Cheltenham and India, and indeed it was a sterling achievement (no pun intended) every single time. John was to regret deeply his failure to formally confirm that stellar service, being hugely appreciated, particularly by the boys as they were always, perhaps surprisingly, flown Business Class! This probably made it easier for the British Airways flight crew to slip them the occasional beer (or spirit!) to ease them to sleep, en route. Which they did!

Discussion within Team Perry concluded that there was no benefit in trying to guess just what challenges their new appointment would bring but recognised that challenges there would be aplenty. In this they were not wrong, but past experience hopefully would prove sufficient to accommodate and overcome, although whilst the politics associated with this new appointment remained an unknown entity, it could not be assumed as non-existent – in their experience! That aside, India was to provide opportunities unique to anything else they had previously known as a family. The Sub-Continent was, of course, known to John having visited Bombay, Calcutta, Madras and Vishakhapatnam Ports whilst at sea with P & O, but these had been shallow exposures, unlike the deeper waters into which John and Ankie were now to venture. Onward and upward, hand in hand. Let battle commence!

India

Arrival to the noise and press of people in Bombay Airport was to bring some neophyte realisation that this was a different World where noise, colours and aromas fought and combined ceaselessly for attention. They would later observe and learn that definition of a 'split second' could be defined as the time between a traffic light turning green, and the immediate cacophony of impatient drivers' car or truck horns. They were met, once through Immigration and Customs ordeals, by Larry Roberts, he who John was to relieve, and once aboard his Ambassador car with all their baggage, driven to the Oberoi Hotel, which was to be their base for as long as necessary, largely defined as, or by, when their container of household goods would arrive. They were also introduced to Anjou, the Country Manager's Driver, with the explanation that to drive oneself in India was not recommended for general reasons of 'safety'. The drive, Airport to City Centre was one that John would take frequently in the future months (driven by Anjou) part of the route in the early hours of the morning often the scene of people defecating close to the roadside, in absence of proper toilet facilities. It was the reality, and just one of the extraordinary, nay startling, contrasts that would define the cultural differences that existed between the relatively well-off and the poor, so evident in India at that time.

The Oberoi Hotel was to prove high in customer focus and attention, with the mini-suite that John and Ankie were to occupy served by, and at a push of the bell, an ever-attentive Butler-like person or persons, seemingly available whenever required, day or night. The restaurants and bars were of the highest order, the Staff always smiling and friendly, and if the intention had been to impress John and Ankie, it had worked. Having done some homework, however, they were both very conscious that ice in drinks was a no-no, salads were to be avoided, and fish never to be consumed during the Monsoon periods, whilst steaks if ordered should always be well done, never rare. It was also discovered that the price of a Gin and Tonic at the Bar was more than a taxi-driver earned in a day, or so it was said, and sight of taxi-drivers sleeping in their cars at night, sobering. It was reality!

Collected the following morning, it was but a short drive to the Maker Towers on Cuffe Parade, wherein was found the Ranadip/SeaLand Office and, as it was later demonstrated, their new 'home', an apartment on the twelfth floor even then in process of re-decoration in readiness for their arrival. It boasted a covered balcony facing the sea and, as it was to be discovered, cockroaches! Ankie would show that the Greek insect spray yet to arrive with their house-hold goods would quickly prove perfectly adequate for the purpose of eliminating said unwelcome beasts.

Holiday in Rhodes, Greece – Duncan (Age 16)

Introduction was made to Dilip De (pronounced as if with an acute accent on the 'e'), Owner of Ranadip Agency, and one-time employee of Mackinnon McKenzie of India, whose effusive welcome to John and Ankie seemed to lack a certain sincerity and warmth, accustomed as they were to the Greek way. He in his turn introduced them to those of his Staff that were present in the Office, to include Ronnie Mandviwalla the SeaLand Accounts Manager, and Prakash Mahadalka the Ranadip Finance man, names that vied with some of those in the Callitsis Agency for their difficulty in pronunciation! A small bit of history that John hoped to find useful was fact that as a P & O cadet, he had been instructed by a Linguaphone course in Hindustani as P & O vessels were Indian crewed, and not all he had learned had been forgotten. Of only passing interest, he also was still in possession of the booklet then issued to all P & O Officers 'The Malim Sahib's Hindustani', written by one C T Willson, of the Bombay Pilot Service many moons in the past. This however was constructed for those who wished "to acquire a working knowledge of 'low Hindustani' spoken by native crews, coolies, servants, and longshoremen generally". De facto, it was best kept well hidden, indeed destroyed, its Preface wording in parts reflecting a curried, colonial diplomacy, even within the context of which it was written! That aside, everyone thus far appeared to speak immaculate English, save perhaps for the Lift Boy!

Introduction was also made to Elizabeth, John's Secretary to be, who would prove extremely efficient, and loyal. In due course Ronnie Mandviwalla would take up a posting in SeaLand's Dubai Office, to be replaced by Sam Bhathena who would work closely with John in the production of a working manual comprising every aspect of SeaLand's activity in Bombay from Service inception in 1979 to the present, something that John had concluded as both necessary and appropriate for submission to the regional Head Office in Dubai, and for the education of future SeaLand appointees to Bombay. Its genesis was fact that, once again, and in absence of any pre-appointment advice or direction, or even proper hand-over by Roberts relative to either Bombay of Cochin activity, it was to be 'make it up as you go along' time. Failure to offer any opinions, guidance, or advice as to his relationship with either Dilip De in Bombay, or the Chakiat Agency in Cochin was unfortunate, but clearly, he and his wife Jodie were more than eager to leave India.

Later, Dilip De would introduce John and Ankie to his wife, Rita, in their Apartment also in Maker Towers, and she was immediately seen as highly intelligent, sophisticated, and gracious in her welcome to India. Medium term events would therefore seem even more horrific, if understandable.

Even later that day, John and Ankie would meet with Larry Roberts and Jodie for dinner at the Hotel, to again be impressed by the service and quality of the food once brought to the table. Evidently, their hosts' time in India had dulled their appreciation, as seen by Jodie's smiling thanks to the waiter and her subtle words, "Gee, this looks like good shit!" Ankie was horrified. It was the last they saw of the Roberts. All in all, not the best start to their new appointment as John and Ankie would later agree, with a steep learning curve to be anticipated and quickly acquired, but as ever they were up for the challenge. It was a new and totally different reality, but new reality was a currency in which they were well accustomed to deal! Cut the pack and deal the cards!

For the first time ever, and as a function of College holidays involving Duncan and Darren, a plan had to be discussed and agreed that would take account of both temperature and humidity in India, and the Monsoon season. With the monsoons starting in Bombay in June, it made sense that the boys would travel to India at the end of the Lent Term (Easter) circa March. John and Ankie would take home leave to the UK to coincide with the monsoon's arrival mid-June and the end of the Trinity term early July, with the boys tasking their second flight to India at the end of the Michaelmas Term in early December, when temperatures and humidity in India were at their most equitable, almost Mediterranean-like. That meant that Duncan and Darren would join their parents in Bombay for their first family Christmas that December of 1981, arriving within the second week of December, and returning to College early in January 1982. Plan agreed and implemented, by Team Perry, and so did Ankie become one of the expat 'Monsoon Memsahibs' so referred, as the wives would invariably leave just before the monsoon broke in Bombay, with the husbands joining them some two weeks later.

Meantime, there was much to be done, and with the eventual arrival of their containerised house-hold goods (John paying the full Customs charge rather than oblige one Officer with a bribe!) Ankie was able to set-to in fitting out their apartment in Maker Towers. This had been preceded by Diwali, the Hindu Festival of Lights, celebrating knowledge over ignorance, good over evil, and light over darkness, the five-day celebrations in Cuffe Parade thoroughly enjoyed by Ankie and John, being able to visit their still empty apartment for comfort breaks. It was during one such brief visit that a cockroach ran up the trouser leg of a now prancing John with Ankie in splits of laughter the while. That roach would soon die, together with its fellows, victims of a Greek insect spray that took no prisoners!

Business there was to conduct however, with John's first visit to the Docks to meet with Captain Simon Bennet, in Command of the 'Boxer Captain Cook', the 576 teu (twenty-foot equivalent) vessel deployed on the fortnightly Service between Dubai, Bombay and Cochin. Noteworthy was fact that refrigerated cargo was one of SeaLand's main exports from Bombay, the 'reefers' being booked to load, believe it or not, considerable throughput of frozen frogs' legs, and prawns, destined for European consumption. What was done with the legless remains of frog was best left unanswered. The cargos would arrive to the Port in ordinary trucks (if one could ever classify Indian road trucks as ordinary!) covered over with burlap and substantial amounts of dry ice. The products should have been fully frozen prior to despatch for loading into 'reefers' waiting in the Port, which had by necessity to be pre-cooled, but John noticed that the taking of 'probe temperatures' were not always taken as routine to check that before being loaded, receiving temperatures were within acceptable proscribed limits. This, he reiterated, had to be done, with Bills of Lading claused accordingly if temperatures were not within those acceptable limits, which caused a degree of Shipper concern which would undoubtedly have reached the ears of Dilip De. As the goods were for human consumption, it was unthinkable that clean Bills of Lading could be issued in the event of inadequate freezing, so unarguable!

Meeting was also arranged with Aadhi Dubash, Owner of the Stevedore Company contracted to work the SeaLand vessel calls, and probably one of the richest men in Bombay, if his substantial home in Bombay, together with his small fleet of expensive foreign cars, was any indication. He was a charming man however, proud of his dual Nationality, Indian and British, and London residence complete with its Rolls Royce car, as he was not shy in mentioning. His plea for an increase in his Tariff, probably prompted by observed change in Country Manager as opportune was, however, rebuffed!

More important meantime was the need for John to make his first visit the Chakiat Agency in Cochin, and with the Apartment now shipshape and homely (some additional rattan furniture had to be purchased to complete the transformation) Ankie chose to accompany him, something that would sometimes happen again when John had business trips to such as Calcutta, Delhi, Bangalore or Madras.

Return to Bombay Airport was to re-visit the organised chaos that there existed, with the check-in desks for the Cochin flight as always ultra-busy, usually with people taking leave from the Middle East to their home State of Kerala. Were it but people, the queues would be seen as normal, but each person seemed to have purchased all that he or she could carry from such as Dubai, including such as bedrolls apparently, so queues were both dense and noisy, as people jostled for position. Although it seemed arrogant and with shades of colonial past, John quickly discovered that the only way to guarantee boarding the flight as booked was to walk straight to the check-in desk waving his British Passport, and thence to the boarding gate. In this case, both John and Ankie waved their Passports, his British, and hers Dutch!

Having done some pre-visit research, they were aware that the indigenous official language of Kerala was Malayalam (pronounced as spelt!) one of the twenty-two scheduled languages of India, and Kerala was also one of the ten Indian States where the slaughter of cows was legally permitted for the human consumption of beef. For the rest, it was a case of wait and see. With the abrupt stopping of their aircraft on landing in Cochin (there was an oil tank at the end of the runway), they were met by P. Narayan, son of the Chakiat Agency Owner, to be driven in his Premier Padmini car first to the Casino Hotel to check in, and thence to the Chakiat Office to meet his father. It proved to be a meeting of the minds, as it quickly became obvious to John that the Agency held and sustained the basic concepts of marketing and was dedicated to the SeaLand cause in their South India bailiwick which embraced the major Port of Madras in the State of Tamil Nadu, and Guntur as they were to both learn and experience in due course, with Bangalore in the State of Karnataka to mention but a few sources of business. The friendship and sense of common purpose with P. Narayan was sealed on that visit, although strangely John would never learn what name the initial 'P' carried, using instead the name Narayan only over the many years of contact that were to follow. He, and the Agency which he would shortly inherit, was without reproach, totally reliable in all that he set out to achieve, both ambitious in his thinking and target setting, and modest in major achievements. More than that, he was trustworthy throughout, in stark contrast to his counterpart in the Ranadip Agency of Bombay, Dilip De, as events and history would bear sad witness.

With business discussions completed, John and Ankie were given a guided tour of Cochin by Narayan, the day ending with a cheerful and laughter-filled (beef) dinner at the Malabar Hotel on the tip of Willingdon Island facing the Harbour. It would become a regular routine during Cochin visits, sleep at the Casino Hotel and dine at the Malabar Hotel, although that night with Ankie, they actually heard, and saw, a cockroach eating from the fruit bowl!

Return to Bombay was made, with collection by the intrepid Anjou and return to Maker Towers, there to prepare for the weekend, and that which would become their weekend bolt-hole, namely the Breach Candy Swimming Club, with its large sea-water swimming pool next to the Arabian Sea, snack bar and sun-loungers, the major meeting point for the relatively small expat community, mainly British and Dutch, with one Norwegian family. Ironically, the Russian and East German presence in Bombay was substantial, although they were forbidden to have any social contact with the 'west' Europeans, so to speak. Further irony was Membership Cards issuance by a Russian.

Their presence at the Club was therefore constrained, but they were able to watch and wonder (gawp!) on those occasions when the 'west' Europeans practised Scottish reels at poolside, in some 30°C and 80% humidity, in preparation for both the Caledonian Night Ball and the Burns Night Ball, two highlights of the social year, held in one of the two main Bombay Hotels, the Oberoi or the Taj Mahal. For Burns Night, British Airways would fly out, gratis, a Scottish Piper and a Haggis, albeit that one year the Haggis missed the flight, necessitating the sourcing and purchase of a replacement in Bombay. Not a lot of guests ventured to taste that night! Ankie and John found much joy in learning and perfecting (well, almost) the reels, and the actual enactment of their nascent skills on the nights. Greek dancing was temporarily forgotten!

Back in their Maker Towers Apartment, which was by then firmly and comfortably established by Ankie, home number ten since their marriage, the Cheltenham Apartment having edged the ninth slot. With window air-conditioning units in bedrooms and lounge, left to them by the Roberts family, all tested and ready to bring relief from Bombay's high summer temperatures and extremely high humidity, they were in. Ankie and John had also inherited, additional to Anjou the driver, his young cousin Francis as house-boy, who would attend daily, largely relieving Ankie (and John!) of any housework, which proved a boon in what seemed to be developing into a busy time, both in work-terms and socially. Anjou and Francis were both of the Christian faith which easier defined their holiday requirements. Ankie had also made firm decision that, unlike many other expats, she would not employ a cook, preferring to both source supplies herself, accompanied by Anjou, and home-sterilise all vegetables. Her decision ensured that the dreaded amoebic dysentery, not uncommon where live-in cooks were employed, would never visit itself upon the family or their dinner guests, once they started to entertain. The Apartment was also, by this time, completely cockroach free!

John had also installed himself in the Maker Towers office of the Ranadip Agency, to realise in so doing that he had no international telephone connection in his small office (that was deployed only in Dilip De's office) and further that the only other means of international communication was by fax machine that took about twenty seconds to print out a single letter! In a few words, the communication set-up was appallingly un-business-like, the word 'communication' verging on the oxymoronic! Dilip De saw no reason for improvement it seemed, 'as one had only the need to adjust'!

John was also informed that SeaLand would underwrite the costs of Club membership, and this too was early-day addressed, with some guidance from other expats, the word having spread that the Perry's' were 'in station' – indeed they had been vetted by two stalwarts of the small British expat community, having been invited to a coffee meeting for just that purpose, as they were to later learn. Very colonial. That aside, membership was granted to the Willingdon Sports Club which boasted an eighteen-hole golf course and other associated means of dining or relaxing, the Sailing Club which offered a very convivial refreshment bar and a lone English resident who claimed he had missed the last boat home after Independence. No sailing was ever involved, however, as thoughts of a possible capsize incident in the polluted coastal waters of Bombay deterred! Finally, the Bombay Squash Club, which brought an interesting interview with the Club's Indian President in the imposing Board Room, with the question being posed, "And what sport do you wish to play, Mr Perry?" His cautious and questioning response, "Squash?" was apparently acceptable, and membership offered. With the Courts having no air-conditioning, occasional games in some 30°C and 80% humidity were more than challenging, and weight reducing. His playing partner, New Zealander David Read, was also resident with his wife, Carol, in Maker Towers, and they would become good friends with John and Ankie. David and John would also play the occasional game of tennis, using a Court close to Maker Towers, the playing surface of which was compacted buffalo dung, pre-wetted before play commenced, which brought an un-fresh meaning to confirmation that it had been a crap game, regardless of the outcome!

Holiday in Rhodes, Greece Darren (Age 14)

Ankie would also join a Bridge group, eventually persuading John to join her occasionally, once her patient tutelage allowed some public exposure to the tables, overall seen as 'continued work in progress'! Finally, and as exercise that they could enjoy together, they joined the many others that would walk around the extensive perimeter of the Bombay Racetrack, and that cost nothing to join! The Bridge group turned out to be rather serious, although one young Brit male in the Banking fraternity, on hearing of his transfer back to London, took too many tinctures of alcohol pre-play, giggling inanely at each of his extraordinary bids, such bids making those of John sound more than thoughtful! It is said that on the actual day of his departure, he hired a horse-drawn gharry to take him to the Airport, leaving a long trail of toilet-paper behind him as the journey progressed, although just what that signified was never explained.

There was work to be addressed however, and with a big customer event organised by Ranadip in New Delhi, P. Narayan, and his wife Suchitra were also invited by John to attend, such that India as a whole would be represented, something that Dilip De of Ranadip accepted, perhaps reluctantly. Accordingly, Ranadip, Chakiat and John mustered at the Taj Mahal Hotel in New Delhi. At some point, and unheard by John, Dilip De informed Narayan that before the Customer gathering, he had arranged meeting with the Secretary to the Shipping Minister, and that Narayan was not, repeat not, invited to that meeting, as New Delhi was 'the Ranadip area'. Reportedly, such was the arrogance and display of ill-will directed at Narayan that he and his wife immediately cut short their visit, returning to Cochin never to speak to Dilip De again, whose behaviour was deplorable and non-contributable to SeaLand's commercial interests. Sadly, it was, too often, his way, a serious frailty that he had successfully managed to hide from those at more senior levels in the SeaLand organisation to whom he owed his employment, and who continued to believe in him.

In late November, however, a more professional gathering was arranged by Narayan of Chakiat Agencies in Guntur, a town central to India's tobacco growing and exports, situated some 400 kilometres to the north of Madras, a train journey of between six to seven hours, roughly following the coastline of Andhra Pradesh, in which State it was situated. Gallahers, Imperial Tobacco and British American Tobacco were large buyers, their Shipping Agent being Sheriff and Son of Madras, and on this occasion, Gallahers had booked with SeaLand London a substantial movement of tobacco to the UK and N. Europe, to be shipped in containers from Cochin. With the information that Gallahers Buyer Richard Digweed, and his second-in-command, Michael Collins were to visit Guntur, Narayan arranged a dinner reception for them, requesting that John and Ankie attend as senior representatives of SeaLand.

Flight from Bombay to Madras was therefore taken, by John and Ankie, and with a four-berth rail compartment exclusively booked for them and Narayan, by Chakiat, it left only a courtesy meeting with Sheriff Dayan, the Managing Partner of Sheriff and Son, before departure from Madras. It proved to be an extraordinary experience, in that Sheriff bred Doberman Pinscher dogs, some twenty of which he kept in a gated and secure enclosure. Proud of his animals, he invited John to accompany him into the enclosure, warning that whilst the dogs were trained to defend their Owner, they would not attack unless so commanded. Mr Sheriff blew his little silver whistle, and immediately the animals stood rigidly still watching him, as he gestured John to follow him into the arena. "Please make no attempt to touch me, Mr Perry, as the dogs will attack you!" Firmly reassured on that count by John, they walked slowly across the enclosure, with only the dogs' heads moving as they intently watched the visitor, who kept respectful station upon their Master, with his hands firmly clasped to his sides. Once out of the enclosure, Mr Sheriff again blew his whistle, and the dogs, not to mention John, visibly relaxed. He would dine off that experience for years to come!

The train journey to Guntur was in itself unremarkable, save that at each stop, vendors would pour aboard the train with assorted food and drinks for sale, which Narayan warned against buying 'just in case'. Sensibly, Ankie had thought to bring some reading material, which sufficed to help pass the time. Once arrived at Guntur, they took up the offered accommodation at the Imperial Tobacco Company guest house, from which in due course they were to leave for the reception venue, rested and refreshed, to take up their Hosting duties. Suffice it to say that the reception was well received and a great success, and with Ankie's poised self-assurance, coupled to John's courtesy call on the Dobermans home enclosure, they felt they had made a small contribution to customer focus so important in the marketing context, and supportive to Narayan's thoughtful perception that had brought the whole event together to ensure future business. As John and Ankie agreed, he was to be trusted, and would undoubtedly go far.

The train ride back to Madras was timed such that some sleep was sought en route, disturbed only by an Indian couple sleeping head to toe on a very narrow bench in the corridor adjacent to the Chakiat reserved compartment, the male clearly snoring for India! While Ankie and Narayan dozed on their respective bunks, John sought to construct a small catapult from an elastic band of a luggage label, fruitlessly seeking to fire small pellets of paper toward the snoring nose but failing in his endeavours which was probably a good thing in diplomatic terms. As the couple were sleeping toe to head, a brief push by the equally disturbed wife to her husband's head restored some calm. Flight back to Bombay after farewells to Narayan, there to eagerly await the arrival of Duncan and Darren to their first Indian holiday from College, just a couple of weeks or so away, as December presented India's coolest and most comfortable weather conditions, comparable to a Mediterranean summer!

There was, however, a celebration to be arranged for December $5^{th}/6^{th}$ among the small group of Dutch expats into which Ankie and John had been invited. It was, of course, the Sinterklaas (remember?) celebration, and with several Dutch children below schooling age in situ, arrangements were set in place. Ton Gerlings, as Representative of a large Dutch bank would play the part of Sinterklaas (no steamboat arrival on a white horse however) and Ankie was persuaded to act as his assistant, the 'diminutive Moor from Spain' (once again, don't ask!) called Zwarte Piet, or Black Peter. With costumes designed and made by the Dutch mums, they looked the awesome part, Ankie even agreeing to be 'blacked-up' with theatrical make-up to complete the illusion. With no air-conditioning in the Apartment chosen for the gifting ceremony, and despite the relative easing of the humidity in December, it was perspiring just to watch the 'actors', and indeed photo of Ankie was taken as she sought to take surreptitious slurps from a can of ice-cold lager! It was a total success! Both the ceremony, and the ice-cold lager, as was later confirmed!

Johann of the Dutch Consulate was also present with his family, and it was to him that that Ankie would direct her question as to the implications of taking British nationality. His response was clear and unequivocal, in that under Dutch law, dual nationality was not permitted, and should Ankie choose to take the British option, she would lose her Dutch nationality. John, Duncan, and Darren were to agree wholeheartedly that she should therefore stay with her Dutch Passport, and as the boys would reiterate, "you are our Dutch Mum, and that's how it should stay!" More of that, however, in a different and future Appointment.

The big day came, the arrival of Duncan and Darren, and Anjou drove John and Ankie to Bombay Airport where they were enabled to take position in a gallery overlooking the Arrivals Hall, "So we can see how they look before meeting them," as Ankie put it. It was a joyous reunion, and quite apart from any Christmas celebrations, plans were afoot to make their visit memorable, with firstly a visit to the Taj Mahal near Agra in the State of Uttar Pradesh, followed by a week in Goa, to enjoy the beach and sunshine in that one-time corner of the Portuguese Empire. The Breach Candy Swimming Club would also feature large in their daily expeditions with Ankie, as John had perforce to daily attend the Ranadip office if only to keep a wary eye on Sales activity or visit the Port when the 'Boxer Captain Cook' hove in sight from Dubai, this last mentioned a valuable source for the occasional bottle of Whisky and/or Gin. NB – Alcohol consumption in India was permitted albeit constrained in some States on varying days of the week. Interestingly, one of John's P & O Officer colleagues, whose father was at one time Commanding the Indian Navy Training Vessel 'Dufferin', would tell of his need to obtain a licence that would define him as an alcoholic, thereby permitting him to buy the occasional bottle of spirits. Strange. That aside, spirits in Bombay were obtainable from smugglers coming in from Dubai, but 'moonshine' alcohol was also sold in genuine whisky bottles, the consumption of which could, and did, result in blindness! This note had little to do with the Christmas holidays of Duncan and Darren, as apart from the probable generosity of British Airways cabin staff, the boys' tastes were still limited to, at most, beer or the Indian version of Cola called 'Thumbs Up', pronounced 'Tums Up', apparently.

Visit to the Taj Mahal was achieved before Christmas, with flight from Bombay to Delhi, and thence a car journey for the two hundred or so kilometres to the town of Agra. The Taj Mahal was commissioned by the Mughal Emperor Shar Jahan in 1632, in memory of his beloved wife, Mumtaz Mahal, to be built about a mile and a half from the southern flank of Agra, on the banks of the river Yamuna, being largely completed by 1643, although not in its entirety until 1653. It was a breath-taking sight, and with scarcely any crowds, the Perry family was free to roam and photograph at will, a far cry from the tourist crowds that would in the fullness of time swarm to this UNESCO World Heritage Site. The visit was well worth-while, truly memorable, although the journey to and from was quickly forgotten in the excitement of a real roast Turkey for Christmas, swimming at Breach Candy, fun with friends similarly returned from Colleges, and many games of Sjoelen, the boys reunited with the 2M x 0.4M Sjoelbak Board (pronounced 'shoolbak board'), or Dutch shuffleboard to the uninitiated. Its size and intended usage had indeed puzzled both the Indian and Greek Customs Officers on its arrival to their respective countries, but to state that in Holland it was known as a Sjoelbak Board seemed to satisfy their curiosity, pretending as they did immediate recognition of its social and competitive purpose!

So, a fun-filled Christmas, with the boys increasingly comfortable wearing lungis, followed by the celebration of Darren's twelfth birthday December 30th, left only the bringing in of 1982 to recognise, with John and Ankie breathing a sigh of relief that 1981 was over. The last quarter, starting with their arrival in Bombay, had proved particularly frantic, and John was hugely grateful that Ankie had taken everything in her stride, pragmatism to the fore, and wonderfully supportive throughout. Their New Year's toast to each other confirmed their mutual commitment, as always, to perseverance in the face of all challenges, come what may!

On the business front, it was apparent that led by P Narayan, the Chakiat Agency in Cochin was fully and successfully committed to SeaLands commercial interests, with John and Narayan bonding well in both the business and social contexts. In matter of Ranadip Bombay, the commitment of Dilip De to SeaLands interests was perceived by many as purchased, perhaps gullibly so, but John worried as to just what was his deeper game, as there appeared to be little attempt on the part of De to engage with John, particularly in business matters. Socially, occasional invitations to his Apartment would result in a few drinks, (he supported and partook freely of the 'wine' of Scotland), but never once would he seek to introduce John to customers, so distinctly unlike Callitsis in Greece, or indeed Narayan in Cochin. That Vice-President Palen had ever considered Ranadip as lead Agent in India, with Chakiat reporting thereto, seemed increasingly bizarre, but thankfully averted by wiser counsel from the Dubai office. A 'stitch in time' perhaps, rather than a 'stitch-up'!

However, that first week of 1982 was committed to their Goa expedition, and once again flight from Bombay Airport had to be undertaken, although with less of the undignified waving of Passports here necessary. As a pleasant surprise, Aadhi Dubash (SeaLands rich stevedore), his family and supporting retinue were similarly flying to Goa, with John and Ankie, plus boys, now invited to join them for an evening at their Baga Beach holiday home. It would prove to be an interesting diversion. Arrival to their hotel on Baga Beach, one of the very few available, was to find that sleeping facilities amounted to four beds in the same open-plan room which, whilst not perfect, was workable under the circumstances, although bringing an exchange of wry smiles between John and Ankie. A shallow river ran past their outside balcony, and they were to learn that on the other side of that river there was an established Hippy colony, which, to their surprise, was partly evidenced the following day by sight of a young woman, naked as the day she was borne and in her mid to late teens (guesswork, obviously!) walking through the shallows of the river, clearly stoned out of her mind. Perhaps she had thought to go shopping, but of a purse, there was no sign!

The weather was perfect, as were the sands upon which they were able to stretch out and sunbathe, so reminiscent of their days in Greece, but with palm trees to climb if so persuaded – Ankie, Duncan and Darren were indeed so persuaded, with photos standing testament to their achievements, and Ankie's continued use of her favoured bikini, as purchased from Harrods of London. Of crowds, there were none, as Baga Beach had yet to be developed for tourist hordes, and the week was to pass in peace and tranquillity, with tans once more the order of the day. Invitation to join Aadhi Dubash and family was reiterated by one of his retinue, and midweek they made their evening way to the Dubash residence. The house was packed with party guests, and to all appearances, looking as if they were from the Bollywood set, all intent on out-speaking each other, a constant high-octane buzz of conversation. Having been served drinks, la famille Perry found itself largely ignored, and after an hour or so, John and Ankie decided that a discrete exit was called for, leaving John to instruct the boys as to the military precision required for such discretion. First one, then the other would slip quietly from the house and muster outside awaiting parents, who would themselves slip out, with John the last to join them. Back to the Hotel, there to dine on beautifully prepared, simple seafood, amid gales of laughter as they reminisced their evening entertainment. Their absence was eventually noted, with Aadhi's man despatched to check if they were alright, being satisfied by a generalised story of tummy pains, for which John apologised.

Ankie and John would spend one long evening together on the sands of Baga beach once the boys had gone to bed and should anyone visiting that area come across a petite wristwatch in the sands, it may well be that which Ankie mislaid. Honi soit qui mal y pense! They were a team, une équipe! The watch, therefore, was mislaid by them both!

Return to Bombay went smoothly, with the ever-punctual Anjou on hand to meet them, and drive to Maker Towers. With only a few days left before return to College in the UK, Duncan, and Darren, together with Ankie, enjoyed the pool, ice-creams and ambience of the Breach Candy Club, the boys to ensure an enviable tan to confirm their sun-drenched Christmas Holiday to those perhaps less fortunate fellow-students of Dean Close College.

Theirs was a poignant departure from Bombay at the holiday close, but more bearable for Ankie and John in knowledge that firstly, the boys would be met at London Heathrow by someone from the SeaLand London office, and thence to a coach for Cheltenham, and more importantly that they would be returning for the Easter holidays come April, when further exciting expeditions would be planned. Meanwhile, loving adieus, and commitment to the careful, if sometimes too beverage generous, hands of the British Airways cabin staff.

January 25th, however, brought event reason to be cheerful, the birthday celebration of the bard (poet) Robert Burns, borne that day in 1759, celebrating also his contribution to Scottish culture, most notably his best-known work 'Auld Lang Syne'. With practised reels faultlessly accomplished (well, almost), and evening of laughter and good will, appearance of the Piper courtesy of British Airways loudly cheered and applauded.

The Australian Ian Blackman, relieved from his Country Manager's function in Saudi, and replacing American Zeb McMillan as the regional General Manager based Dubai, made his first visit to Bombay early in the year, his cheerful presence seemingly satisfied by all that he heard and saw, suggesting that there would be a Dubai meeting planned shortly that John would be required to attend, to meet the team there assembled. His arrival back to Dubai brought news that he had left his hand-tooled leather cowboy boots in his Hotel room, with request that they be rescued and re-united with him in Dubai come the planned meeting. The boot's rescue was indeed made to happen, although return to their Owner was thwarted by fact that John's suitcase, committed to the tender care of the Cathay Pacific desk in Bombay, failed to make the flight to Dubai, being eventually located in Bangkok, bereft of the boots, among other things that had also gone adrift. As Ian Blackman was heard to loudly lament, "If it rained bloody film stars, I'd get bloody Lassie!" That Dubai meeting was, nevertheless, brought to a successful conclusion, ending with a beach Barbie, Australian style. John was also invited to the Blackman home, there being introduced to Ian's Japanese wife, Chigusa, who had prepared a splendid dinner, accompanied by a few tinctures of wine.

Back in India, business life took its usual routine path, but with more effectively organised customer meetings usually accomplished during visits to, and with, Narayan of Chakiat Agencies Cochin. One such visit was to Alleppy, there to meet with Mr Prasad, Managing Partner of the Travancore Mats and Matting Company exporting coir products, and main supplier of such to IKEA, and US specialist importers of coir products. Highlight of that meeting was to be invited to dine at his family home, an unusual honour indeed.

An amusing incident in Bombay was sponsored by John tasking the Company's chosen legal Firm to come up with definition of certain Corporate legalise which, after some six weeks, had still not been achieved. His question as to why the delay, delivered in the Solicitor's office evinced the following response – "Mr Perry, it is the case that the British invented bureaucracy. What we in India have done is to perfect it!" Judging by the Dickensian appearance of the many shelves in his office groaning under the weight of dockets pleading for attention, he spoke unto the truth!

Intrigued by discussion with one of Ranadip's Salesmen as to a potential customer in Poona (Pune since 1978), John made arrangements to visit the named Company, a car journey of some two hours from Bombay, and requiring an overnight Hotel stay in the town, situated on the Deccan plateau. Clearly, Ankie needed their car and driver, so hire car with driver was necessary and duly achieved, although the age of the driver was cause of some concern. The products being produced for export were the glass inners for vacuum flasks, actually blown to shape individually from molten glass, and exported to Germany for eventual flask completion. Suffice it to say that the sight of those near naked men, imported from another part of India reportedly for their large lungs, manipulating and blowing the molten glass was akin to a film scene from Hades, not Venice, all fire and brimstone, awesome to watch from a safe distance. Invitation from John to have the Manager join him for dinner at the Hotel was trumped by insistence that John join said Manager at his favourite restaurant 'that served the best prawn cocktail in town', a dubious accolade for a place so far from the sea. Indeed, the resultant tummy trouble a couple of days later was the closest to dysentery that no one would wish to be, but glass inners for vacuum flasks to Germany went in SeaLand containers! The car ride starting back to Bombay approached the terrifying though, as the very elderly driver attempted to race trucks through the steep downward ghat, or pass, on leaving Pune, totally ignoring John's shouts to slow down, and the rolled-up newspaper finally deployed from the back seat about the driver's shoulders to emphasise the order! Once satisfied that he had out-driven the trucks, he smiled and resorted to more chauffer-like demeanour, honour satisfied.

The very friendly, yet highly professional, relationship with the Callitsis team in Greece was, by odious comparison, missing with Ranadip in Bombay, the Managing Director Dilip De clearly unwilling, or mentally unable, to believe that John's presence as Country Manager could potentially be beneficial in that, and to quote Aristotle, "the whole is greater than the sum of the parts," relating in this case to the effectiveness of the two interacting with each other in a marketing capacity, being potentially greater than acting individually. By direct comparison, Narayan in Cochin had recognised that potential benefit, and worked accordingly where he perceived benefit could accrue. This reluctance of De to concede to such marketing basics was reflected in his obvious disapproval of John seeking to have group discussions with the Sales team, themselves somewhat subdued by his disapproval. Being averse to something could also manifest in an impulsive reaction, as evidenced in his apartment on one after work occasions. John was there introduced to a friend of Dilip who was ecstatic in having been able to purchase a much sought-after concert ticket, the concert featuring a famous American entertainer visiting Bombay. Dilip asked to see the ticket, which was proudly produced, only to be ripped to shreds by Dilip, declaring the concert to be rubbish. He had, by then, downed a few tinctures of Scotland's finest, but nevertheless scarcely conducive to supportive friendship! Or rational thinking! That aside, John and Ankie's evenings were usually bespoken, the social round in the small expat community being busy. John's Bridge ability had also been somewhat honed by Ankie, with occasional games being played with Brian and Margaret Dalby, him being the Representative for the Standard Chartered Bank. It was a friendship that would last long into the future back in the UK, with occasional golf between John and Brian bringing much amusement and badinage. Dinners with friends who employed a live-in cook were also enjoyed, but with great care taken not to eat salads, or take ice in drinks, which at times tested diplomacy. Entertaining guests to dinner also required great care in terms of sterilising vegetables, whilst ice blocks were made using bottled water. Occasionally, the lift to their apartment would break down with just the top half of the lift having risen above the floor level, with guests being placated by passing their drinks of choice into the lift, whilst repairs were undertaken. To employ a much-used euphemism to events in Bombay, an 'interesting' adjunct to entertaining!

 A quick trip to Calcutta was the next business travel commitment, asked to meet with a gentleman purportedly working on behalf of SeaLand and presumably appointed by Ranadip. It proved to be a wasted journey, with no obvious benefits accruing to Sealand which, if nothing else, begged the question of what benefits accrued to Ranadip, a question that would remain unanswered. Lunch was offered at the Calcutta Club, and before return to the Airport, a bottle of quality Scotch whisky was pressed upon John which, perhaps, brought a slight return on time invested. Long flight delays back to Bombay prompted vague thought of broaching the bottle, but that particular day was the strictly enforced so-called 'dry day' of the week in Calcutta,

Capital of West Bengal, and once, Capital of British India. It also explained why the Bar was closed! John, therefore, contented himself with memories of his first visit to Calcutta in 1956, then a first-trip Cadet aboard the P & O cargo vessel 'Cannanore', enthralled by the Hooghly River up which Calcutta is situated, and amazed by the sights, sounds and smells of the city, once experienced, never forgotten.

With the Easter break from Dean Close College came the much-anticipated return to Bombay of Duncan and Darren, once more their arrival into the Arrivals Hall observed from a convenient gallery to assess delivery condition from the tender care of British Airways. Regardless, their emergence from the arrivals process was greeted with joy and enthusiasm by Ankie and John, and so back to Maker Towers. The highlight expedition planned for this holiday was a seven-day visit to Kashmir, there to enjoy the hospitality offered by the Dutt family aboard a rented houseboat moored to the banks of the Dal Lake in Srinagar. Origins of this particular tourist attraction dated back to the late 1880s when Kashmir was ceded to the Maharaja Singh who, whilst happy to support the British Army in various military operations, nevertheless forbade the building of houses by foreigners in Kashmir. To circumvent this Law, and as the State offered such wonderful walking, fishing, and shooting respite from the heat and dust of the Indian plains, houseboats were built instead (who said the Brits were not innovative!), residences eventually to be developed into hotels and guest houses.

So, on the appointed day, flight first to Delhi, and thence to Srinagar, having met en route a young British couple intent on playing golf on the world's highest golf course. Sadly, for them, it turned out to be covered in snow, the same snow that neither John nor Ankie had anticipated in clothing terms. Consequently, the horse-riding organised for John and the two boys turned out to be a chilly couple of hours wearing only light summer clothing, and even chillier with some later tobogganing! It should be noted that both boys had taken riding lessons in the heat of their time in Greece, whilst John had similarly taken to horse in the summer heat of Adelaide, in Australia, when with P & O. Ankie, meantime, had located a hot pot-bellied stove in the riding facility, to which she sensibly paid homage, as her menfolk defied the elements, and prayed that they would not be unseated from their, thankfully, docile steeds. The houseboat was a joy in vaguely Victorian style, and whilst the menu was somewhat constrained for each and every dinner, at least they were asked every day just how they would prefer their mutton cooked for that particular evening. An extended trip around the Lake was chartered in, aboard the so-referred Shikara boat, their Helmsman making sure they were comfortable in the scattered cushions beneath the awnings, and Duncan and Darren managed to find a small rowing boat one day in which they rescued a stunned Kingfisher that had collided with an open window of the houseboat. All very aquatic! There was also a two-day fishing trip organised, in that it was authoritatively promised by Mr Dutt that even if an old glove were used as bait, trout would be caught aplenty thus bringing gastronomic relief from the daily mutton. Sadly, a bomb had been exploded the day before in a Mosque, reportedly somewhere in the Middle East, and reportedly by an American citizen. Accordingly, Mr Dutt cancelled the trout fishing as anyone of other than Indian appearance passing through Srinagar would be judged as somehow involved or responsible by some lengthy, mental association with skin colour, perhaps an early example of crime profiling? Discretion was though the better part of valour, and certainly the distant noise of an angry crowd could be heard.

Evenings would see card games played, and one evening, when some time was taken to look through the visitors' book, behold there was entry made some years before by John's older brother, Michael, he and his wife, Joan having similarly holidayed aboard the self-same houseboat! Bets were taken that they probably had mutton for dinner every evening! Return to Bombay at the end of their week, which had been voted a great success, meant happy days again for Ankie and the boys at the Breach Candy Swimming Club, with John relatively busy in the office during weekdays.

Return to the office always brought disgust with the lack of up-to-date communication equipment, a source of constant irritation seemingly without remedy, which made any contact with the Dubai Head Office both difficult and frustrating for both Bombay and Dubai, further adding to Sealand's seemingly inbuilt poor showing in information dissemination. This meant that regular visits to talk with Captain Bennet in Command of the 'Boxer Captain Cook' did bring added value in news terms, quite apart from any liquid assets, the while keeping a close eye on the loading of frogs' legs and prawns to the refrigerated containers, and the logging of pre-loading probe temperatures, inevitably bringing protests when less than acceptable receiving temperatures resulted in the clausing of Bills of Lading.

There was also a growing awareness, if not concern, on John's part that to place a foreign national in India as Country Manager, be that American, Australian, European or whatever, was probably an unnecessary indulgence on the part of Sealand in that an Indian national would be perfectly capable, given the opportunity and support. There could also be a considerable cost benefit, bearing in mind not only the two so referred 'Rest and Recuperation' absences that were additional to standard expat allowances, but also annual home leave. John's appointment had reduced these costs generated by the three expats previously 'in-station', American, Australian, and Dutch (placed there to set up operational and documentation procedures) even with agreed Boarding College fees taken to ledger, but operational cost benefits were there for the taking. That apart, 'in-country focus' would gain from sustained 'in-company presence'. John and Ankie would discuss this, in the realisation that were Corporate thinking to reach similar conclusion, they would again be on the move, but for now the Corporate scene seemed set, with no obvious expectation of change. Buddhists like to say that peace comes when expectations end, but experience said that life is a series of the unexpected, so press on regardless was their agreed conclusion, and they would deal with the future as they had with the past. Together!

Their most immediate future was to bid sad farewells to Duncan and Darren, as they left Bombay for return to Cheltenham and Dean Close College for the start of the Trinity Term, Ankie's sadness somewhat leavened by the knowledge that with the monsoon's arrival circa mid to late June in Bombay, she too would be making similar tracks to the UK in anticipation of the boys' Summer holidays, which would not be in India as a function of relative weather conditions, and as previously planned and agreed. They would also be hosting brief visit by John's brother, Michael, and sister-in-law, Joan, en route back to Japan where Michael was there engaged as Chairman for Unilever Nippon, they too having returned their offspring to Cheltenham Colleges, post Easter holidays. That would prove to be one of life's unexpected events too, in its own way.

With one thing or another, and including business, the year's second quarter would prove to be unexpectedly busy with events, however, unrelated to business. It commenced with the anticipated and welcome visit by Michael and Joan Perry to Bombay, planned for some forty-eight hours, before continuing to Tokyo, but despite their First-Class travel from the UK, they arrived with Joan suffering considerable back pain which, on medical examination and diagnosis, found her hospitalised in Breach Candy Hospital, adjacent to the Swimming Club. There she had to endure the use of a simple device devised by the Hospital to, quite literally, stretch her back-bone! It was nursing in the good old-fashioned way, and with Joan's pre-marriage background as a State Registered Nurse, she was fully appreciative of the efforts expended on her behalf. This stretched (no pun intended) to other thoughtful attention too, in that her regular daily visitors, Michael, John and Ankie, would smuggle in small quantities of Scotch Whisky in tiny bottles, sufficient for her 'sundowners', fortunately not detected by the very epitome of a traditional Matron, firmly but kindly authoritative beneath her high, starched headgear. The forty-eight hours lay-over stretched out (no pun intended) to about ten days, but so effective was the simple equipment devised for the treatment, that Mike and Joan purchased it from the Hospital for future use as perhaps needed.

Michael, meantime, had made his number with the Chairman of Unilever India, the most affable Ashok Ganguli, and had otherwise managed to enjoy his enforced 'holiday', with the Unilever communications, undoubtedly better than that of SeaLand, fully advising of reason for his enforced absence from Japan. In due course, and with Matron's blessing, they were enabled to leave Bombay, with tentative idea exchanged that a visit to Tokyo by John and Ankie would be welcomed, if it could be slotted into their otherwise involved travel planning. Food for thought indeed, and as chance would have it, an unexpected visit to Bombay later in the year by one Will Middleton would provide that opportunity he, interestingly, being en route to Rotterdam to take over from Scot Palen.

Late May produced yet another unexpected move, this time for John and Ankie, in that the owner of their Apartment in Maker Towers was returning from Dubai and would require that his property be vacated accordingly. That, at least, was the story spun by the 'committee' that in effect monitored the comings and goings in Maker Towers, the real reason more probably related to John's strong complaints concerning noise levels emanating from the Apartments above and below that of John and Ankie. Influenced by Dilip De? Possible, but never defined. So, once more into the matter of another home move, from home number ten in Maker Towers to home number eleven, an Apartment fortunately available in the building known as Rhamba', situated in

Napeansea Road, Malabar Hill, virtually the other side of Bombay from Cuffe Parade, but (small bonus) the area where most Dutch and Brit expats resided. The move necessitated the removal and re-location of the portable air-conditioning units as well as the usual household goods, and in that the ambient temperature exceeded 30°C, and humidity (pre-monsoon) 80% plus, they were fitted as a first requirement, and turned on as the furniture was in process of being installed. Entering the scene came a panicking Apartment Manager asking that the units be turned off as the supply wiring was in danger of causing a fire, being close to melting. Not convinced that he was technically correct, but good reason not to have all units running simultaneously in the future! Request sensibly honoured, Project Manager Ankie displaying her usual calm control. Plus, of course, she was content with the ambient temperature being in excess of 25°C! Within a couple of days, the move was finalised, their new home ship-shape and Bristol fashion, and not a Cockroach left standing either! All that remained was to affix their engraved nameplate to their front door which read 'John & Ankie Perry, + D2' (D squared), simplistic maths attempt to relate again to Aristotle, and the need for the boys to look after each other, 'the whole being greater than the sum of its parts' at College.

An intriguing feature of Malabar Hill was that it contained the fifty-five acres of land in which the Dakhma, or Tower of Silence, was built for the unique funeral rituals of the Parsis, one of the most successful minority groups in India, having originally settled in the States of Gujarat or Maharashtra. Towers of Silence were built for excarnation, the exposure to the elements of human dead bodies to decay in order, according to ancient custom, to avoid contamination of the soil with the corpses. Bodies are placed on stone beds, or gratings, on the roof of the Dakhma, with a central ossuary pit beneath, into which remains of the corpses drop once the scavenging birds, usually vultures, have done their work. Bodies disintegrate naturally, assisted by lime, with that remaining washed off by rainwater into multiple filters of coal and sand until finally reaching the sea. It was also the ancient belief that this was a final act of charity, providing birds with that which would otherwise be buried or cremated.

With mid-June came the annual monsoon to Bombay, constant heavy rain that invariably brought some flooding, but also some relief from the high humidity that preceded the downpours. They were also the cause of not in-frequent electricity outages, often anticipated, as Ankie and John found, by watching from their Napeansea Road windows as successive sections of Bombay fell to darkness, until their section of Malabar Hill also blacked out, with multiple candles then necessarily deployed. For them, it was their first experience of the conditions, and rather awe-inspiring it was too, although it must have spelled an annual disaster for the thousands of Indians living in the spread of slums that existed in the City.

For Ankie, it was approaching the time for her to leave for the UK, to open up the Cheltenham Apartment in anticipation of the end to Trinity Term at Dean Close College, and the boys release for the summer holidays. Not surprisingly, she was in a state of high and gleeful anticipation of her Monsoon Memsahib role to be, with flight scheduled for departure during the last week of June, which for John came all too soon, as he would not be joining the family in the UK until the end of July, for pre-arranged home leave. Their parting at the Airport followed none of the 'don't look back' routine favoured in past occasions, but what followed their final lingering embrace would long be remembered, amid gales of laughter in the re-telling. Once through the Emigration line, Ankie turned to face John, then to execute a perfect and very athletic 'star-jump', with a grin across her face that clearly stated 'Whoopee, I'm out of here', or words to that obvious effect. She was totally focussed on seeing her two sons, and cared not a jot for who knew it, although she did later confide her thankfulness that she had not ended up on her bottom, post 'star-jump'! She would be collected from Heathrow by John's parents, a source of relief to both Ankie and John.

For the first time in their marriage, John felt a strong sense of loss, but determined to stay busy, he made plans to visit Cochin again, there to receive the usual professional up-dates on business developments, and a social evening with Narayan at the Malabar Hotel. That proved more than usually interesting, in that there was a dance performance by a very graceful female dancer, watched avidly by a visiting Arab judging by his traditional clothing, who insisted on repeatedly attaching rupee notes to her gown, as his expression of appreciation. She too appeared quite happy with the donations, probably the reason she was there in the first place! Back in Bombay, July end loomed, and John's anticipation for the family reunion in the UK mounted accordingly. There was, however, an incident that brought great sadness prior to his departure, the sudden death of Rita De, wife to Dilip De. Formal explanation was that whilst cleaning in her kitchen using a solvent, a fire had somehow developed, severe burns bringing about her death. To John's ears came a different version purportedly from a house-servant claiming to have watched in horror, but the formal explanation would of course prevail, with sincere condolences offered and accepted. Case closed, no questions.

By July end and leaving Anjou and Francis in charge of the Napeansea Road Apartment, John took flight to London and hire car to Cheltenham, there to be joyfully reunited with Ankie, Duncan and Darren in Flat 7, Cedar Court, their base for the next too few weeks. For a holiday, some ten days had been booked for Portugal, in a villa within a small enclave of holiday homes near a beach, and with its own pool. It would prove to be a superb break, with sand, sea, swimming, and sardines, with sunbathing supported by steadfast, super sunshine (25°C+) that summer of August, just to lay emphasise with a touch of alliteration! Some horse-riding for the menfolk, a visit to a Bull Fight (in Portugal, the bull is not killed), visit to a golf-course where Ankie also tried her hand on the driving-range (to conclude that it was not a game for her) and a trip in their hire car to Cape St Vincent Lighthouse, that singular navigation mark so familiar to Navigator John during his P & O days. The boys would make friends with others of the age in the enclave pool, which led to John and Ankie meeting socially with other parents, which on one occasion brought about a friendly rubber of Bridge after refreshments. Here it should be noted that John had brought with him a small selection of Bridge reference books, determined as he was to improve his game knowledge in preparation for return to Bombay's occasional Bridge evenings, and daily encouraged by Ankie to so do for an hour, on the villa's flat, sun-drenched roof. All went well in the (fortunately) friendly Portuguese rubber until John, recognising a total lack of points to his hand of cards, nevertheless, and bizarrely, made a call indicating that he had a surfeit of points, to which Ankie rightly bid in anticipation of a slam. There was complete silence at the end of the game during which John had lost every trick, save for a weak and chastened 'sorry' from himself! Ankie would later embrace and console him, but after short analysis and reminder of bidding calls! Work still in progress!

Back to Cheltenham tanned and relaxed, visits to John's parents, and some necessary shopping before John's return to Bombay, sadly before Ankie who would follow him a week later, after seeing the boys back into College. It was all a bit messy, but with Ankie's constant self-confidence and expertise, nevertheless achievable in their general scheme of things. Necessary shopping included such luxuries as HP Sauce, Military Pickle, Pork sausages and suchlike, but also a new suitcase for which visit to Debenhams was made. There they witnessed two salesmen jumping up and down on a 'Delsey' suitcase as demonstration of its robustness which seemed unharmed by the assault, so an obvious purchase. Sadly, when it appeared on the Bombay Airport luggage carousel a week or so later, it looked as if a Boeing 747 had rolled over it, albeit that the luxury items as above referenced made it unharmed, being well wrapped. Subsequent letter of enquiry to the Delsey Company, suggesting that the weight of two salesman was scarcely comparable to that of a Boeing 747, received a masterful sales response, encapsulated in the final sentence which read 'Just imagine how bad the damage would have been if it had not been a Delsey product!' Touché!

With Duncan and Darren safely, perhaps reluctantly, back to Dean Close, and Ankie safely, perhaps reluctantly, returned to India (did she leave a birthday card for Duncan's fifteenth Birthday September 22nd?) life briefly steadied back to some sort of routine, both in business and socially. Occasional Sealand visitors came and went from either Rotterdam (David Tyler) or Dubai (Anthony Gaskell), neither of whom seemed capable of explaining their purpose in the visit, and whilst John knew Tyler to be part of the Mid-East Sales team in Rotterdam and ex-Ferrymasters UK, Gaskell's function in Dubai remained unexplained, or offered, other than he had been resident in Dubai for some considerable time. De facto, neither brought any obvious weight to bear on either Sales or Operations, or in more trenchant reflection, the Marketing of SeaLand in India. John was beginning to feel increasingly exasperated by lack of modern communication means, and senior Corporate contact, simply because successful marketing required, very simply, excellent communication!

Perhaps on the plus side came there no expressed complaints as to either Sales or Operations deficiencies concerning the Bombay or Cochin performances, per post, fax, or rare telephone call, nor indeed during the occasional visit to Dubai by John. Nevertheless, the sheer lack of communication felt increasingly like isolation from the Divisional team if such a thing existed. The opening line of Shakespeare's Richard 111 briefly flickered, "Now is the winter of our discontent", but in the heat and humidity of Bombay, how would that be classified? Classically oxymoronic?

Notwithstanding, weekends continued to be enjoyed with friends at Breach Kandy's welcoming facilities, and for John, the occasional weekend golf outing at the Willingdon Club with fellow expats, usually from the Banking fraternity. Caddies were not obligatory (John never employed one), but some did, even with an 0630 tee-off in order to avoid the heat of later hours. What was necessary though was the employments of ball watchers, engaged to watch the fall of the golf-balls, particularly if, as was too often the case, that entailed playing out of the rough, where snakes were to be found sunning themselves. During one such four-ball match, a Banker known for his slight eccentricities, and seeking his ball chipped over the green, suddenly reappeared on the green whirling a long snake around his head, which he then proceeded to stuff into his golf bag which, in golfing terms, further handicapped his caddie! No explanation was even given!

November brought another unexpected, although pre-advised, visitor to Bombay, in the person of Will Middleton who, as it would transpire, was en route from Japan to take over from Scot Palen in Rotterdam and was therefore taking the opportunity to see part of his future area of responsibility which would extend from Europe as far east as Bangladesh. John and Ankie entertained him at their home, together with invited guests, and in discussion with Ankie, was persuaded to join her the following day when she made her weekly visit to the Crawford Market (always with Anjou in attendance), for meat and vegetable supplies. Crawford Market was a place of raucous denial to any resemblance of hygiene, with birds and humans in apparent competition as to which species could get to the raw cuts of buffalo meat first, and Middleton expressed himself as shocked and horrified by that which he there observed as Ankie slowly but bravely completed her purchases. Her description of the Market on the previous day had been heard with respectful disbelief by him, but seeing, hearing, and smelling was believing indeed! So much so that in the more formal conversation with John that was to follow, Middleton advised that with immediate effect, John and Ankie would be granted a third 'Rest and Recuperation' break as part of their relocation package. This brought a serendipitous probability to a Tokyo visit sometime in the early New year, provided Michael and Joan were still there. It would be fair to suggest that, even though Ankie's 'Buffalo Bourguignon' was deserving of a Michelin Star rating, Will Middleton would have probably declined the dish, if offered!

He undoubtedly had meeting with Dilip De, although John was not present, nor advised as to discussions held. History would suggest, however, that Middleton, as others before him, had been gulled by the usual charm offensive and smooth talking, as the Ranadip Agency would survive a few more years to come. Narayan also flew in from Cochin for discussions, undoubtedly bringing a more measured picture of his Chakiat Agency activities and aspirations to the fore, being pleasantly surprised to receive gift of a Schaffer Pen Set, engraved with his initials PN, so WM had not come unprepared. He would leave for Dubai and Rotterdam shortly thereafter, where no doubt his India exposure would be discussed and analysed.

He and John would meet again in Rotterdam during the third quarter of 1983, just before John was scheduled to return to India, post the summer home leave of John and Ankie for that year.

With December fast approaching, and therefore, end to the Michaelmas Term at Dean Close, John and Ankie gave thought to the up-coming return to India of Duncan and Darren for the Christmas holidays, their expedition this time chosen to be to the Republic of Maldives, its 26 atolls situated in the Indian Ocean, some 430 miles from the Indian coast. Interestingly, as they found, the Maldives had gained Independence from the UK in 1965 but had become a member of the Commonwealth during that July of 1982.

Delivered from the customary tender hands of British Airways, the boys quickly adapted to their first exposure to the 'Rhamba' apartment, and reacquainted themselves with Breach Candy's ample pool, sunshine, and ice-creams. They would later enjoy the company of John and Ankie's friends, Dutch, and New Zealanders, for a Christmas dinner repast, as always superbly prepared by their Mum, and just a little help from the Crawford Market! There would follow loud games of Sjoelen, not unnaturally played on the Sjoelbak Board, as individuals each sought to master that famous Dutch game of skill that demanded much noise additional to the staccato clack of the wooden pucks. Correct pronunciation of Sjoelen or Sjoelbak continued to impress the Dutch guests.

Post-Christmas, flight was taken to the Maldives Capital City of Malé, followed eventually by a boat trip to the particular atoll of their choice, name of which has been lost in time mists, under overcast skies and through rough seas, hardly welcoming under the circumstances. A Frenchman aboard had better anticipated the weather, in that he wore a heavy northern climes raincoat. Darren fell asleep on deck, to awaken just as the boat started to plunge into a deeper wave trough, prompting an alarmed bellow from Darren in Dutch, a common expletive that may well have shocked had he said it on an Amsterdam

Canal boat! Arrival to the atoll was to find a clear newness about their hotel, with Staff apparently still under training. That, combined with the thirty-six hours of rain that followed, combined with little culinary flexibility from lobster or fish, and a walk around the atoll that was all over within twenty minutes, brought about a change of plan. The Maldives vacation was vacated, and with telephone connection amazingly available, flight was booked from Malé to Colombo, in Sri Lanka, and return boat trip from Atoll to Malé undertaken post-haste. Arrival to Malé airport was well before flight time, but eventually la famille Perry mustered at the check-in, finding themselves at front of a queue that had yet to form. To their surprise, however, a Maldivian citizen, as it would transpire, seemingly unaware of queueing etiquette, took position in front of the afore-mentioned family, at which John offered the welcoming confirmation that it was of no concern to them, as they were not in a hurry. Ankie nodded agreement, noting the honey deployed. In response came the immortal words, charged with a strong Maldivian accent, "We don't need you people here, so just get back to Blighty.", possibly indicative that he had read a few 'Boys' Own' magazines. He actually did use the word 'Blighty', requiring some explanation for Ankie and the boys.

Suffice it to say that the remainder of the holiday spent in Sri Lanka was excellent, with the boys enjoying some lake water-skiing (cautiously aware that crocodiles were there too) the bathing of elephants, visit to the Temple of the Tooth at Kandy, visit to Trincomalee and stay at a Tamil run Hotel where Darren was helped to celebrate his thirteenth birthday. A gifted hotel-baked cake, a massive black spider in the bedroom that hid itself 'somewhere' and being briefly trapped in the lift that broke down, prompting a brief few swear-words, but in English! Sadly, that cheerful Hotel would be burned down during the territorial Civil War (how can war be Civil?) between Tamils and Sinhalese that commenced in 1983, not ending until 2009 with death or disappearance of over 200,000 civilians, and over 50,000 fighters, mainly from the Tamil minority.

It was back to Bombay, with Breach Candy Swimming Club for the boys' tan accumulation before time came for the Junior Team to return to Cheltenham for the 1983 Lent Term. As time would tell, this was the last Christmas/New Year spent in India, as the Perrys' would resume their peripatetic existence come the third quarter of 1983, with the year ending in fresh and unexpected challenges that would test both their resourcefulness and, indeed, patience. Meantime, much water would flow 'neath various bridges. Duncan and Darren would, nevertheless, be returning to India for the Easter holidays at end of the Lent Term, having been out on two exeats from College as was usual each Term by John's mother and stepfather, known affectionately as Oma and Opa, being Dutch for grandma and grandpa. This nomenclature had been introduced by Ankie, being gratefully received by the grandparents, as it made them sound younger!

Once the boys had left for the UK, John attended meeting in Delhi with potential customer(s), one such meeting being in the home of an important industrialist, so described by Dilip De, in which one large room had been converted into a clear replica of an English pub, its Bar complete with beer pumps. No clear reason was given for the meeting, but a convivial couple of hours passed, perhaps somewhat marred by a whisky-inspired retort from the Indian Host suggesting the only reason that John had been allowed to the home was 'because of the colour of your skin'! DD tried to laugh it off, but forms of racism apparently knew few defined boundaries, with John merely inclining his head in brief acknowledgement of attempted humour. Honey can be deployed wordlessly. The following day, after Dilip's early departure back to Bombay, John who had chosen to take a later flight, was privileged to watch part of the Dress Rehearsal for India's Republic Day Parade, which would take place on January 26th, as every year since Independence. It was a stunning sight, moving through Rajpath the wide ceremonial boulevard, through India Gate, to Delhi's National Stadium, where the President would take the salute on the actual day of enactment. Some eighteen to twenty-four different Regiments of the Indian Army, together with Naval and Air Force units marched past in all their finery and decorations, to include elephants, and the camel-mounted Border Force, unique in the world. The colours, sounds, and discipline were extraordinary, and a massive credit to the Nation. Sadly, Ankie was not present on that occasion, as she would have been as delighted as John, who, unfortunately, was unable to observe the whole breath-taking event, having a flight to catch.

The next important event come February was the selection and purchase of a new Company car, the (in)famous Ambassador, the sit-up-and-beg built by Hindustan Motors Calcutta, in technical collaboration with Morris Motors, to manufacture their version of the UK's Morris Oxford. That which had been handed over by the departing Larry Roberts had seen its day, displaying definite signs of growing malaise. It was not a World-beater, it was drivable and roomy, and with the obligatory addition of air-conditioning (not standard) it became acceptable, as John would learn on those weekends when he would drive himself and Ankie to Breach Candy, or the rare occasions when he had to take his life in his hands and drive from Malabar Hill to the office in Maker Towers. The cost was in the region of £10,000 equivalent, and as Ankie would so succinctly and sweetly put it, "I have never gained so little pleasure in spending that amount of money!"

With March came further meetings with customers in Calcutta, and as Ankie had yet to visit the Capital of West Bengal, one-time home to the British Raj administration of India, she chose to accompany John, checking in to the Oberoi Hotel as they did on arrival thereto. By sheer and cheerful coincidence, they would there meet up with Alan Boxer, good friend from their Greece days, himself on business in India, where he had responsibility for a sizeable manufacturing plant at Dum Dum just outside Calcutta, as part of his wide territorial Management brief.

On leaving Greece, Alan had been appointed Managing Director International EMI Music, and whilst the 'International' bit did not include Europe, North America, or Australasia, he was kept travel busy by his Countries of involvement including Argentina, Brazil, South Africa, Nigeria, four SE Asia countries, India, and Pakistan. He was staying but a few days, the Oberoi being his base. They had met only briefly the previous year in Bombay, when John and Ankie had entertained him at their Maker Towers home (plus visit to Breach Candy), but this was an unexpected bonus, enabling them to take dinner together and a lazy evening sitting by the Hotel's outside pool reminiscing as to their Greek days, with coffee and the occasional smidgen of Indian brandy (recommended), and exchanging some amusing details of their local experiences. He would depart the following day to further his busy travel schedule, and eventually they made their farewells, with John and Ankie passing their best wishes to him, and his wife, Pat. Their concerned thoughts for Alan were, however, diverted to John as they prepared for bed, as John was to find his backside a mass of mosquito bites, with Ankie's concerns more than tempered by her outbursts of laughter at the sighting. He had felt nothing during the evening, nor had there been mosquitos heard or seen, so perhaps Indian brandy dulled the senses to local concerns. As John would ruefully observe, he knew of fish that were known as bottom dwellers, but Indian mosquitos?

Post business, most of a day had been left to explore parts of Calcutta, but the over-powering sense gained was one of over-population and therefore substantial over-crowding, with air quality concerns arising from, among other issues, the use of dried buffalo dung for home-fire heating, adding to the not unusual times of air temperature inversion, which could shroud the city in pollution. Sighted reminder of the River Hooghly's polluted state would remind John of his Cadet days at sea with P&O on the Indian run, when the Hooghly's pollution would give rise to cynical suggestion that the river was the arse of India, therefore questioning how best to describe Calcutta's geographical position. It looked worse in 1983 than in 1956!

Return to Bombay, to routine office and social commitments was to, once more, bring home to John and Ankie that their day-to-day existence was largely mundane, the lack of interest particularly felt by Ankie who had little to compensate for the absence of their two sons, save for the excitement in anticipation of their return to India twice a year, or for her extended monsoon Memsahib home leave during the British summer. For all that India had to offer, and there was much daily reminder of the grinding poverty of many, in stark counterpoint to their own privileged position, was source of increasing and concerned mental conflict.

From a business point of view, John felt trapped within an established environment that neither brooked, nor encouraged, any form of entrepreneurial activity, and save for the relationship with Chakiat Agencies in Cochin, was politically worrying! In the round, their lifestyle was an antithesis of that experienced with SeaLand heretofore! That they had each other was a saving grace, and regular discussion as to how best to cope brought some relief to the situation, in their determination to see it through, together!

They must have been enjoying something however, for suddenly the much-anticipated return to India for Duncan and Darren to enjoy their Easter holiday was upon them, and with no plans this time having been put together for an expedition, it would turn out to be many visits to friends and the Breach Candy pool, which seemed to happily fill the bill. Not to forget rounds of back-gammon. There was, however, one last call to assemble to the world famous 'Hash House Harriers', that extraordinary cross-country event introduced by Brit expats, seemingly wherever they settled. In essence, a small group of trail blazers (using kitchen flour) would set off, laying the trail for those that would later set off in noisy pursuit in a motley array of clothing, with shouts of 'On,

On' and blasts on a bugle, eager to reach the defined destination, there to enjoy ice-cold quaffs of beer, the race having been sponsored by Bombay's main brewery, providing its brew of London Pilsner. In Bombay, the small British contingent was augmented by Scandinavians, Dutch, a Swiss, New Zealanders, and enthusiastic Indian devotees, and of course, their holidaying off-spring, Duncan and Darren being keenly involved. To take a short cut, or to otherwise default, was penalised by requiring the miscreant (a surprising number of overheated, self-confessed miscreants there were too) to sit upon a large block of ice in penance, drinking their beer, whilst ignoring any haemorrhoidal downsides, or perhaps one should say, backsides! Was it this run that came across a trio of Indians, naked as borne, tending in the hot sunshine their still of illicit hooch, to watch astounded a bunch of mad foreigners blowing bugles burst en mass past them? Surely one would have observed to the others that he must have inadvertently been drinking their brew, as he had just had an illusion!

The boys' holiday would pass all too quickly, but return to the UK they had to, in ignorance that indeed this would be their last venture to India, but in the knowledge that the summer holidays would see the family reunited again, with something bound to persuade toward a beach somewhere. In fact, Ankie had already had a brief discussion with John in that regard, and although no final decision had been made, their thoughts had turned to Greece, to the island of Rhodos. It would come to pass!

Brief early May visit by Gaskell from Dubai, during which he had discussions with Ranadip's sales personnel whilst totally ignoring John, brought forth no tangible benefits. However, the spontaneous and generous bestowal of a third 'Rest & Recuperation' break by Middleton post his Crawford Market experience engendered plans for John and Ankie to visit Tokyo during May, there to visit brother Michael and sister-in-law Joan, decision that proved prescient with relocation changes for both the Perry families to come about during the last knockings of 1983.

Their flight to Tokyo would be via Hong Kong, enabling brief stop-over there to meet up with past SeaLand friends and colleague Mike Morris and his wife, Joanne, their one-time next-door neighbours whilst living in Oud Beijerland, Holland, Mike meantime having switched his allegiance to a rival container ship operator. They would also meet with Dennis and Rowena Minns, both childhood friends and neighbours of John in Eastbourne, Dennis having achieved his luminary position with HSBC (Hong Kong and Shanghai Banking Corporation), and Secretary to the Hong Kong Golf Club, a more particular achievement. It would be a busy, helter-skelter series of visits to various parts of Hong Kong and Kowloon, so well-known to John from his P & O days, but an eye-opening and interesting diversion for Ankie, even although the weather was less than inviting, with rain never far away. The flight into Kai Tak Airport was its usual breath-taking experience for Pilots and passengers alike, as the line of washing passed close under the descending aircraft's belly. For Pilots, it was technically demanding as the steep low altitude right hand turn (sub 600m feet) into the final approach could not be instrument-flown. It was rated the World's seventh most dangerous Airport.

Arrival to Tokyo was more comfortably routine, and with Mike and Joan's full involvement, a memorable programme over several days was able to be enjoyed, with a car specially laid on to take the visitors from India on several chauffeur-driven rides through extraordinary scenery, and to view not a few temples. To accompany Joan to a supermarket was to see prawns so fresh that they were still moving in their sealed packaging, whilst dinner one night at the Hilton Hotel was to realise just how well Michael was respected in his Unilever capacity. Dinners at their home, a western-style house, were always an event full of laughter, no more so when their Canadian neighbour recounted her careful preparations to mark the return of her husband from an extended business trip, to include the special purchase of satin bed-sheets – the which, as she so feelingly described 'turned out to have no damned traction'!

They were also taken to watch a series of Championship bouts between vast Sumo wrestlers, their all too brief and sudden encounters preceded by much ceremonial salt throwing and belly slapping, the final winner that night being, as one recalls, a substantially large Hawaiian whose salt throwing and belly slapping had clearly stood him in good stead.

It was an interesting and laughter-filled few days, mood enlivening for both Ankie and John, and with farewells made, came return to Hong Kong for brief two hours or so (the washing line still very much in landing approach evidence!) and onward to Bombay's routines and challenges. In fact, and as a function of upcoming yet unknown changes, they would all meet again that year for Christmas at The Mill, UK home to Michael and Joan in Worcestershire, close to the country town of Malvern that nestled in the Malvern Hills.

With mid-June came the invariably predictable monsoon rain to Bombay, with its equally predictable heavy downpours, which brought to a seasonal halt the exercise walks that Ankie and John enjoyed on the Racecourse circuit. Breach Candy too was lost as a social rendezvous, and somehow pool swimming in heavy rain remained an unattractive option. To Ankie, however, these annual constraints meant that homeward bound loins were to be girded, and London flight to be booked, with the Dean Close Trinity Term soon to end, thus marking the start of the summer holidays, and her need to be back in the UK accordingly. To John, it would mean a few lonely evenings and weekends before he too could join the family on his annual home leave, although in truth friends of various nationalities and menu choices tended to issue a wealth of supper invitations. There was Squash to be played, and customer contacts to be made, particularly in the Cochin area with Narayan, where he was always made most welcome. Ankie's departure late-June would be followed, nay, eagerly followed by John's departure on home leave come late-July, for joyful reunion in Cheltenham, leaving Anjou and Francis once more in charge of the Rhamba Apartment, not to mention the new Ambassador 'sit-up-and-beg' car!

Arrival home to Cheltenham found Ankie and the boys engrossed in plans for the briefly discussed holiday on the Greek island of Rhodos, and John brought his enthusiasm wholeheartedly to the planning. There would, however, be visit to Dutch Oma and Opa in Amsterdam (did their more natural nomenclature Oma and Opa make them feel younger?), to include a return visit to Maduradam, to the home of Ankie's sister Nel, and boat trips on Amsterdam's canals, all in bright sunshine, a far fling from monsoonal Bombay. Rhodos, however, could not be denied, and with visits to the increasingly youthlike English Oma and Opa, they were off to the welcoming arms of their, as rated, second home, Greece, into which they comfortably resettled. It felt as if they had never left, with rented, red, open-air beach buggy, water skiing for the boys (again proudly overseen by totally impressed parents), sea swimming and lazy taverna meals, all embraced within the Mediterranean's summer sunshine, the natural charms of Greece, and hospitality of their Greek hosts. John and Ankie reminisced laughingly about their brief call into Athens en route to a Rotterdam meeting during the first year in India, when, having taken a taxi for quick foray into the city between flights, the vehicle had broken down just outside the airport, at which point the driver abandoned his taxi, and left! Then too, they had turned to each other, and smilingly observed 'we've come home'!

Departure from Faliraki, for that was the small coastal village that had afforded the Perrys such welcome, was reluctant but inevitable, as time was drawing close when John would have to return to India that August of 1983, to be followed some two weeks later by Ankie. Faliraki would, as years advanced, progress (if that is the right word) into a fairly major tourist attraction, so the family was indulged by its nascent recognition, and was so remembered. Back in the UK, tanned and relaxed, but time perhaps to commence sourcing the basic comestibles to assist life in Bombay, such as HP sauce proudly original since 1899, pork sausages from the local Butcher, and cheddar cheese to mention but a few, with no requirement this year for a new Delsey suitcase! However, message was received from Rotterdam that John's presence was there required on a fairly urgent basis, to meet with VP Will Middleton, so shopping per se was temporarily abandoned. John and Ankie discussed the summons, noting that their return to India would mark a two-year sojourn thereat, and mulled the possibility, therefore, of a further relocation, to conclude the inevitable 'wait and see, react accordingly' position that they had had to adopt so often in the past. Notwithstanding, the water ashore was about to become deeper, as John was to discover.

Arrival to Rotterdam was to be first introduced to the Personnel Manager, an American named Ed Donald, replacing in post the previous Dutch employee. He would prove to be that which is known in American parlance as a 'gopher', or in British parlance, a 'dogsbody'. Pleasant enough, but enough said. Meeting with Middleton was joined, for John to be bluntly advised of that which had reportedly occurred in Bombay in his absence, namely that the Reserve Bank of India and Customs Authorities had raided the Ranadip Office, there to discover documentation proving conclusively that before John's arrival in India, SeaLand had imported chassis without paying duty, but as John was now the titular head of SeaLand in India, his return to Bombay would see him arrested, and imprisoned, pending investigation. "This," solemnly declared Middleton, "means two things. Firstly, of course, we cannot allow your return to India. Secondly, we are in the midst of a substantial and very necessary cost reduction exercise here in Europe, and as such there are no positions into which we can place you, so must regrettably let you go." Another euphemism!

This was immediately recognised by John as a devious scheme set up by Dilip De who, and to quote, an American colleague, "was quite a schizophrenic character with a terrible vindictive quality about him, and little else to commend him," which fell neatly into John's experience and opinion. He seriously doubted that such a raid had taken place uninvited, if at all, or indeed that any incriminating evidence had been located regarding chassis importation some four years, four whole years, before John's arrival in Bombay. Sadly, Middleton now saw this as a God-given excuse for a substantial operational cost reduction during his watch, and it was therefore fait accompli. A done deal, and John took no trouble to hide his contempt accordingly, from he who had so wilfully chosen to utilise the bizarre story, and to hell with honey. His face said it all! That aside, there was also to come a feeling of relief in the ending of life with SeaLand, but not before Middleton had agreed to John's forcibly put suggestion that his salary should continue unchanged through the remainder of 1983, and that Boarding School fees for Duncan and Darren should continue to be paid by SeaLand until such time as both had taken the GCSE exams, i.e. thru mid-1986. Middleton's agreement brought his gopher back into play, and necessary arrangements were finalised.

So ended some fifteen frenetic years with SeaLand, during which John and Ankie had learned much in business terms, operational, marketing, and financial, and had also learned the extraordinary importance of good communication, something that SeaLand had so inadequately grasped throughout. These lessons would stand in good stead with persistence and determination remaining omnipotent, but first challenge was how the heck to get their household goods back from India?

Return to Cheltenham was to convene an Extraordinary Meeting of Team Perry, this time to include both Duncan and Darren, to discuss in detail that which John had briefly imparted to Ankie in phone call from Rotterdam. Having already analysed and recognised their vulnerability in India, the situation had come as no great surprise to John and Ankie, despite the convoluted methodology, but to the boys, it brought anger and distress, which manifested in the destruction of treasured SeaLand baseball caps! Of necessity, however, was need to discuss just how they were to retrieve their worldly goods from Bombay, and it fell to Ankie to vocalise that which appeared to be the only solution, forced upon them by, if true, the threat of arrest should John reappear in Bombay. "There is no other choice," she began, "in that I am the only one that can safely return to India, and who knows what has to be done – after all, I have some experience in moving homes, and there is no way that we can trust Ranadip to do it on our behalf." She was, of course, absolutely right, and despite John's qualms, he knew instinctively that Ankie was fully capable to successfully undertake the mission.

Accordingly, Rotterdam was informed of the decision, and effectively charged to ensure Ankie's safety whilst in India, and SeaLand London was instructed to book Business Class return flight, the return date to be left open. Message was also to be sent from Rotterdam to Ranadip, to ensure that car and driver (Anjou) were always available to Mrs Perry, as was all co-operation that Mrs Perry might demand. The die was, once again, cast! Bizarrely, it was now John seeing Ankie off to India, and their embrace as they parted at Heathrow was both whole-hearted, and hearts-felt! To John devolved the responsibility to see the boys back into College, and in knowledge of the poor communication with India, to worry constantly as to how Ankie was progressing. In the event, she would return in triumph after some ten days, job done, bringing with her the bosom of the family, and surprisingly, four small silver ashtrays, each one intriguingly cast around a silver Indian rupee, dated 1877, 1903, 1918 and 1919 respectively, and engraved as hereunder:

'John Perry, with best wishes from your friends in Bombay', and dated September 1983, almost as if it had been pre-planned! Cynical? Perhaps.

Some six long years were to pass before SeaLand finally had to recognise the need to dispense with the services of Dilip De, and with extreme secrecy, a company was registered in India with SeaLand holding a 74% stake, and Chakiat Agencies the balance of 26%. It was called Sun Transport Company Pvt Ltd to maintain the requisite secrecy, with office space leased close to Churchgate Station in Bombay, and after full recruitment, Dilip De was given termination notice during the third quarter of 1991. The company name was subsequently changed to SeaLand Agencies India Pvt. Ltd., and whilst De took SeaLand to Court, claiming SeaLand's chassis as his own, he eventually had to pay damages in excess of Rupees 2.6 million, to SeaLand. His career in shipping was finished, but as far as John and Ankie were concerned, his vindictive deviousness back in 1983 had, inadvertently, given John's business career an unexpected burst of fresh energy, upon which Team Perry was able to capitalise!

In December 1999, SeaLand was bought out by the Danish company Maersk, and to its credit, and indeed that of Chakiat Agencies, SeaLand ensured that the Chakiat shares were bought at a return of 18% over nine years, a well-deserved reward for Narayan's honest and steady support over the years, not to mention his thoughtful investment!

So, with worldly goods regained from India, and the family reunited in Cheltenham, knowledge as to where the next square on the board was positioned had yet to become apparent. Surprisingly perhaps, neither John nor Ankie felt any disquiet, so set about enjoying their new-found freedom!

United Kingdom

It duly came to pass, however, that thoughts turned to the fiscal future, and whilst Cheltenham was a welcome reward after Bombay, it appeared to be less than fallow ground to harvest employment for John, his qualifications and experience suggesting that focus on the London market might offer greater opportunity. Here fate yet again took a hand, in that word of his parting from SeaLand had apparently beaten the intended distribution of numerous copies of John's CV, as demonstrated by receipt of invitation to meet with the owners of Johnson Stevens Agencies, a Company about which John knew little. On investigation, it turned out to be a major and progressive London Agency representing a substantial portfolio of shipping Lines, serving a wide variety of the world's trade-lanes. It sounded interesting, and after contact had been established, John and Ankie travelled to London for a November meeting with the joint managing Directors Derek Johnson and Tom Bax-Stevens, the former a one-time Sales employee of SeaLand, as it turned out.

It was explained that indeed they were the appointed Agents for a variety of Lines with strong growth potential, and for one major Line, namely Yang Ming of Taiwan, they had responsibility for the appointment of Continental Europe Agencies. Such was the growth potential that they felt their UK Sales organisation required major restructuring, and their Continental involvement re-emphasised. The appointment on offer was designated as Director of Sales and Europe, with the task to successfully implement a country-wide marketing and sales structure sufficient to develop strong business growth, and expansion plans. A salary was identified, together with confirmation that a BMW 500 Company car would be provided. They had reviewed John's background and experience, and having met, offered him the position, requesting that he advise them of his decision within the following few days.

Returned to Cheltenham, Team Perry convened to discuss the offer, not least of all the defined extent of the function, noting particularly the carefully worded 'to successfully implement' a marketing and sales structure. On balance, they agreed that with a clear definition of required outcomes, it was well within John's capabilities and experience, and the salary acceptable. Timing became a matter for discussion as clearly a move from Cheltenham would be necessary, as well as the identification and acquisition of yet another new home. Johnson and Bax-Stevens proved amenable to the matter of timing, and noting that their Head Office was in Barking, Essex, made suggestions as to potential search areas. The job was accepted. They were back in business!

Meantime, it was agreed that John would spend some weeks getting to know the people at the Agency in both their Sales and Operational capacities, the latter at the Port of Felixstowe. In particular, to review the current Sales structure, and evaluate the personnel involved. This meant driving to Essex each Sunday evening for the week, with residence at the so referred 'Ilford Hilton', a fleabag of an hotel, and back to Cheltenham each Friday evening, some 125 miles and two and a half hours drive each way, even in a BMW! These weeks would also bring knowledge that none of John's predecessors had lasted more than two years in their appointments, and the opinion that if Britain would ever require an enema, then Barking would be where it should be inserted! He would also conclude that both Johnson and Bax-Stevens were salesmen rather than marketeers, although to describe them as salesmen using the epithet 'pure and simple' would be to misread them, as they were neither pure, nor simple! They were, without doubt, excellent salesmen, outwardly theatrical, enthusiastic, convincing, and business-like, larger than life and well versed in promising to achieve or exceed required volume and revenue targets as defined by their Principals. At the same time, and as required, intelligent deviousness could be deployed, and when necessary, ruthlessness!

This conclusion, drawn after just a few weeks, would stand John in good stead, as it enabled him in turn to deploy appropriate diplomacy, or indeed apparent respect to their egos, as to cross either of them would invite instant reprisal. Deeper water demands appropriate buoyancy, as John and Ankie would agree at weekends, with experience supportive to their survival planning.

Christmas 1983 was celebrated with a full-on family gathering at The Mill, home to Michael and Joan, with matriarch mother and husband Alex also now resident there. Younger brother, Brian, and wife, Lesley were present with daughters, Sara, Lindsey, and Victoria (aka Tia), to join with cousins, Andrew, Caroline and Debra, off-spring of Michael and Joan. John and Ankie, now more accustomed to an Indian summer for Christmas, completed the gathering with Duncan and Darren, to enjoy the rich feeling that, pro tem at least, they were once more resident in Britain. Darren's fourteenth birthday would be celebrated at the Cheltenham Apartment, and then en famille, they decamped to Gerrards Cross, invited thereto to join their good friends from their Greek days, Alan, and Pat Boxer, to bring in the New Year. Delightfully, more good friends from Greek times were also present with their children, the Cooper and Revel families. It was a night to remember, with much noise, dancing and cheerful laughter, happy memories of Greece exchanged, and for off-spring to be amazed at just how much school friends from St Catherine's School had grown and developed!

That aside, and more importantly, Ankie was both happy and content to be back in England, with her two sons now close and contactable at will, Duncan now aged sixteen as of September, and Darren now fourteen. Together, she and John would spend time house-hunting, and it was purely by chance that, on passing through the pleasant town of Epping one weekend, they discovered a tiny estate of new-built houses in Tower Road, with one house still to be completed, and unsold. It would become theirs and in due course, and come early April 1984, the house-plate 'Orcades' would take pride of place above the front door. Just twelve miles from Barking, adjacent to the Epping Forest and close to the M25, number 1A, Tower Road (only slightly modified by Ankie in the late building stages!) would become their twelfth home since marriage in 1967, just under eighteen years before. Welshman John Davies, with his poem 'Leisure' inadvertently caught the spirit of their eighteen years with his opening lines; "What is this world if full of care, we have no time to stand and stare," thus relieving them of the onerous task to find words to rhyme with peripatetic!

Ankie would swing into full 'house-move' action yet again, this time further complicated by furniture returned from India being stored in Malvern, and Cheltenham furniture to be either retained or otherwise disposed. Yet again, her clear thinking and experience to date proved sufficient to ensure smooth collection, collation, and despatch to Epping, with John abandoning the 'Ilford Hilton' for two weeks to join Ankie in her endeavours, and sadly, the pending sale of their current home. Duncan would leave Dean Close School at the end of June 1985, followed by Darren at June-end 1986, no doubt bringing a sigh of financial relief to SeaLand!

John would take on the full role as Director of Sales and Europe for Johnson Stevens Agencies (JSA) as from April 1st, the day's significance not escaping him. Potentially some storms to follow the calm, but with forewarnings already taken aboard, weatherable with judicious sail trimming, perhaps collectively generalised as 'work in progress'!

John's few weeks of advanced attendance to JSA Barking had not gone unrewarded, in the sense that evaluation of the Company's current Sales structure, centred largely in Barking, and regionally in Birmingham and Glasgow, was in itself generally sound, if somewhat top-heavy in the South. The southern region was divided into six sub-regions, each with an allotted Sales Representative, ostensibly reporting to a southern Sales Manager, presumably based in Barking. This incumbent was charged with overview of Sales Representatives' interface with customers, and their booking figures, together with responsibility for contact with certain major Accounts, as identified by the Directors. That he resided some two hours' drive from Barking suggested that his attendance thereto was, perhaps, less frequent than was necessary.

Both Birmingham and Glasgow had a simpler organisation, each with a Sales Manager and small office contingent sufficient to allow appropriate customer interface as required. Ireland was operated as a JSA subsidiary, its independence robustly championed by its Manager, but outwith John's purview or responsibility.

Within the Barking office, each Line represented had a Line Manager, with a supporting team responsible for taking bookings and producing appropriate documentation to pass to the Operations Manager and his team based in Felixstowe, handling despatch and receipt of containers, and distribution of necessary information to the Port's largely computerised vessel working systems, now much advanced from John's experience in 1968/69. Lines represented included Yang Ming (Far East), ABC Line (USA), Neptune Orient Line (India), Iscont (Israel and Med) and Nile Dutch (West Africa), with others constantly being sought. Yang Ming was by far the largest operation, including the overseeing of Continental Agents on behalf of Yang Ming.

The apparent downsides, and impediment to potential growth, were functions of inadequate in-house communication, coupled to the unusual factor that there was no central register of exporters to the various trade-lanes, with Sales Representatives (at least some) claiming 'ownership' of his (there were no female Reps at that time!) portfolio of Accounts, possibly seeing this as a safeguard or protection against potential dismissal, a fear factor. In fact, personnel 'churn' was a function of an occasional display of the Board's ruthlessness, as previously mentioned.

Another communications issue was that Line Managers' interface with the Sales force was either intermittently direct, or equally intermittent with the appropriate Sales Manager, depending on the vessel schedules relating to each Line. In effect, there appeared to be no formal responsibility placed upon the Line Managers to advise Salesman as to the on-going contribution by Accounts, nor indeed centralised records, Line by Line, of Shippers' export bookings, or indeed lack of bookings.

That good communication within an organisation is paramount between each component involved in achieving required outcomes is a basic imperative within the marketing concept and this was clearly absent and requiring resolution. This in turn would require application of yet another basic, that of good Management, namely "Planning, Organising, Leading, and Controlling," but first a presentation to Johnson and Bax-Stevens, to achieve their understanding and acceptance.

As was their wont, John and Ankie discussed these conclusions, within the context of presentation approach, concluding that timing and diplomacy were cardinal requirements, along the lines that despite the obvious strengths of JSA, increasing demands upon the structure to achieve enhanced growth required some centralising and accumulation of Account data Line by Line, in turn, requiring the upgrading and streamlining of communications twixt Line Managers and Salesmen, thereby bringing enhanced customer focus to all levels of involvement. Potential touchpaper? Possibly.

In essence:
- All known Account detail to be downloaded by all Sales Reps to a central data base in Barking.

- Line Managers to issue, post each sailing, a "Missing Shipper Report" to Sales Reps/Management, thus enabling appropriate investigative contact.
- Line managers to liaise closely with Director of Sales in matters of concern or requirement.
- As Director of Sales, John would assume responsibility for interface with all Sales personnel as necessary, or as directed by the Board.
- Position and functionary of Southern Sales Manager to be re-evaluated.
- Seek to have all Departments of JSA buy in to the marketing concept, in that all Company activity must be part of customer focus, in order to achieve required outcomes.

Meeting with the joint Managing Directors was joined, and perhaps surprisingly, their agreement was forthcoming, to the extent that Johnson would throw his weight behind the imperative to centralise an Account data base, and the implementation of the 'Missing Shipper' identification, post each vessel despatch. This amounted to playing the fear factor! Again surprisingly, re-evaluation of a Southern Sales Manager position, and functionary, would be for John to undertake and bring to a conclusion. Buoyancy test? Perhaps.

Simultaneous to all of this was activity at a Tower Road Epping to unpack and distribute/wash/burn the contents of many cardboard boxes full of household accoutre from India, so carefully organised by Ankie, and now delivered and stored in the garage. John's mother and stepfather had arrived from Worcestershire to assist in settling into the new home, stepfather with his superb knowledge of DIY, and a very professional toolbox very much involved. In the garage, John extracted an evil smelling blanket from its box, and gave it a very vigorous shake and, as he did so, a brilliant flash illuminated the garage. "Hell's teeth!" he shouted, bursting into the kitchen. "You must have packed part of the monsoon too, darling," only to be brought up short by sight of stepfather Alex still quivering in shock, having inadvertently shorted the power supply whilst exploring a ceiling light with his screwdriver! The main switch board was sited in the garage! Much subsequent laughter over G & Ts, but factually every item of clothing, or bed linen, had to be washed or dry-cleaned to dispel the retained aroma of Bombay, so long had the goods been in transit or storage. Also now positioned in the lounge was a beautiful teak escritoire measuring 43 inches in height, 30 inches I breadth, and 17inches in depth purchased from the Bombay 'Flea Market for next to nothing, clearly furniture from the Raj past, and as demonstrated by the combined efforts of John, Ankie and driver Anjou, able to be carried on the back seat of the redoubtable Ambassador motor car! Just!

Of immediate business need was to be introduced more formally to Yang Ming's UK Management, themselves also resident in the JSA offices, namely Oliver Yu, and his second-in-command, Captain Shee, both making John feel most welcome. This developed into a respectful working and social relationship, albeit that Oliver Yu would never hold back if he felt that his Company's interests were in any way neglected. Introduction to the owner of ABC Line, Svee Rosenfeld, would follow shortly thereafter, as well as the Allalouf family and Schlomo Nadar of Iscont Line, all of whom would feature largely in John's involvement with JSA, and from whom he would learn much over the coming years. Another pleasant surprise was to learn that the Neptune Orient Line (NOL) representative was no less a person than Grant Whillance, he, and John as P & O Cadets aboard the vessel Shillong having each towed a rickshaw together through the streets of Kowloon, with the rickshaw owners as reluctant passengers exuding unmitigated concern! Happy days!

Introduction was also formalised with JSA's Felixstowe Operations Manager Brian Boreham, and John Foord who looked after the marine operations. John's appointment was accepted with scant obvious enthusiasm by the former, he and John having crossed swords, so to speak, in India, and equitably by the latter. The Felixstowe operations were well run, and therefore complimentary to the customer focus concept. JSA also boasted a small Travel Agency in Felixstowe, although its contribution to the overall enterprise was of no concern to John, other than getting his frequent travel arrangements together.

One Board member yet to be formally introduced was Derek Robson, the Company Secretary, and that too took place as soon as possible. His main claim to fame, quite apart from the fact that he knew where all the Corporate fiscal bodies were buried, related to a drive that he had taken, after dark, in the New Forest, Hampshire when he had the misfortune to run into the rear of a New Forest pony, such that the rear end of the poor animal broke through the vehicle's windscreen. As the animal was in a state of shock, its bowels reacted accordingly, depositing content onto Derek's lap, whilst at the same time bringing damage requiring later medical attention. Derek would laugh the incident off, saying that he forever after found dried effluent in his jacket pockets, no matter how often cleaned, and it was assumed that the pony had been put down. All that aside, he was a cheerful if cautious person, fond of his lunchtime beer, and always ready with words of thoughtful advice, or indeed caution. He was a survivor!

Finally, visits to both Birmingham and Glasgow were important and undertaken, there to meet the Sales Managers and their small teams, and to sell the objective of centralising the Accounts data in Barking, in pursuit of better communication and hopefully, export throughput yield. Both Tom Campbell (Glasgow) and John Frearson (Birmingham) impressed John, and whilst Scottish resistance to change was slow in fading, fade it did to good purpose. With the agreement of Johnson and Bax-Stevens, John would make an early visit to the USA, ranging between New York and New Orleans, to meet with the main importers of Scotch whisky, and other British brands of alcoholic beverages, hopefully to equal good purpose.

Ankie & John Family Wedding in Worcestershire

Duncan (age19) and Darren (age17) Attending Family Wedding in Worcestershire

With the summer months approaching, and 1A Tower Road now fully habitable with its many Dutch, Greek and Indian artefacts suitable deployed, not forgetting the much-travelled Greek terrace furniture first purchased on arrival to Athens back in June 1976, thoughts of a holiday began to focus, with Duncan and Darren being collected from Dean Close School for their summer break. In truth, both Ankie and John felt the need for some respite after so many months of re-establishment challenges to overcome, although the choice of Croix-Valmer, a small commune in the Var Department in SE France seemed to be an unusual departure from their beloved Greece. It was, nevertheless, an enjoyable and relaxing ten days, made only slightly remarkable by the discordant sounds of the boys singing the British National Anthem returning late one evening from, it was assumed, a local tavern, as they strode the road back to the holiday residence, said road fortunately otherwise deserted! Just what prompted this choice of (as rendered) almost-music was never really explained, rationalised merely as 'boys will be boys' with the 'Entente Cordiale' remaining apparently unsullied.

Return home brought the growing realisation to John and Ankie that whilst their last thirteen or so years had been that of Expats, bringing a degree of discipline, timing, and accepted custom to their activities, they were now beholden to themselves to govern the pace and content of family aspirations. In John's case, there were new rules of engagement to be decided upon with a possibly capricious Board which, if wrongly deployed, would prove disastrous. Sobering thoughts indeed!

On the new home-front, however, work to be done in late August of that first year was inspired by Ankie's conclusion that the lounge of 1A Tower Road Epping was too narrow (railway carriage-like was mentioned), and with planning permission gained, went about cajoling the appointed builders into finishing the expansion work both on time and budget, all of which proved timely for the busy Christmas to follow that year. Unexpectedly busy Christmas? Not a bit of it, as Ankie was determined to have Christmas in her newest home and wanted to invite pre-determined guests. It just needed a little extra lounge space to accommodate plans!

Meantime, and with so many freight bookings over a wealth of Line Principals, Saturday morning attendance to the Barking office was often necessary, and on one such day, John was to witness the arrival of Bax-Stevens with his dog, a Dobermann Pinscher which, as TBS would confide, was a 'gay' Dobermann (no shades of the Madras Dobermanns there!), a state of affairs unknown to the attendant Porter to the building, home to the JSA offices. "You can't take that animal in here," he said to TBS, barring his way. Bax-Stevens smiled, and in his acquired American Mid-West accent softly responded, "You goin' to tell the dog?" offering the dog's lead, resulting in the lift soon ascending to the JSA floor with gay canine presence included!

Such gentle diplomacy was not necessarily the forté of Bax-Stevens, however, as was to be demonstrated much later in John's first year. From some unknown, and certainly unconfirmed, source strong rumour had reached the ears of TBS that JSA was about to be dismissed as the Iscont Line's UK Agents, and without any consultation with his business partner Johnson, sent electronic message to the Iscont Management in Israel, ending unbelievably in these exact words: "…and you can stick your Line up your arse!" The very next morning, John was despatched by Johnson to Israel, there to pour diplomatic oil on much troubled waters which, thankfully, was in its turn, diplomatically received by the Allalouf family, with whom John established a

213

sound working relationship, learning much in the process as to the positive determination inherent in the State of Israel.

As a barometer of business success, none better than to see good humour displayed by Johnson and Bax-Stevens, because that meant that the tills were ringing up in Agency earnings. In fairness, both were delightful company and hosts when in good humour too, so the year moved toward its end in reasonably cheerful fashion, despite the occasional challenge from Svee Rosenfeld of ABC Line to reduce his costs, ofttimes calmed by his British secretary Ruth, always pronounced 'Root' by her employer! Cheerful lunches at the local Chinese restaurant in company with Oliver Yu and Captain Shee, with TBS in hearty voice, his portly frame shaking with laughter when, on loudly suggesting that the Chinese owner must exercise well judging by his slim frame, came strong response from the proprietor with the words 'not exercise, just poverty!'

Christmas invitations were issued, and 1A Tower Road Epping echoed with the high spirits of assembled family members, John's mother and stepfather Alex, brother, Brian with Les, and their family, together with Duncan now seventeen years of age, and Darren to notch up his fifteenth birthday come December-end. As John and Ankie's twelfth home, and Ankie's hugely successful cooking, it was well christened, even with the wine(s) not being blessed!

The New Year was equally well celebrated, and as Ankie and John offered their customary toast to each other, they embraced with the words, "So far, so good, the Team is still in the running," or words to that general effect after some small indulgence in champagne. McDuff was again enjoined to 'lead on', and let the Devil take the hind-most!

1985 brought more involved interface with the Line Managers, as the establishment and usage of a centralised data base, coupled to introduction of the so referred 'Missing Shipper Reports' began to produce positive results. Feed-back to the Sales force became focussed, which in turn brought about a more identifiable Customer targeting in planning and application, now routinely available post each Line's sailing. It was a beginning.

Regular visits to Yang Ming Scandinavian and Continental Agents were also programmed, their purpose initially to be more a matter of orientation, leading to liaison as appropriate or sought by the Agents involved, all of whom proved to be highly professional, and alert to changing needs of their markets.

John would learn much from these visits, appreciating both input, and occasional need for discretion in any associated reportage. Learning of John's Dutch connections, it also brought the occasional invitation from the Dutch Agent's Principal to attend horse-trotting races in Holland, which indeed John and Ankie would usually accept.

In discussions also with the Midlands and Scottish Sales managers, target Accounts were identified and where appropriate, John would either make joint calls with the District Manager, or alone as evidenced by the USA visits to Scotch importers, and as would eventually be undertaken in interface with selected Accounts in Israel, as suggested by the Allalouf family.

Time also had to be spent in Barking, and with his office sandwiched between those of Johnson and Bax-Stevens, John was conscious that he would be under continuous outcomes assessment, unlike his fifteen years with SeaLand where assessment was probably at very best sporadic, and appraisals either formal or informal, non-existent. Actually, not exactly true, as in final 1983 interview in Rotterdam, Will Middleton had observed in passing that John was 'an average employee', having met John but once in Bombay, which notably failed to ring the 'faint praise' bell, whilst damning by inference! In Barking, John mused of Homer's mythical sea monsters, sited in Greek mythology on opposite sides of the Messina Strait and rationalised as nautical hazards, between which sailors would have to pass, giving adjacent preference to neither between Scylla and Charybdis or, as the French would have it, 'Tomber de Charybde en Scylia', and the more pragmatic American terminology 'Between a rock and a hard place'! Interestingly germane!

Barking was also subjected to some research in effort to discover a trace of historical value, to learn that Captain James Cook RN, famed explorer and hydrographer, married Elizabeth Watt in 1762, in what became St Margaret's Church in Barking, she being the daughter of Samuel Watt, keeper of the Bell Inn, Wapping. Historical value indeed, with local rumour or suggestion that he, Cook that is, had started one of his intrepid voyages from Barking remaining unsubstantiated!

Ankie, meanwhile, with the latest home now spick and span, was busy creating new opportunity for herself, enrolling in a College not too far from Epping to allow daily attendance, there to attend lectures and practical applications in matters of Aromatherapy, Electrology, Beauty Therapy and Advanced make-up. In July 1985, she passed the examinations with her usual flying colours, being duly presented with resulting Certificate in name of the Wendover College of Beauty Therapy, whose curriculum had conveniently been taught at her chosen College. A small bedroom at 1A Tower Road was transformed under her thoughtful guidance into a fully equipped treatment room, and before long, her reputation as a skilled beauty therapist brought her a steady clientele, enchanted by her skills, personality, and intriguing Dutch accent! John, having sustained muscle injury at the Epping Squash Club, would himself submit to her magical applied massage, and marvel at the results.

Her July exams triumph had, however, been preceded in June by son Duncan's final departure from Dean Close School Cheltenham, and the return to Epping of both Duncan and Darren for the summer holidays. With one large school trunk suitably re-housed, and contents inspected, passed for washing/dry cleaning or potential landfill, and Ankie's July exams expedited, family thoughts turned to summer holidays.

To John's pleasant surprise, it had been revealed by Johnson and Bax-Stevens that they owned an apartment in Marbella, Spain, part of a complex that included a large swimming pool, and a golf course. Moreover, it was offered to John and family for their summer vacation, an offer that was accepted with grateful alacrity and eager anticipation. A Company car was also garaged there, so flight was booked to Marbella, an airport last utilised by John in June 1976, just days prior to taking up his Greek appointment.

It was a grand holiday that summer, with Spain's weather at its best, much time in the pool and sunbathing, a round of golf for John and Darren on one of the hottest days, which suggested the need for cold beer(s) when re-united with the much-tanned Ankie and Duncan at the pool, and some exploring done by car as the mood took them. An incident upon which the family dined out for years involved topping up the car's petrol tank at a wayside garage. With the tank filled, John proffered travellers' cheques in payment, then a widely accepted form of purchase abroad, to have it indicated that only cash would be acceptable. John's rather 'take it or leave it' response to the elderly pump attendant lacked diplomacy, and without a further word, the attendant sourced a length of rubber tubing, the end of which he inserted into the tank, and commenced sucking out his recently delivered petrol! A hurried 'tarpaulin muster' was initiated with Ankie and the boys emptying any and all spare cash about their persons to the fund, which thankfully just matched the petrol's cost, probably to the attendant's relief too, sangria being more to his taste. Situation saved, but by luck rather than any judgement. Lesson learned, never underestimate or seek to patronise those less fortunate than oneself! Plus, cash is a simple commodity, understood by all, so keep some handy!

By 1985, the Port of Felixstowe had grown considerably from that which John had experienced back in the late 1960s. Interestingly, much of the land upon which expansion had taken place was owned by Trinity College Cambridge which, in the 1930s, had bought land near Felixstowe which then included a small scarcely known Dock, handling such as grain and coal. By 1985, that insignificant Dock had become a major Port, with three fully operational container Terminals, substantial Ro/Ro facilities, was already the largest, privately owned, container Port in the UK, the first sea Port in the UK to introduce computerised customs clearance, and with work already started on construction of the large Trinity Terminal, phase 1 of which would open in 1986 with the ability to handle the largest container ships in the world. Insofar as Trinity College was, throughout, the Landlord collecting rent, the Bursar who decided to make that 1930's purchase 'punt' could well be called visionary or forward thinking. He too could have been a full-on advocate of Antoine de Saint Exupéry, and his observation that "as for the future, you have not to foresee it, but to make it possible." Bullseye! Johnson Stevens Agency was, in terms of representing Lines calling Felixstowe, a reasonably major player, and indeed was focussed both on gaining further representation, and bringing such business to Felixstowe. Additionally, of course, to ensure that Lines so represented received first class service in vessel operations and despatch, the final link in the marketing chain so important for customer retention. In this last-mentioned, John had little to criticise, in that JSA Felixstowe maintained both good working relations with the Port authorities, and a sound professional grip on container despatch and receipt, which in turn brought strong truth to JSA's overall sales pitch. It was, de facto, with strength in depth, a sound marketing tool.

As such, few complaints from Lines' Principals, or indeed from the joint Managing Directors for John to address, thus enabling full attention to advancing both Sales activities, and European responsibilities, to successfully see out the year of 1985, success being rated as continued employment and accordingly, retained self-confidence as to the immediate or short-term future. So enabled, and with Ankie's business enterprise in good shape, Christmas would be enjoyed with Duncan and Darren, once again at The Mill in

Worcestershire, home to brother Michael and sister-in-law Joan, together with the cheerful company of brother Brian and Les, matriarch mother, and Alex.

Come New Year's Eve back in Epping, John and Ankie would again raise their charged glasses in toast to each other, as they pondered their good fortune thus far, and being reunited again as a family, noting that Darren would also leave Dean Close School in the coming June (more fiscal joy for SeaLand) to continue for a final year at the Bancroft School in Woodford Green, a short distance from Epping. However, 1986 had other surprise events to capture their attention, some business-associated in John's case, but resulting in a splendid, totally unexpected, family return to their beloved Greece.

Between the usual hurly-burly of life with Johnson Stevens Agency, requiring constant alertness for mood-swings of the joint Managing Directors that might require evasive action of diplomacy, came news of an event with ABC Line. As advised by Johnson and Bax-Stevens, the Owner of ABC Line, Svee Rosenfeld, had engaged with a Member of the House of Lords, who would attend on board the next ABC vessel to call Felixstowe, there to meet with Mr Rosenfeld, and both Johnson and Bax-Stevens. After they had been introduced, they would in turn introduce John should time allow, and he should therefore ensure his availability on that day. Events, however, would take a different turn, and with the JSA group of three duly mustered on the arrived vessel's Bridge deck, Mr Rosenfeld led his guest thereto to effect introductions. To John's amazed surprise, the guest turned out to be none other than Euan Geddes, or the Hon. Euan Geddes as he had been in September 1960 when sent by P & O to their tanker 'Maloja', aboard which John was then serving as Third Officer, to gain some first-hand vessel experience. Being about the same age and disposition, he and John had enjoyed a sometimes-bibulous friendship over several weeks, but fact that Euan had succeeded to his father's title in 1975 had totally escaped John's notice, busy as he was within the SeaLand organisation.

The now Lord Euan Geddes, on seeing the JSA reception, cried, "John, how good to see you again after all these years," shaking John's hand, which turn of events had John, with studied diplomacy, introducing his joint Managing Directors to his Lordship! He would later drive Euan back to London, a journey livened with much reminiscing and laughter, parting in good spirits. Sadly, their paths would not cross again, and his Lordship would eventually assume, among many other attainments, the role of Deputy Speaker to the House of Lords. Subsequent serious discussion with Mr Rosenfeld in matters of his targeted sales requirements ended with him springing another major surprise, completely out of the blue. "I gather you like Greece," he started, "and I own a villa on the island of Mykonos. Would you and your family be interested in using it for your summer holiday? There may be a little cleaning up to do, but it's yours gratis if interested, and there is also a small car garaged there to be used." Suffice it to say that John's response was hugely enthusiastic, but before bringing the news to Ankie, he telephoned Rosenfeld's Secretary Ruth (aka Root) in Belgium to be sure.

"John!" responded Ruth. "He would never have made such an offer if he had not meant it – enjoy!" Ankie and John would share a bottle of champagne that evening, whilst anticipating their fantastic good luck! Duncan and Darren were equally overjoyed!

Before the summer holiday, however, a trip to Taiwan with Tom Bax-Stevens to meet the senior Management of Yang Ming Line. He seemed better disposed to long-haul travel than Derek Johnson, and usually chose a more leisurely pace, so hence a stop-over in Hong King was scheduled on the return. They were well received in Taipei, wined, and dined, with Bax-Stevens at his most engaging and sincere self as befitted meeting with JSA's main business principals. Altogether an interesting and first-time exposure to Taiwan for John, adding much value to his understanding as to the energy and independence of its people.

With the aircraft's low-level bank over the ever-present washing lines for the usual final approach to Hong Kong's Kai Tak airport, the brief one-day homeward stop-over began, the island to John being a well-known and much visited jewel of past experience. For Tom BS, the opportunity to search out and purchase Rolex watches for his daughters, or rather extraordinarily good Rolex imitation watches, which reportedly were later received with less, much less, daughterly approbation than he had anticipated, as in "but they're not real, Dad!" which boded, potentially, pocketbook ill!

Safely returned to the UK, and with necessary account of the trip shared with the Yang Ming UK Representatives Oliver Yu and Captain Shee, together with the JSA Line Manager, family focus switched to a much closer island, situated in the southern part of the Aegean Sea, and part of the Cyclades group of islands. Mykonos! It turned out to be the family holiday of a lifetime, able as they were to once again embrace the much-loved Greek ethos, courtesy of Svee

Rosenfeld. Whilst July and August were usually the hottest months of the Greek summer, Mykonos was seasonally cooled by the 'meltemi' wind, bringing a pleasantly dry and relatively cool 27 degrees centigrade to the island, which fell neatly into Ankie's preferred temperature range!

The villa was situated a short drive from the main town of Chora, (Greek for 'town', a Greek linguistic device used when both the island and its main town share the same name) on the south coast, the south-facing terrace a mere fifty or sixty metres from the sea, at the bottom of what was probably the garden at some time. The resident car, a small VW saloon of doubtful age, surprisingly came to life on keyed request, and once the villa's refrigerator had been cleared of its old and much congealed content, and suitably cleaned, so could the family go shopping. Other cleaning was certainly an immediate priority, and indeed as was the unblocking of all waste pipes. This last mentioned was reluctantly undertaken by John who, vaguely versed in Greek plumbing experience from the past, managed so to do.

Swimming off the small sandy beach in the warm Aegean Sea was much indulged by all, with Duncan and Darren, having teamed up with a Greek couple from Athens, literally under-water herding a shoal of whitebait into waiting nets. John watched proudly, floating on the water's surface, his goggles allowing total vision through the clear water. Ankie, with equal pride in their achievement, cooked the three or four kilos of fish for lunch, served with a suitable chilled bottle of Greek white wine, a classic piscatorial example of 'freshly caught'. It was idyllic, itself a word derived from the Greek language! Visits to Chora were regular, there to waterside dine, explore, and be amazed at the large resident Pelican that appeared to own part of the beach. Outings also to several of the small villages and beaches scattered throughout the island, all thanks to the robust, if scarred, VW car in which, at the ages of 19 and nearly 17, respectively, Duncan and Darren sought to 'have a go'. Ankie too would seek her 'mummy roads' to explore as in their Greek days, and at her age of forty-five years, looked no older than a svelte 18-year-old, in her newly acquired miniscule bikini, her chosen casual wear around the villa. If pride was indeed to precede a fall, John as husband and father was in big trouble, but blissfully ignorant! The two weeks passed all too quickly, their return home being marked by letter from the family to Mr Rosenfeld, expressing deep gratitude for his generosity. It was back to business.

Back to business indeed, although John had the pleasure of meeting up with Grant Whillance in his capacity as the Neptune Orient Line Representative at 1A Tower Road, there to initially discuss the Line's activities and requirements, but later over dinner and a few glasses of wine, reminiscing over their days together as Cadets aboard the P & O cargo Liner 'Shillong', way back in the late '50s, and their Port calls to such as Hong Kong and Shanghai to mention the two most notable shared experiences. There was the usual friendly rivalry as to their pre-sea training, Grant having attended HMS Worcester in the Thames, (as did John's younger brother Brian) and John HMS Conway in Anglesey, North Wales. They would remain as families in close touch over the years to come.

Ankie meanwhile resumed her Beauty Therapy business, her deep summer tan now, no doubt, a strong feature of her customers' envy!

That, apart from the usual day-to-day need to focus on JSA's growing business, would bring Christmas, this year to be enjoyed together as a family at home, and welcoming in 1987 in the customary fashion, now over two and a half years since joining JSA in April 1984. That in itself was cause of some self-congratulation between John and Ankie as their champagne glasses were raised, this year enthusiastically joined by Duncan and Darren in sharing the bottle!

1987 would mark several new beginnings, some more obvious or impactive than others, but starting with visit to Holland in January to attend the wedding of Ankie's sister Thea to Paul van Wier. This was followed, for John, by a 'business trip' to Sri Lanka with, and arranged by, Bax-Stevens, its claim to mention being fact that no business was conducted, which begged the question as to its purpose, in that the Ceylon Shipping Corporation was firmly contracted to the Cory Brothers Agency, and the Line was already a customer of the Port of Felixstowe. Notwithstanding, it was for John a brief, unexpected but welcome break to an island so well known to him over many years, bringing the opportunity for some winter sunshine, and indeed to purchase a few Sri Lankan Batiks for Ankie. For return to the UK, John wore his usual long-haul garb of tracksuit, whereas TBS was, surprisingly, extremely well turned out in suiting, and very nervous as their taxi hied them to Colombo's Airport. Juggling with his departure documents, he bade John to hang on to a small packet which he had dropped as he searched for his Passport, which John stuffed into his tracksuit pocket, and promptly forgot about it. Return of the packet was sought by TBS on exiting Heathrow, its contents proving to be but a few Sri Lankan gems, which perhaps explained John's required presence on the TBS visit to the island, known to ancient Persian traders as Serendip! To quote a political paraphrasing, "No man has greater love that he who lays down his friends for his life," and it had not gone un-noticed that TBS had chosen to stand well back from his colleague going through the Customs area!

For the Port of Felixstowe, 1987 would be remarkable in that the P & O Group purchased the Port from the then owners European Ferries, and the Port succeeded in handling one million teus (twenty-foot equivalent container units) as a United Kingdom first. Son Duncan concluded that his Slough course in Accountancy had run its course and, unbeknown to his father, had in April interviewed with JSA, to receive job offer to work in the Accounts Department, which in later life would prove useful experience. Son Darren would be taken out of Bancroft School, consequential to his parents' conclusion that the then Headmaster chose to put his personal success ahead of his pupils' success, and with Darren deciding on a career in the Hospitality Industry, he would later in the year enrol at Huddersfield Technical College, soon thereafter to become a University.

Another notable first was that there would be no possibility of a family holiday that year, so come late September, John and Ankie took a ferry voyage to Spain, crossed into France at Hendaye, enjoyed a casual visit to Biarritz, and then 'spur of the moment' direction changes that took in, among much else, Bordeaux, Perigeux, Poitiers, Tours, the Paris périphérique, Reims, Belgium and finally Amsterdam, there to spend a few day with Ankie's parents, their first visit thereto for some considerable time. They had graced an abundance of hotels en route, and taken a plethora of fine food, and for both it brought relaxation from what had been a year-to-date of increased work-related stress for John which had taken its toll. It was two weeks of reaffirming their strong bond, and determination in continued persistence. They also religiously shared the driving, two hours about! What a team!

Christmas of 1987 was once again in Epping, a close family affair, but this year with the added pleasure of hosting Geoff and Luttie Langfield, staunch friends since their first meeting back in 1968 Southminster, giving both Ankie and Luttie the opportunity to re-embrace their shared native language of Dutch. The New year was again seen in at the home of Alan and Pat Boxer, together with other assembled good friends from their Greek days, and gracious, how all the children had grown into such pleasant young adults!

1988 loomed large, John conscious that this April would not only mark Eastertide, but also his four years tenure as Director of Sales and Europe for JSA. In general business was good, with the tracking systems for bookings and volumes put into place working well, were properly bedded in, and enthused by the Line Managers, and Sales force. European and Scandinavian Agencies were performing to Yang Ming's satisfaction as far as could be judged! Affability is a reasonable indicative, but not on those occasions when it fails to reach the eyes. As Playwright R.C. Sherriff's 'Journey's End' may have put it, based on his experiences as an Officer during WW1, "It's quiet out there, too damned quiet!" John would ponder this, and as in both his Greece and India days, ask himself whether there was something that he was missing that, in this case, Johnson and Bax-Stevens had not! Their most efficient Secretary of many years, Eve, was often a good bell-weather as to their mood swings, but no deeper water seemed currently in the offing, no sudden flood tide.

Epping, meanwhile, brought yet another disappointment, in that E837NMP, the BMW allocated to John, suffered its second criminal assault, the car radio having been torn from its site overnight, with the vehicle carefully parked in the home driveway. The first assault had taken place some months previously, when the car had been parked at Epping Station, north-eastern terminus to the London Underground's Central Line. Both these assaults were, however trumped in their nefariousness by the early 1986 incident when, with John and Ankie attending a Freight Forwarders Dinner in Glasgow, thieves had broken into 1a Tower Road, stealing items of Ankie's jewellery, the Queens Gold Medal awarded to John in his final pre-sea Term at HMS 'Conway', and various pieces of musical equipment belonging to Duncan and Darren. Epping Police had on that occasion contributed their studied opinion that John and Ankie had been fortunate in that the miscreants had not defecated on their carpets! In none of the three incidents did the Constabulary appear to take much interest, other than to suggest that Epping's adjacence to the M25 offered a good getaway route! Files closed. No stolen goods ever recovered. The town was becoming less than enchanting!

January 18th, however, marked John's 50th birthday, joined by Greece friends, Brian, and Jenny Cooper, for a celebratory lunch laid on by Ankie, with Duncan (now 20) and Darren (now 18) in close support roles, with business and Epping concerns temporarily forgotten.

Nevertheless, demands of business development and growth continued, and to John this meant the continued application of as many aspects of marketing that would support the constant need for growth in Sales. First class communication within the JSA organisation, with all sections buying into Customer Focus was a must! This, together with excellent communication by the Sales team, and Line Management groups, to both current and targeted business accounts. All basic stuff but requiring constant attention and polishing where appropriate. Public Relations, or PR, remained exclusively the retained domain of the joint Managing Directors, and was rarely evidenced by other than occasional industry advertising, although undoubtedly both Johnson and Bax-Stevens entertained key Accounts, and sought continuously for new business opportunities.

Easter was spent en famille in Holland, Duncan wearing his 'Mission' tee-shirt, and 'Cardiacs' leather jacket, thus displaying his then acquired musical tastes. Events to come would suggest that this jacket was somehow mislaid by Pickfords during a relocation move, thuswise so convinced, albeit unconvincing, were Ankie and John, in consequent loss analysis. Fortunately, by that time, Duncan had been enthralled, in the listening, to the sounds of Pavarotti the Italian tenor! Not converted, but now cognisant of other musical choice. Quality time was spent with Ankie's parents, sisters, and brothers-in-law, not forgetting niece Maaike, and tentative arrangements mooted for sister Nel, brother-in-law Hille and niece Maaike to spend Christmas in Epping. Come May, Ankie would, in her usual pursuit for further interests and qualifications, gain from the RSA Examining Board her Certificate for 'Word processing, Stage1, Distinction', thus further justifying earlier purchase that year of an electric typewriter. This was prompted by John's growing interest in, and application to, the writing of a book, with Ankie's immediate and enthusiastic interest to both proof-read each completed page, and thereafter, bring it to full typed and readable expression. The book would be entitled 'Quit Ye Like Men', although subsequent events (what else?) would not see it brought to full publication until 2008! Time and Tide, or perhaps the Shakespearian 'To be, or not to be?', that was the question.

July 1988 would bring the family back to one of their favoured Greek islands, then still unspoiled by over-enthused tourism, Skiathos, where Darren had first learned to water-ski, and where both Duncan and Darren would demonstrate their continued skill on the water. The usual two weeks of sheer joy at being back in Greece was this time enhanced by day trips to the adjacent islands of Alonissos and Scopelos, and 'twas with reluctance that return to the UK had to come about. Once home however, with containers and Beauty Care businesses to look to, life's rich pattern continued to unfold, richly leavened by an August invitation by good friends Alan and Pat Boxer to join them and others for frolics in their pool, and barbecued lunch, followed on August 14th by a cricket match between the JSA Barking team, and the JSA Port team led by John Foord. As chance would have it both Duncan and Darren would play for one side or the other, although John foolishly agreed to John Foord's (sly!) suggestion that the LBW rule should not be applied, thereby encouraging the match win by JSA's Port team! Ankie reviewed her latent knowledge of cricket gained during their Holland appointment, choosing to spectate, rather than preside over the score book!

Meetings in London with the Allalouf brothers and Schlomo Nadar of Iscont continued to be arranged and enjoyed by John, their enthusiasm for London clearly enhanced by the fact that the UK business was flourishing, and not a little by their enjoyment of a full so referred 'English Breakfast'. A further visit to Israel was also undertaken, only slightly diminished by John's arrest on arrival to Tel Aviv, based as he would subsequently be informed, on his close resemblance to a known UK agitator or some such. His release some four hours later, sponsored by reassurance from El Al London as to John's authenticity, came as a relief, despite his temporary incarceration having been courteously managed, and apologetically ended. Sales calls had been arranged and were carried out, ending what had turned out to be an interestingly different visit to Israel, with unfettered return home.

The recounting of all this to an enthralled Ankie brought forth much laughter, as did John's description of a light, post-jog, lunch taken at his hotel one day, starting with his decision to order a cold roast chicken salad. "It looks like ham." John observed to the Waiter, who reassured him it was chicken. "It smells like ham too," John continued, and taking a small portion to his fork added, "and it tastes like ham, so on balance, could it not be ham?" The Waiter's continued insistence that the meat was chicken brought John's diplomatic praise for said chicken as having been 'tastefully garnished', at which point Ankie smilingly offered a small newspaper article she had kept that seemed to bear witness to John's observations at table.

For all of this activity, however, John was becoming increasingly concerned as to the sparsity of new business development, in the form of additional Lines as Principals, apart from the gaining of a small start-up' service from Norway to the UK which looked promising. Its longevity however was brief, in that the giant DFDS would bring that competitive challenge to a close after a few brief months of operation.

However, September saw an extended weekend spent in Cornwall by John and Ankie, continuing the long friendship with Keith and Jenny Robertson established aboard P & O's 'Orcades' way back in 1966/67, they now being comfortably resident in St Agnes. Thereafter, with Keith and Maureen Davie, now almost 'second family' so many years had their friendship lasted since Cadet days with the P & O, their home being in the tiny hamlet of Nancenoy, situated some half-way between Gweek and Constantine. A long way to drive even for an extended weekend, but as always sharing the driving two hours about made light work of it, although Ankie preferred to navigate when in the narrow lanes of Cornwall.

Christmas was to be a major event this year at 1a, Tower Road however, as Ankie had confirmed the Dutch presence for Christmas Day, added to which they would be joined on Boxing Day by brother Brian with Les, their three daughters Sara, Lindsey, and Tia, together with matriarch mother to John and Brian, and of course Alex. Sadly, brother Michael and wife Joan were otherwise engaged, somewhere in the world! For all of this, Ankie had purchased seemingly the largest turkey in Christendom, to be deployed over the two days with a sumptuous spread of seasonal gastronomical delights, with John told off to ensure adequate supplies of spirits and fine wines to complete the family entertainment. Duncan and Darren in their turn were deployed to ensure the Sjoelbak Board was ready for many games of Sjoelen, otherwise known as Dutch shuffleboard! It was to be the Christmas of all Christmases, which indeed it so turned out to be, with much laughter, badinage, and good cheer, all in perfect harmony with Ankie's superb organisation and preparation. Well, save for the occasional inter-age, inter-cousinly provocation.

As it transpired, the size and quality of that Christmas would turn out to be most appropriate, for between Christmas and the New year, the fickle finger of fate would once again beckon-in the winds of change – it would be, de facto, their last Christmas and New year in Epping, as events would but shortly demonstrate. Antoine de Saint-Exupéry on stage yet again, his New Year message loud and clear – "As for the future, you have not to foresee it, but to make it possible." Hallelujah!

By now long accustomed to being called for meetings or social events by the Port of Felixstowe, it nevertheless came as a surprise to receive the late-year call from Derek Kingston, Director of Personnel and Labour Relations thereat, asking John to join him for an evening meal and discussion at an hotel in Marks Tey chosen, as he put it, as roughly halfway between the Port and Epping. The meeting was indeed joined and Derek, as was his wont, came quickly to the meeting's intent, taking John completely by surprise. His words may be paraphrased by the passage of time, but not much.

"As you are aware, John, the P & O Group acquired the Port of Felixstowe in 1987, and I am here today representing the Chairman Robert Guille, and the Board of Directors. In short, we seek to recruit a Head of Marketing, someone capable of taking us successfully into and through the last of the 1990s, and into the 2000s. We have carefully analysed and researched the market options, and have narrowed it down to two persons, yourself, and a Scot, and we would be interested to hear as soon as possible if you are willing to come for formal interview before the Board of Directors?"

To say that John was astonished was the understatement of Anno Domini 1988 and, not unnaturally, completely unprepared for such an unexpected approach. His immediate question however, sought reassurance that the meeting was indeed a closely guarded secret, understanding as he did that his joint Managing Directors expected nothing else but total loyalty, and would not be constrained in their reaction if that were in doubt. The reassurance was given, with further information that the Board of Directors was eager to expedite the appointment as early as possible in the New Year. Potential salary and benefits were outlined, with the potential for Board appointment in due course, circumstances related, held out as a possibility. Finally, the successful appointee would be required to re-locate nearer to the Port, for which all reasonable expenses would be reimbursed. All in all, a succinct, crisp, and professionally delivered outline of that which the Port of Felixstowe had to offer, should John agree to be interviewed, and able to convince the Board of Directors that he was indeed right for the position 'Head of Marketing'.

Whether or not dinner materialised is lost in time mists, but in immediate response to Derek Kingston, John pleaded for time to consider the overall ramifications of the offer, with the promise that he would respond within the next forty-eight hours, one way or the other. This was agreed with some reluctance, and so back to Epping through the increasingly misty evening, and time for Team Perry to reconvene for yet another career review, to consider current employment opportunities or otherwise, and Ankie's Home Beauty business. Indeed, the irony of the situation was not lost to Ankie and John, in that having resigned from the P & O Group as a relatively senior sea-going Officer in May 1967 to, hopefully, pursue a business life ashore, this 1988 invitation to interview for a return to the P & O group, in a senior Marketing role, had not been foreseen or anticipated in the intervening twenty-one years. Success, apparently, is a journey, rather than a destination!

Both were well aware that over the past months, the stress factor for John had increased in direct proportion to the perceived lack of new challenges at JSA, added to which the bonhomie factor emanating from the joint Managing Directors was also perceived as weakening which, opined John, could be seen as a potential deep-water hazard, approaching as he was his fifth year in JSA situ. In counterpoint to that was a first-class opportunity to interview for a major Marketing role in a business in which he was well versed, with huge potential should he succeed. "In essence," agreed Ankie, "it's too good an opportunity to miss, and we should go for it, potential advantages well outweighing any contribution my Beauty business brings. You have brought strength to the JSA organisation, and you owe them nothing further."

The following day, confirmation was passed to Derek Kingston, and a confidential date for early Board interview agreed. The most important throw of their career dice had been cast! The sharing of their New Year champagne tasted none the less for it, their confidence in each other unabated!

There remained the need to retain secrecy, and in knowledge that any clear sighting of John in Felixstowe would almost certainly be passed to JSA Barking, certain devices were brought into play to disguise the planned journey from Epping to Felixstowe on the day agreed for the Board interview. The Company BMW was booked in for a routine major service, and a courtesy car taken, whilst a flat cap, never usually worn, was purchased for the occasion, and added to the dark sunglasses, an improbable combination for January, but nevertheless a comfort, affording Ankie rueful smile as she waved him off.

The journey was uneventful, and called into the Board Room, sans flat cap and sunglasses, he was introduced to the Chairman and Board of Directors, to include the Director of Operations Calum Begg, the ambitious Scot that John had employed on opening up SeaLand's service to Liverpool those twenty years before, in July 1969! The allusion to sowing and reaping briefly crossed John's mind, to then face a barrage of questions as to his qualifications and experience, and how he had been drawn to marketing. The Chairman, Robert Guille, continued to press for an answer to his question, "and what, Mr Perry, do you consider to be the main problem facing the Port of Felixstowe, in marketing terms?" to the extent that a direct response could no longer be avoided. "Well, Mr Perry," spoke the Chairman appearing from behind a cloud of cigarette smoke, "that was my fourth time of asking." Taking a deep breath, John responded, "Operationally, Sir, you have much to offer, but it is my opinion that in marketing terms, the Port suffers from what I would describe as rural complacency!" Silence came, as pencils moved across note-pads, and with but few questions remaining, the interview was shortly brought to a close.

It was a pensive drive back to Epping, and not to put too fine a point to it, John felt that he had probably been too honest in his expressed opinion to the Chairman, to the extent that he would not be offered the position, subject of interview. Ankie would later disagree, suggesting that the Board was surely looking for honesty, and that they just had to wait now for the formal outcome. Many years later, they would learn definitively that once he had left the Board Room, the Chairman had posed the question, "Was he right?" to receive affirmative agreement from all present! However, in the immediate present, three of four days were to pass before brief telephone call from Derek Kingston was formally confirmed by letter that John had indeed been successful, and that the P & O Group's Port of Felixstowe would wish that he took up the position as Head of Marketing as soon as possible. In the event, it was agreed his appointment would commence April 1st, leaving John the unenviable task of submitting his resignation to JSA's joint Managing Directors, almost five years to the day since joining the Company. Meantime, a surfeit of euphoria to be shared between Ankie and John as they celebrated this newest challenge and opportunity, now able to share the news with sons Duncan and Darren, and the wider family both in the UK and the Netherlands. Later would come the sober realisation that, yet again, they would have to find a new home, this time in Suffolk, the move that would come about marking their thirteenth home in just twenty-one years! In the event, it would prove to be the most frustrating of them all in execution, but the most satisfying on completion.

With John's office sandwiched between those of his two Managing Directors, formal meeting was easily established, and his resignation delivered, together with disclosure as to the approach by the Port of Felixstowe, and his acceptance of the offered position. Their congratulations were honestly given, despite their obvious surprise, and on March 17th, 1989, Ankie and John were given a farewell party presided over by Johnson and Bax-Stevens, who presented John with a silver mug, inscribed with the words, "To John. Good luck from all your friends at JSA." In truth, John was able to reply with thanks that he had learned much during his tenure with the Company, and in turn wished them continued success, together with his assurance that he would keep in close contact in the upcoming future. It was onward to the next square for John and Ankie, with persistence and determination!

Although the lifestyle over the past twenty-one years had brought many benefits, wonderful experiences, and indeed accrued knowledge, almost by definition friendships gained, and there were many, were so quickly lost, ease of communication via information technology or social media yet to be developed. An incident during their Epping tenure rather underlined this, as Ankie decided to check with the Dutch Embassy in London, by telephone, whether Dutch law had changed, to allow dual nationality. She addressed her question, in Dutch, to the official who had taken her call, to be astounded by his amused response, "Hello, Ankie, and no, nothing has changed from the advice I gave you in Bombay seven years ago!" It was friend, Johann, who, transferred from Bombay through other Embassies since, was now resident in London. Friendships that pass in the night indeed, to give it a nautical twist!

P & O Group's Port of Felixstowe

There appeared to be three priorities to address, to be introduced to the Port's current marketing team, to search for a property near Felixstowe and secure it, and to sell the Epping property, the last two hopefully in some form of close tandem. Ankie and John had agreed that their target area for home purchase would be Woodbridge, and with house sales in Epping in high demand, foresaw little difficulty in expediting both sale and new purchase. In this they were wrong, as four-bedroom houses then for sale in Woodbridge seemed rarer than the proverbial hen's teeth, whilst combination of a collapse in the Epping housing market, coupled with their chosen Sales Agent's devious inadequacy, ensured that eventual purchase of the Woodbridge property would not be completed until December 1st of that year, whilst the Epping property would remain unsold until a few weeks into 1990. Their new home-to-be was eventually located as Plot 29, Saxon Way Woodbridge, a new-build already under offer, which fortunately came back to the market. As soon as it was sighted, Ankie knew it was to be their new home, despite being fatuously described by the Developers as being situated in the "Valley of the Ferns." It was to become 'Orcades', 1, Saxon Way, Melton, Woodbridge, and although purchase was not finalised until December 1st, Ankie had meantime ensured a variety of changes within the property, reluctantly agreed by the Developers, and an earlier move into the house for carpets and furniture. It was, after all, a part of her extensive and impressive curriculum vitae, so succinctly phrased in its final section entitled 'Lifestyle'. It read: "Since marriage in 1967, husband's career and family commitments prevented carrying on own career. Became expert in moving house (needs a certain flexibility!)" In truth, she could have added that without her total commitment to the family cause, their degree of success, such as it was, would have been severely curtailed!

Although John's need to meet and appraise the Port's customer facing team was important, his overall mission was now to inculcate throughout the Port's departments his acquired understanding of marketing and customer focus, emphasising that the mix embraced in the 'marketing umbrella' – forecasting, budgeting, pricing, advertising, sales, public relations, account management and research – was never constant. It was the art of identifying and understanding customer needs, and coming up with solutions that satisfy the customers, and produce profit for the stockholders. Market leadership would be gained through customer focus, bringing satisfaction, product innovation, quality, and service, not to forget first class communication. If these were absent, no amount of advertising, sales promotion or salesmanship would compensate. In effect, to help other Management to see that customers were the foundation of the Company's business. No small challenge, but one of paramount importance. For starters, the Chairman required a marketing plan, and an annual budget, with no evidence that such had been achieved in the recent past. Back to zero base budgeting, but first to meet and appraise his team as currently existed. It would prove to be enlightening!

The team appeared to exist under the doubtful nomenclature of the 'commercial group', although to John's critical eye could have been better described as the 'inconspicuous group', save for she who had the secretarial role, Clair Noye, whose clear instincts for progressive change were frustrated by lack of any professional leadership, or directional impetus. That would change, with Paul Davey, and eventually Martin Woor who was destined to join the group, allocated with specific marketing functions for which they proved entirely suitable and able, while John Minns, very close to retirement, would indeed shortly retire. Polly Mullett, who for no rational reason had been allocated a Public Relations (PR) role for which she was clearly unqualified and untutored to perform, felt she reported directly to the Chairman, which left the most senior of the group, Mike Mitchell, self-styled as responsible for sales. "What do you do," questioned John, "prior to visiting a customer, or potential customer?" Thoughtfully, Mike put his finger in his mouth, and then raised it. "Right," said John, "so you've wet your finger, and now what?" The response came as no great surprise. "I'll see which way the wind blows and take it from there!"

Appointment announcement by P & O Group

In the event, Mullett's title and failure to contribute to the marketing regime proved to be unassailable, in that the Chairman chose to retain PR unto himself, which by definition meant no PR, presumably as a function of P & O's policy, or lack of attention to that important and consequential detail. Her position was perhaps best described as impregnable, as well as non-contributory in any business sense. As Ankie would observe in home conversations, "probably diplomatic to leave well alone!" Mitchell's background was operational, but John would soon conclude that experience as outdated by the Port's growth and eventually, months later, persuade Neil Hollis, then managing the burgeoning Trinity terminal, to join the marketing group, his knowledge and extraordinary memory bringing a wealth of up-to-date operational experience to the group's expanding role.

Meantime, and with Davey in newly designated important informational research and support roles, it was established that prior to any visit to a client or potential client, whosoever making that visit would, from now on, be thoroughly briefed as to all aspects of the client's business. Further, that each and every client, large or small in volume and revenue terms, would be visited at least twice a year, once to encourage social contact and relationships, the other for necessary contract negotiations. For the latter, pre-planning would be mandatory, with necessary P of F 'red lines' established and agreed, with areas of possible compromise equally established and agreed. Wet fingers, from now on, were unacceptable in any marketing sense! Supportive to this, and as all agreed in due course by the Chairman, a series of bespoke advertisements, crafted in English, German, Dutch, and French, would appear in Lloyd's Lists, or equivalent publications, in each appropriate country, outlining the Port of Felixstowe's main attributes. Budget for the entirety of the annual programme was signed off by the Chairman and brought in plan form to the attention of the Board of Directors, and those senior Managers reporting to the Chairman. As was the need for all departments to recognise their important contribution to the overall marketing effort. As the Musketeers of Alexandre Dumas would have it, "All for one, and one for all." It was a beginning. Notably, Lloyd's List made an error shortly after this, in that the French edition appeared in the UK publication. Robert Guille came steaming into John's office waving his paper, ready to question the advertising project which, as was being reported, was attracting wide attention. "Got your attention though, didn't it Mr Guille," being the best riposte that John could laughingly muster, later to upbraid Lloyd's List for allowing it to happen.

The daily travelling between Epping and Felixstowe, some 75 miles each way via Ipswich, was a drudge to be borne, but John was keen to spend as much time at home as was possible, to enable discussion and planning with Ankie relative to their need to relocate home, and indeed each day's experience at the Port. Teamwork was their forté, with current changes in circumstance bringing that, once more, into sharp focus.

Next in order of need was to be formally introduced to fellow senior Managers, which included John Bubb in Operations, another Master Mariner that had swallowed the anchor, having first attended the HMS Worcester pre-sea college and subsequently sailed with the Cunard Line. This brought into play the traditional banter between Conway/Worcester, P & O/Cunard, and he and his wife Liz would become good friends with John and Ankie over the years to come. Chris Lewis too, he being then in charge of the Port's computerisation programmes and would rise to much greater things in time. Others too, in the engineering, accounting and personnel functions, and then on to meet the Terminal Managers for Landguard, Dooley and Trinity Terminals, not forgetting the Warehouse and Rail Division Managers, all busily engaged in the growth and expansion of their areas of high responsibility. The Port also boasted its own Police Force, and the Senior Officer thereto was sought out and introductions made. Noteworthy is fact that the Walton Terminal, owned and operated by Orient Overseas Holdings Ltd (OOHL) of Hongkong, was not included in the P & O Group's purchase of the Port of Felixstowe, their operations mainly involving the Orient Overseas Line's UK calls. That would change with time!

A surprise visitor seeking meeting with John was introduced as Pasquale Formisano of the Mediterranean Shipping Company (MSC), the formidable right-hand-man of Gianluigi Aponte, founder, and owner of MSC, headquartered in Geneva. Reason for his visit, however, came as no surprise, in that MSC had a problem, unrecognised and unaddressed by the so referred 'commercial department'! He, as a consequence of MSC's growing use of the P of F, required guaranteed berthing on arrival of his vessels. Having done some quick research into MSC's vessels and call frequency, it was clear that the fleet comprised of a range of assorted container ships, with a call frequency anything but based on a regular schedule, and of this he was reminded. Discussion went back and forward, until finally Pasquale, as John was now invited to address him, spoke thus: "John, watch-a my lips! Our ships are-a shit, our schedule is-a shit, and that is-a your (expletive with an F) problem!" Recognising the depth of Pasquale's frustrating operational conundrum, and the increasing quantum of MSC's revenue contribution to the Port, it was time to apply marketing principals, to both understand MSC's needs, and to come up with a solution. "Pasquale," John responded, "now that we understand each other, let's agree a means of working that will minimise or eliminate any berthing delays for your vessels, and I will work closely with our operational people to ensure they are working with us on this." Further discussion focussed on MSC tightening up on their pre-advice of any vessel's delayed arrival, combined with frequent up-dates to each month's intended/planned calls to Felixstowe. This brought John into close contact with Roy Davies, owner of the MSC Agency in the UK, and Mike Chambers his operations Manager, both of whom would also become good friends, and occasional golf partners. It was also advised that John would shortly visit Geneva, and that his visits thereto would be at least two a year, or more if required. MSC was to become a major customer in a few short years, with Pasquale having no further need to travel to Felixstowe with concerns. Such was the increase in their business that Captain Nicola Mastro was sent to Felixstowe as MSC's permanent representative, being warmly welcomed, and respected for his professional involvement.

Another customer whose volumes were to increase to major levels was the Maersk Company of Denmark, and point was made to ensure frequent meetings with Maersk's representative in Felixstowe, Knut Stubjkaer. Meetings with Agencies within the Port representing substantial container volumes through the P of F were also initiated, with much learned and questioned, not least of all, just who is this Head of Marketing, and how will he affect their business, or ways of going about it? The most searching and in-depth questioning came from Mike Watson, Operations Director for Anglo-European Agency, and it was from him that John was able to gain a wider perspective of the Port's 'politics' that prevailed. He and his wife Biddy were to become close friends to John and Ankie over the years, with Ankie and Biddy also having a common interest in the playing of Bridge.

Any thoughts that John may have occasionally harboured in either Greece or India as to his functional position being a sinecure was here almost impossible to contemplate, as already the job was shaping up as full-on, and full-time, and a challenge to be embraced. There were two obvious issues to be addressed as soon as practically possible – the first was to re-locate the family home from Epping to Woodbridge, and this was being addressed at, often extended, weekends, with Ankie and John both fully focussed on this imperative. The second was recognition that the Marketing group, as now referred, needed refreshing, and strengthening to bring about greater emphasis on research, Account management, forecasting and budgeting. This was brought to the Board's attention, with the eventual result that Martin Woor would join the team post his introductory management training on joining the Port in 1989. He would work in tandem with Paul Davey. There remained the need to increase the depth of Sales expertise, with the conclusion that up-to-date operational knowledge was key to this, which in due course brought about approach to Neil Hollis, then Manager of the rapidly expanding Trinity Terminal, who eventually joined the team circa mid-1991, bringing notable, and invaluable, contribution.

As to the re-location matter, and with the property in Saxon Way eventually targeted as available, financing its purchase became elusive, with a surprising lack of interest in the offered sale of the Epping property. This would resolve itself in the first quarter of 1990, but meantime the Chairman, in order to resolve the financial impasse, authorised a substantial interest free loan to secure the Woodbridge property, way in excess of his Memorandum and Articles of Association limit, but with a 3% penalty if not repaid within a set period. This allowed Ankie to swing into contact with Pickfords, with less than immediate (but achieved!) co-operation from the Developers of Saxon Way, Valley of the Ferns, for her required changes within Plot 29 and, finally, access to 1, Saxon Way, soon to be named 'Orcades'.

All of this, however, was to happen after late June of 1989, as John and Ankie were to take themselves off for a well-earned two weeks of holiday in France. Son Duncan, who had also resigned from JSA, was employed elsewhere in a credit control function, whilst Darren was attending Huddersfield University, so this would be the second holiday without the boys. With the route again planned by Ankie, ferry was taken to Le Havre, with destination the small village of Caperstang on the banks of the Canal du Midi, in the Region of Languedoc-Roussillon. Here they would spend a relaxed and gloriously happy week alone, aboard a cabin cruiser motoring between Caperstang and Marseillan, situated only a few kilometres south-west from Montpellier. They would learn that politeness in French to the lockkeepers (les éclusiers) would ease their passage, not to make fast their mooring lines to a bollard when the lock's water level was to drop (they watched as an éclusier had to take an axe to the lines of one unfortunate boat left hanging by its mooring lines!) and wonder at one of the main tourist attractions in the region. This was the flight of staircase locks, known as 'Les 9 écluses de Fonséranes' at Béziers, which lifted craft to a height of 21.5m (71 ft.) over a distance of 300m (980ft), requiring constant close attention to mooring lines! Ankie, whose helming skills were very good in the Canal, chose to let John navigate the staircase locks, as she very professionally took responsibility to handle the mooring and letting go. Teamwork personified!

Return to the UK, refreshed and raring to go, was for John to resume his introduction to the Port's current customer base, both in the UK and in Europe, whilst Ankie sought to enliven the Estate Agent charged with selling their Epping home, and at the same time having, sadly, to evaluate when and how she was to wind down the Beauty practice that she had so successfully established. With appropriate deposit made on Plot 29, Saxon Way Woodbridge to secure the property, she was also enabled to put pressure on the Developers which would eventually bring about agreement to gain earlier occupation of the property than legal title would suggest, such legal title not being formally agreed until December 1st, in the year of our Lord 1989! In summation, indeed the most frustrating of the thirteen home moves made in the twenty-one years since leaving the P & O Group as a sea-going Officer, but as time would tell, it would be the last, on re-joining the P & O group! Olé!

With Finland's 'forest products' importations into the UK focussed strongly on Felixstowe, it was appropriate to acknowledge the importance of this traffic, and indeed considerable time would be in due course devoted to visiting Finland, and the many Mills producing these products. More immediately, visit was made to Finanglia, headed by John Ashley from the Company's then Head Office in Dock Street, situated in London's Whitechapel area which, in those days, was not the most salubrious. Having studied at the

Sir John Cass Nautical College for his Second Mates Licence, as was the means of transition from Cadet/Apprentice to Officer status in the Merchant Navy, the name of Dock Street stirred vague memories in John's mind, only to find that the Finanglia office was sited in the very building in Dock Street that had accommodated, thirty-one years before, the Examination Hall and office of the Chief Examiner, a man of fearsome reputation to aspiring/perspiring candidates, as he conducted the dreaded Oral Examinations. John Ashley's office was actually that of the aforementioned dreaded Chief Examiner, so was entered with memories of deep apprehension, and the barked instruction from the Examiner to 'take a horizontal sextant angle through the window' between observable and indicated objects. John Ashley was, however, a pleasure to meet, and would offer both friendship and thoughtful information over the coming months as John came to better understand the forest products industry.

Finntransit was another major user of the Port, and although name of the resident Finnish representative in Felixstowe in 1989 is time-misted, Pasi Piperenian was a person never to be forgotten in his ever cheerful and professional conducting of visits to the many Mills in Finland, and his sobriety throughout despite an obvious enjoyment of vodka.

Last, but by no means least, was the Forest Lines Agency, ably represented by Geoff Dickman in Felixstowe, and his immediate superior based in Rotterdam, Jeremy Fletcher-Morris. Their forest product cargoes arrived from the United States, mainly from New Orleans via Rotterdam per Central Gulf Lash vessels, thence to Felixstowe per a smaller Lash feeder vessel 'Spruce' which, as the vessel type suggests, carried Lighters aboard, or barges as more usually called, which would be floated out from the mother vessel 'Spruce' which had partially submerged, to bring about the birth-like appearance of up to twelve barges containing a mix of break-bulk forest products to be discharged alongside Landguard Terminal. Impressive, but fortunately not too frequent an occurrence where speed of vessel despatch was service paramount, and critical for berth, rather than birth, utilisation! Occasional containers would also arrive per OOCL. Geoff and Angela Dickman would become good friends over following years.

Late 1989 brought about visit to Marseilles, there to meet with Jacques Saade, Chief Executive of the CMA Line, seeking to understand why the Line had given notice to leave Felixstowe in 1990 for Thamesport, the newly created container Port in the Medway. John's reception was cool in the extreme but heated in language as Jacques Saade repeatedly pounded his desk as he berated P & O's attitude in denying him a sought-after reduction to his contracted rates, thus giving him no choice but to sign-up with Thamesport. Fortunately, this was all before John's arrival to Felixstowe as Head of Marketing, so invitation to lunch was eventually and cordially offered by Saade, to be thankfully accepted by his impressed visitor who, it must be said, had recognised mission impossible, having seen and indeed heard it!

A weekday visit to Woodbridge to once again meet with the Saxon Way Developer was achieved, with Ankie keen to impress upon the site Manager that a serving hatch twixt kitchen and dining room was a 'must-have' feature. Despite his protests that it was unusual, and awkward to include in planned fittings and decoration, he faced determined Dutch demands, and the hatch was duly constructed to order. It would be their first Christmas in their new home and what better inauguration of this unique feature that would service much entertainment over the coming years, its origin the result of Ankie's not unusual prescience!

A relatively quiet new-home Christmas it was, with Darren home from college, and Duncan from his current place of work, and both of them seeing 'Orcades' in Woodbridge for the first time. Duncan sported a well-developed moustache which, happily he forewent early in that New year of 1990, which new year entry was celebrated once again at the Mill, home to Mike and Joan, mother and Alex, another full family event with Brian and Les, together with their offspring, completing the merry gathering.

For John, 1990 would prove to be yet another full-on year with a surfeit of travel necessary to maximise his meeting with customers, based as they were in Finland, Scandinavia, Germany, Holland, Belgium, Switzerland, France, Sri Lanka, the Middle East, India, the Far East, and Mexico. His planned aim to visit each customer at least twice a year became a reality challenge, realism having to recognise that objective as better spread over eighteen months, even two years, as 'events' inevitably caused planning reappraisal and programme changes to accommodate to changed circumstances. Fortunately, this was recognised as a normal function of business life, unlike in politics when any change from proclaimed 'manifest' intent is howlingly greeted as a 'U-turn!'

Ankie enjoys home visit from Duncan (age 33) and Darren (age 31), November 2000 - Her Boys!

Ankie spent the first quarter of that year in planning and implementing the change from builders' rubble to landscaped garden for 'Orcades' as now named, having first received from a local first-class garden centre a proposed lay-out. "I am pleased to inform you," started the Representative, "that the plan will cost much less than originally thought." That begged the obvious question of how much, and his response of £15,000 was sufficiently jarring to prompt the next question, "How much for the plan itself?" The reply of £100 was quickly acted upon with the plan being purchased, a jobbing gardener hired, and landscaping with but a few necessary Ankie changes implemented, for the approximate final cost of £3000! Job done, with Ankie's garden destined to become her pride and joy, and much admired by many. She also concluded, during one of John's overseas visits during these early months, that the brand-new fencing stretching some 300m metres around the property was 'too glary' and donning one of the boy's Kashmiri coats and a bobble hat, she stained the entire fence, inside and out! Determination unmatched!

On March 26th, her application to join the Suffolk Coastal District Council's employ was realised, where she would yet again demonstrate her acumen, ability and common sense working in the Public Relations department, her cheerful application much appreciated by all that came to know her. Definitively, an asset to the Council's reputation. It was about this time too that their Epping property was finally sold, thus saving many miles of driving back and forth, hassling the reluctant Agent, cutting the grass, and general worry. It also brought great relief to the Port's Chairman, finally recouping the considerable bridging loan to the Perrys, prior to any auditors questioning this unquestioned largesse with Corporate funds.

For the first time in years, and in the realisation of a more settled life, John and Ankie were now able to appreciate that they could enjoy and develop friendships with their new neighbours in Saxon Way, rather than viewing them as ships that pass in the night, and this became a great comfort to them both, particularly with John now so involved in travel. By sheer chance, they were also to meet up, and become friends with, Mike and Marian Garnett, it later coming out in general conversation that when John was serving aboard HMS Keppel and witnessing the 1967 court-martial of HMS Palliser's Commanding Officer in Rosyth, Mike was at that time serving as Weapons Specialist aboard HMS Palliser! One of life's many extraordinary coincidences indeed!

Every customer visit, whether socially or for contract negotiations, were memorable, just some more so than others. One such "more so" was with DSR. the East German Line based in Rostock, then firmly embedded within the communist bloc. In line with John's marketing philosophy, he together with Mike Mitchell who accompanied him, had prepped for the meeting as best possible within the bounds of probability, loosely defined by a quasi-understanding of communism in business. It was, however, a surprise to be confronted by the DSR team of some eight persons, some apparently acting in a control role over others, so making it difficult to know just who was leading the negotiation which, thankfully, were conducted mostly in English. Their grasp of detail appeared unlikely to enhance their negotiating position which prompted John to seek a break for brief private discussion. Taking refuge in a nearby toilet area, and with all water taps full on as to confuse expected bugging, the Port's original plan was revised with more emphasis to be placed as to the importance of concessions now to be made available, but with the clear need for the DSR team to identify he who was leading on their behalf, and that he had authority to sign off any final agreement. Meeting was eventually concluded to the apparent satisfaction of all, appropriate signature(s) gained, with good will prevailing.

Return to the hotel was accompanied by a pleasant and openly friendly keeper, and he was invited to join John and Mitch for a beer, which he gladly accepted. In that all the tables in the Bar area had but two chairs allocated, John repositioned the third required chair from an adjacent table, at which point the very large woman in charge of the Bar strode forth, to aggressively shout "Nein!" and reposition the chair back to its allotted table. "Come the revolution," said John, "you will be one of the first to go!" Fortunately, her grasp of English was non-existent, but friendly keeper from DSR was visibly afeared that she might understand. It was a stupid thing to say, and belated thoughts of honey and vinegar flitted through John's mind. Another lesson learned and returning past the controlled border was further reminder that both discretion and forbearance were of paramount importance in this part of the world. What little of the city of Rostock they had seen was truly impressive, although the atmosphere was unforgiving.

Friendship prevailed within the Port environment, with the Chairman's predilection for a gin and tonic at the end of a busy working day *occasionally* assuaged by John Bubb (Operations) and John Perry (Marketing) when either or both were present in the office. They would dine off the time when, Operations John having already been visited, he rang to advise John of Marketing that the Chairman was en route toward him. With the Chairman already arrived and in situ, the call was thoughtlessly put into speaker mode, with the loud message that the Chairman had already had one gin and tonic causing John of Marketing to make embarrassed lunge to end the call, with subject of the message raising a quizzical eye, and his glass in the general direction of the Operations office!

Away from the Port, John and Ankie became active members of the Deben Yacht Club (DYC), John in a sailing and safety boat helming capacity, and Ankie soon drafted in for her calm personality, diplomacy, and organisational skills as Secretary to the organiser of the Deben Week Regatta as it was then, the annual event when Felixstowe, Waldringfield and the Deben Yacht Clubs were all deeply involved in making a success of the organised racing. John would also join the nascent Ufford Park Golf Club and Gym (one of the first members), with Ankie taking up yoga, and weekly Bridge sessions held at the Woodbridge Community Centre. Friendships blossomed, and dinner parties proliferated, with John and Ankie at their happiest since leaving Greece in 1981, content in their new environment and their studied decision to take up the Port of Felixstowe challenge. John had full delegated responsibility for customer contract negotiations with obvious requirement to keep the Chairman fully advised and, in keeping with marketing philosophy, all those in Operations and elsewhere with the need to know. That Ankie was kept very much in the loop as to John's concerns and reactions to situations was a given because that was their way, teamwork! So far, so good!

1990 saw continued development in the Port, with Trinity terminal Phase 2 opened, whilst later in the year the millionth container was handled with the working of Yang Ming Line's 'Ming Energy' (ceremonially attended upon by Johnson and Bax-Stevens of JSA!) bringing the year's total of teus handled to 1.44 million, an achievement unique to the Port of Felixstowe as a UK first.

Interface with customers continued apace, with John's knowledge of Heathrow and Gatwick Airports unsurprisingly in tandem with his travel commitments. Checked baggage became a time-consuming hindrance and purchase of a Samsonite suit carrier (expensed!) became his only form of travel accoutre, always accepted as hand baggage, allowing swift departure from most airports. This ease of passage was, however, disturbed in that whilst visiting the Mexican Line in Mexico City with John van Bergen of Cory Bros, close of negotiating play was marked by presentation to John of a Mexican Line golf umbrella gratefully (but ruefully) accepted, rueful as something else to carry. This in itself was not a substantial problem with only one anticipated flight back to the UK, had not late message from the Port's Chairman arrived with the questioning instruction, "Can you just nip down to Buenos Aires to meet with…" naming John's point of contact. Fact that Argentina was not a nip, but rather a whole continent away had probably not escaped the Chairman's notice, but clearly seen as detail of no great importance. The instruction was diplomatically answered in the affirmative, with added request that Ankie be advised, and substantial steaks were in due course consumed once required meeting concluded. Return flight to the UK from Buenos Aires was eventually booked, and the BA Jumbo boarded with golf umbrella once again passed as safe, followed by emergency order to disembark as function of a bomb aboard scare. Aircraft towed to safe part of the airport, there to discharge luggage for passenger identification. By now, the flight crew were out of hours, but thankfully chose to ignore their Union's rules, agreeing to fly the 'plane home.

Note to file: never fly a series of long-haul flights with a golf umbrella that cannot be carried in checked in baggage, being seen as suspicious in absence of golf clubs or intent to play golf! Plus, a bloody nuisance!

The Mexican Line's European Representatives were actually based in Hamburg, and therefore readily accessible for regular visits, but it was to the Hamburg Office of Hapag Lloyd that the Chairman sought to join John on a non-negotiating visit, and to Hamburg they travelled together. Once ushered into the Line's Boardroom, the Chairman chose to light his habitual cigarette, unfortunately timed as their hosts chose to enter the room, which boasted not an ashtray. One was tactfully obtained, and the cigarette extinguished, with the Chairman being cordially greeted in excellent and unaccented English. To John's concern, his chairman's response was in slow, abbreviated English usually reserved for those with small grasp of the language. Not pidgin, but close! Fortunately, and as discussions progressed, he relaxed and gave good account of himself, his English improved meanwhile, with the meeting coming to an amicable and productive end. John would, in the fullness of time, find the Hapag Lloyd contract negotiators less inclined toward amicable meetings, being more Germanic in their beliefs as to their contractual rights, and the Port's obligation to agree, although generous in their hospitality once negotiations were, usually, mutually agreed as to outcomes. The overnight stopover in their hotel was preceded by a cheerful meal in a friendly Bar close to the hotel, with the Chairman fully relaxed away from his UK duties joining a few new German acquaintances in the singing of 'Lilli Marlene', the wartime song made famous by Marlene Dietrich. Prudently, and diplomatically, John retired to the hotel, and to bed.

Returning briefly to the matter of negotiations, it is a fact that being unable to speak German, John found himself at a psychological disadvantage in negotiations with the Germans, but not so with Dutch or French negotiators, in that his grasp of those languages was adequate to ensure that if private conversations were required by those on the other side of the table, either they would leave the room, or ask John to so do. He requested, and was granted, permission to employ a German language teacher to take on a class of Port employees, which happened. Unfortunately, general interest flagged after a time, and sadly the course was abandoned, a lost cause.

During 1989, the Port's main approach channel dredging to a depth pf eleven metres had been completed, together with further development of the

Port's computer system, renamed FCPS (Felixstowe Cargo Processing System), all this being grist to the mills of those several Lines intent on increasing the size of their deep-sea container vessels. This was evidenced by the steadily growing container traffic over Felixstowe, now firmly established as one of Europe's major container Ports and bringing a wealth of information to impart to customers during social calls, as planned within the overall marketing concept.

Since his meeting with Pasquale Formisano in Felixstowe, John found that his welcome to the Geneva office of the Mediterranean Shipping Company (MSC) was always assured, with both Gianluigi Aponte, the Chairman, and Pasquale Formisano, generous with their time, hospitality, and questioning. He would learn of their Saturday mornings Management meetings, when scheduling of their growing fleet of vessels and trade commitments would be vigorously discussed, debated, and assigned, with an occasional operational Rubicon necessarily crossed in scheduling terms!

Welcome and hospitality for contract rate negotiations were no less gracious, albeit that between welcome and hospitality, Il Signor Formisano would vigorously, professionally, passionately, and sometimes theatrically, defend against any rate increases or contract changes unless he was satisfied as to the validity of proposals, and strength of purpose in presentation. Notwithstanding, anything in excess of two percent would never be agreed. On one memorable occasion, he bade John to wait as he exited the room, to reappear moments later with a large bowl of peanuts which he slammed down onto the table. "This is a-what your offer is a-worth!" he loudly postulated, before asking John if he would like some more coffee! Compromise was finally reached, and lunch taken overlooking Lake Geneva, or in a favoured, quaint village restaurant a short, but always fast, drive from the office. He was larger than life, and an outstanding credit to MSC!

Neither Ankie's Dutch pragmatism, nor John's purchase of a Samsonite suit carrier, belied the fact that his travel commitments were far in excess of those experienced in their twenty-one years of business involvement, with consequent time spent away from family life. This gave time together greater meaning and relevance, although travel and work necessary to bring 'Orcades' in Saxon Way to a state judged to warrant a two-week holiday combined to argue against the idea for this year. John also fretted at the loss of contact with their sons, and their progress in work and play. Notwithstanding, November 6th marked the 50th Anniversary for Ankie's parents, Johannes and Aleijda, and arrangements were put in hand to ensure a few days in Amsterdam to mark the occasion, and to meet up with sisters Nel, Joke and Thea with husbands Hille, Ron and Paul respectively, sister Nanny as yet to marry, and brother Jan also single. A few days before departure however, they had a brief visit from younger brother, Brian, and wife, Les, accompanied by their three fast growing daughters Sara, Lindsey, and Victoria (known as Tia), to inspect John and Ankie's (largely Ankie's) new home-making progress, another very welcome diversion. The Amsterdam venture was a great success, and the visit of Brian, Les, and family led to Christmas that year being celebrated at their home in West Farleigh Kent, with much good humour, bonhomie, and just the occasional bottle of wine to toast absent family and friends!

Darren would celebrate his 21st Birthday come December 30th, to receive his gold signet ring engraved with his initials, but in Greek Cyrillic lettering, as had been Duncan's presentation two years before. The similarity between the two signet rings was unremarkable, both boys' initials being DP, as a function of slight brain-fog experienced by John and Ankie those years ago, over-excited by being parents to two wonderful boys. That the rings commemorated their earlier formative years in Greece was, however, the important factor, where friendships, happiness, summer sunshine and winter snow all combined for very happy memories! Happy days indeed!

Entry into the New Year of 1991 was, as ever, celebrated by Ankie and John in champagne style, and once again counting their blessings that had brought them to Woodbridge. There appeared to exist many opportunities, or challenges, for further business development as the Port of Felixstowe developed and grew, and if John and his marketing team were able to capitalise upon this, the immediate to medium future looked bright. One matter that continued to puzzle John was, however, something about which he appeared unable to influence, being the total absence of any Public Relations activity, an important panel of the overall marketing umbrella which was being ignored. That the Chairman saw this as his 'part of ship' was clear, but failed to explain the neglect, be that a personal antagonism toward PR, or a P & O Group policy. It also begged the question as to the continued employment of she that boasted the PR title, her close, indeed touching, association with the Chairman supporting her overt claim that he was her direct reporting line. Brief visit to the Port by Sir Jeffery Sterling (if in late 1990) or Lord Sterling of Plaistow (if post his elevation by Thatcher to Baron Sterling in February 1991) she saw as her spotlight moment, although her obsequious attention paid to this Chairman of the P & O Group was, at best, a public embarrassment, regardless of which year it was. Coming events, as yet unrecognised, would see her swift demise. For John, his brief introduction would mark the second P & O Chairman to whom he had been introduced, the first having been Sir Donald Anderson during the maiden voyage of 'Canberra' in 1961, where John served aboard as Snr. Third Officer. Sir Donald's presence aboard, however, bore faith in continuity.

Return visit to Taiwan, by now familiar territory for John, was this time in the company of his Chairman who, despite the flight(s) duration, wore his usual office suit throughout, whilst John relaxed in his habitual long-haul garb of a tracksuit. Unfortunately, on eventual arrival to Taipei in the early evening, the Chairman's suitcase had gone adrift, and with meetings scheduled with Yang Ming and Evergreen Lines starting the following morning, purchase of some clean clothing for him became necessary from their hotel shop. This proved to take longer than anticipated as, although short in stature, he was broader in beam than most Chinese, but eventually tailoring compromise was achieved, leaving only the well-worn suit to be over-night dry-cleaned. As chance would have it, midnight found his missing suitcase delivered to the hotel, which in due course would carry the additional burden of newly acquired and expensed clothing homeward. Meetings with both Yang Ming and Evergreen went well, every courtesy being extended to their visitors from the UK, who carefully avoided enquiry as to the commodities served during their very Taiwanese lunch, and with ignorance delivering bliss, they were enabled to declare it delicious!

With expansion of forest products warehousing much on the cards, visits to Finland were undertaken, and on one such visit, John was accompanied by George Steele, a senior within the Engineering department. They would together take up fishing! One overnight stay was in a log cabin adjacent to a large lake, and next to the lake was a sauna, and a 'magic tree', so described by their hosts which, on invited closer inspection, boasted a tap which, on turning, dispensed vodka! With some time to be filled prior to the evening meal, and vodka to be avoided, George and John took up their host's invitation to take some time afloat on the lake with fishing rods, and with each siren call from the shore to 'come in to try the magic tree', they would mutter together, "Keep bloody fishing!" With dusk approaching however, ashore they had to go, then into the sauna to be beaten with bits of leaf bearing twigs, and thence back into the ice-cold lake for a pre-dinner heart stopper! Oh, and finally, offerings from the magic tree! All in the name of marketing!

In truth, involvement with all those in this Finnish industry bore witness to their fine hospitality, and ultra-generosity in expounding their depth of knowledge in all matters relating to the production of forest products, and their nation's extraordinary attention to re-forestation as an environmental priority. No explanation in this instance was offered as to how they plumbed in vodka to that particular tree, but what a unique forest product!

With a cold and snowy start earlier in the year, and a brief window of opportunity in workload identified for mid-May, invitation to visit friends in Plouer-sur-Rance, a small commune in Brittany between Dinan and Dinard, was seen by Ankie and John as a chance for some early sunshine. The commune inhabitants of some 2.5 thousand now included Jeff and Luthie Langfield who, it will be remembered, became their good friends in the Essex village of Southminster way back in early 1968 Luthie, as Ankie, hailing from Holland. Jeff was, as always, busily engaged in his Civil Engineering career in the UK, so their reasons for locating to Plouer-sur-Rance were not straightforward, but no doubt cost focussed as was Jeff's wont. Ankie set to as was customary to plot their route, which again took them from Portsmouth to Le Havre, and thence southward past that most impressive of landmarks, the Mont-St-Michel, to soon enjoy four sun-filled days with the Langfields visiting the town and beaches of Dinard, and the town of Dinan among other things. Their home was an impressive place, with Luthie's French well developed as a function of expedient necessity, but both she and Ankie clearly enjoyed reverting to their native tongue of Dutch.

From Plouer-sur-Rance, decision had been made to take up a further invitation en route home, namely, to visit John's goddaughter, Karen, and her French husband Daniel, now living in Le Pecq, a commune within the Île-de-France region, situated in the suburbs of, and some eighteen kms from, the centre of Paris. There they would spend two days, arrival thereto having offered an overcome challenge to Ankie's navigation, to spend some time visiting the Palace of Versailles, a mere twelve kms from Le Pecq, the one-time home of Louis XV1 and his wife the Archduchess of Austria, Marie Antoinette, better known however for her (probably) misunderstood reference to cake for the peasantry, and eventual appointment with Madame Guillotine! More importantly, they were able to enjoy Daniel's cooking, and reminisce as to their hosts' splendid wedding

of October 1990 in Mawnan Smith, Cornwall where, in the tiny church some members of their Parisian choir had rendered their tribute in Capella music, so beautifully sung in French.

From Le Pecq, it was back to Le Havre and Portsmouth, with perhaps another sun-filled holiday to arrange as was their custom, come August or early September. In that regard, John was experiencing some slight discomfort from a hernia, and recognising that August was a month when few customers welcomed or expected visits, and with appropriate medical advice to hand, he booked himself in for corrective surgery under the BUPA plan for early August. It was to be a decision which prescience could have forestalled, but probably best for its absence on this occasion, as events proved.

June, meantime, allowed for a brief visit to the nearby Centre Parks facility in Elveden Forest, there to meet up with son Darren who was in residence, on a four-month work placement from Huddersfield Poly/University (as it was, and to become) where he was studying for Hotel Management, then in his second year. Son Duncan was at that time working in Southend but would return as prodigal son later that month to welcoming arms, home in Woodbridge. Darren too would have the occasional weekend free, with Ankie and John delighted to have both sons around the house again. Duncan would later that year have a few months with the Maersk Company Felixstowe in a Credit Control function, thereafter, to join the NHS in a broader financial function, based Ipswich.

Friends and family visits aside, customer visits remained a priority, with John finding that this too often developed into new friendships, the London office of Bulcon, the Bulgarian Line, a case in point. Captain Roumen Georgiev there resident would become a good friend, together with his wife Detalina and daughter Roumena, all of whom would visit Ankie and John at their home in Woodbridge. John would also visit Bulgaria, to be taken on a tour of Bulgarian vintners, seeking to attract, successfully as it turned out, increased shipments through Felixstowe, enjoying in the process some excellent Bulgarian wines sadly vilified by cheap over-exposure to UK University students! Others too, of course!

August 1991 was to become a memorable month, its start for John and Ankie marked by John's brief admission to a private hospital in Ipswich the evening before his planned hernia operation, having been told that it would be quite acceptable should he wish to bring a half-bottle of red wine with him, to accompany his evening meal, as surgery would be early the following morning. Home soon after to convalesce for a week, with telephone in almost constant use, whilst enjoying the August sunshine, and doing as he was told by Ankie! Meantime, Neil Hollis would transfer to the Marketing team, bringing with him a breadth of operational experience and knowledge that would add much benefit to the team as hoped. This, coupled with his excellent memory and cheerful disposition, brought him strong welcome and, more importantly, customer appreciation. This period was, quite literally, the quiet before the storm, such storm unannounced by any meteorologist, and its arrival kept a closely guarded secret by the P & O group in which one must include Robert Guille, the Port's Chairman. Had meteorologists been involved, it could well have been dubbed 'Storm Derek'!

On John's return to the office, driven there by son Duncan as medical constrains still applied after his seven days of convalescence, the storm broke! The P & O Group, led by Lord Sterling of Plaistow, had sold seventy-five percent of the Port of Felixstowe to the combination of Hutchison Holdings and Orient Overseas of Hong Kong, for the reported sum of £80 million. The remaining twenty-five percent, owned and operated by Orient Overseas Holdings, would subsequently be purchased by Hutchison Whampoa in 1994, but meantime it was to be amalgamated with Trinity Terminal, operating under the collective name of Trinity Terminal as from December 1st, 1991. Derek Harrington, entrepreneur, and businessman long involved in port and associated operations, as well as the Tung Group, then owners of Orient Overseas, would assume operational control of the Port of Felixstowe as Managing Director, being the first overseas Port acquisition of Hutchison Port Holdings, requiring therefore strong and experienced leadership. He would bring with him Peter Bennett as General Manager, himself a long-time associate of Harrington and the Tung Group, and Douglas Barr as Operations Director, position that he had held covering the Walton Terminal and others. He would also introduce and transfer Paul Wright from his position as Managing Director Walton Terminal, and Q.C. Huang from his assignment as Marketing Director, Walton Terminal, and other associated duties as ofttimes directed. Finally, Anita Hamilton, who had reportedly left her trainee accountancy course unfinished and untested, would be assigned as replacement

Public Relations person, surprisingly still outwith the Marketing group, where she would demonstrate a continued high degree of functional ineptitude, which she sought to off-set by working flat-out to please him to whom she was to report, gaining herself a derisive sobriquet, and becoming a laughingstock within the Port. As one major port customer put it: "I know what her title is, but what does she actually do?" Her position too seemed impregnable, and to question her continued employment, dangerous in the extreme.

To John's surprise, Wright and Huang turned up to his office, seeking to assert themselves as now being part of the Marketing group, although John whose position remained thus far unchallenged had received no advice of this. Notwithstanding and in absence of any formal guidance, it was obvious that Harrington had thuswise assigned them, and shortly after that, John was advised that he would be required to accompany both Harrington and Huang to the Far East, there to meet with Yang Ming and Evergreen Lines of Taiwan, and the Hanjin and Hyundai Lines in Seoul, South Korea. His question to the Managing Director as to whether he should undertake such a trip a mere ten days after his operation received the response, "Well, it's up to you," offered in undertones of potential career appraisal, which rather settled the matter! The visit went ahead, with John cautioned by Ankie to remain diplomatic throughout for obvious reasons, although Harrington's request that he allowed Huang pride-of-place in discussions with the Lines 'to preserve his dignity' was both surprising and unnecessary. Notwithstanding, Harrington was charm and good will personified throughout the trip, even to the extent that when John's company car came up for renewal, it would be from the Hyundai stable in order to bring truth to Harrington's assertions in Seoul! Return to the UK would for John be via Sri Lanka to enable a courtesy call on the Ceylon Shipping Corporation, whilst Harrington and Huang in all probability staged Hong Kong into their return. In due course, and after necessary discussion, John assigned the Far East to Huang, with Mexico and South America being assigned to Wright. John would remain responsible for Scandinavia, Europe, the Mediterranean, the Middle East, Sri Lanka, and India, not forgetting the USA, with all three, John, Paul and QC, taking the title of Regional Marketing Director. In effect, assignments to both Wright and Huang would border on sinecures, but with neither of them either students or practitioners of the marketing concept, it was a job sometimes enhanced doing work for

Harrington, although Huang's predilection to rate reductions in defence of popularity was unhelpful.

Peter Bennett was sharp, and hugely supportive to Derek Harrington throughout, whilst bringing appropriate caution or suggested change to some of Harrington's sought-after outcomes. He was also polite, and perceptive, when he asked John if he had any objections to the Marketing secretary, Claire Noye, transferring over to work for him and Derek Harrington. Although John certainly did have objections, he rationalised the approach as being good for Claire in financial terms. In the event, her assignment proved of great value and worth to the Company in many ways, not least of all in turning some of Harrington's more adventurous sought-after public relations outcomes to practical achievement. Peter was also good fun, ever ready with good humour, and supportive to those with a genuine business concern. John had practical experience of this when returning back to Felixstowe with Harrington in Derek's chauffeur-driven car. They had both been invited to dine with Captain Georgiev of Bulcon, in London, to be royally fed and wined, and were nearly back to Felixstowe when Harrington openly expressed his interest in appointing Anita Hamilton as Operations Director, which John found astonishing. "Do you think that she is right for that job?" he questioned, briefly losing his senses. There was an explosion of temper, his subsequent dismissal of John from the Port preceded by his shout, "When will you people understand that I am God here," and followed up by telling John to report to him the following morning when dismissal terms would be addressed. John's immediate action on reaching home was to telephone Peter Bennett at his home for advice, to be told two things. "Firstly, do not mention me as being involved, and secondly, do nothing in the morning." Finally, bid to attend upon Derek the following afternoon was to hear him ask what it was they were to discuss, and why, to which John adopted a discrete puzzled look, to be told, "Never mind, probably to make sure you thank Captain Georgiev for a splendid dinner," and that was that. John would remain gainfully employed, and Anita H would never aspire to an operational function, as it was probably the wine speaking the previous evening!

A Day at the Races. Newmarket, October 1996

In truth, Derek Harrington's arrival to the Port of Felixstowe was a breath, nay, a gust of fresh air into the Port's PR sails, so long flat-aback under the P & O group ownership, bringing customers, Agents, and many besides to horse racing at Newmarket and Goodwood, Golf days, tennis debentures, Snape Maltings concerts that the Port undertook to sponsor, and even Royalty and military bands to announce the opening of new and important Port developments. He was by no means devoid of faults, but at the same time unexpectedly generous at times, personally sponsoring one of his driver's private medical costs as example. De facto, he was fiercely devoted to the success of the Port, and as such, supportive to the concept of marketing espoused by John since joining the Port, and occasionally ruthless in weeding out those that were demonstrably falling short of his high expectations. Mike Mitchel, barely hanging on to his marketing job in John's eyes, would very early on in the game pay the price when, on entering Mike's place of work, Harrington found him to be reading a novel, consequently being dismissed on the spot. Harrington's reporting lines were to Canning Fok in Hong Kong as Chairman of the Ports Group, and ironically to John Meredith, a one-time P & O sea-going Officer of about John Perry's seniority who had left the sea to join the Whampoa Dock Company in Hong Kong, now in the ownership of the Hutchison Group.

Just prior to the Port's sale by the P & O Group, John had been contacted by Eddie Green, who headed up Norfolk Lines Ferries based in Great

Yarmouth, from whence the Line operated a roll-on, roll-off service to Scheveningen in Holland, a relatively small Port, catering largely in shipping terms to the Dutch herring fleet and other fishing enterprises. John and Ankie knew Scheveningen well having visited the Port many times during their SeaLand days in Holland, if only to watch in (close-mouthed!) amazement as the Dutch swallowed whole the Hollandse Nieuwe Haring (the raw herring!) during the herring season that started each June, a common sight in the Port area.

It seemed that Norfolk Line had serious growth aspirations for which the Port of Great Yarmouth appeared unable or unwilling to encourage, coupled to the relatively poor road infrastructure in terms of access and distribution connections to the Port, so important to a growing Ro/Ro operation. In this context, Eddie Green had made contact with Felixstowe, Harwich, and Tilbury, and it fell to John to present to him an operational cost and service capability analysis in light of the vessel size and frequency envisaged by Norfolk Line. Interestingly, early 1992 would see the completion of the Dooley Terminal re-surfacing, thereby forming an enlarged, purpose-built Ro/Ro facility, becoming the second largest in the UK. Road infrastructure was, of course, excellent by comparison to either Harwich or Tilbury, and with frequent Ro/Ro traffic with Finnish forest products already in situ, John was confident that this new business could be secured. The analysis would be put together by the Marketing team, in close consultation with Operations, to ensure that nothing, but nothing, was overlooked, to include the re-surfacing schedule which, in turn, would have a bearing on scheduled start-up, if the Port of Felixstowe bid were successful. Naturally, Chairman Robert Guille was kept informed, although in light of approaching events, his mind was probably focussed elsewhere!

Not unnaturally, the bidding process was to remain highly confidential, and a series of meetings over a couple of months between John and Eddie Green were so arranged to ensure such confidentiality, more so when it was finally agreed that Felixstowe would be the best option. It remained only to agree the rates' structure which, with changes required By Eddie Green finally agreed by John, the Felixstowe bid was accepted, and contract signing to be completed in Great Yarmouth during the final quarter of 1991. Derek Harrington had been kept fully appraised of the negotiations after taking over as Managing Director, and with a date set for contract signing, he advised John that he too would be present at that gathering. Douglas Barr, once in situ as Operations Director, was similarly advised of this potential new business, and with his reputation for dedication and effectiveness, and enthusiasm for change, it came as a surprise that he was more guarded in his support for this potential operational addition, with Felixstowe's main function being focussed on containers. Fortunately, and with negotiations well advanced, he recognised the business opportunity for what it was, giving his full support to the project.

Welcome by Captain on board M S C 's "Melody", September 2000

BWelcome Aboard M S C 's "Melody", September 2000

Signatures were exchanged as planned, with only a last-minute, slight change unexpectedly insisted upon by Harrington, that the rate per unit handled should be dropped by a further £1! It was, after all, his to give. In January 1992, Norfolk Line commenced service from Felixstowe, the Line's owners, Maersk of Denmark, already a valued customer of the Port! Today's Information Technology floats the suggestion that the Port of Felixstowe 'poached' Norfolk Line from Great Yarmouth, whereas history defines that Felixstowe was able to respond to market needs by offering a long-term sustainable solution to the Line's growth aspirations. In marketing terms, this is not referred to as 'poaching', but rather 'customer focus'!

Negotiations with the United Arab Shipping Company (UASC) as potential customers would also start in late 1991, these being particularly memorable to John as first taking place in the Middle East, then coming face to face with the Line's two negotiators. One was Dutch, and the other from Denmark, those two nationalities having proved to date to be the most difficult with which to negotiate, due to a perceived stubborn streak in their genetic makeup that would deny compromise until the very end. Notwithstanding, negotiations would prove successful albeit drawn out, as the Line would not commence calling Felixstowe until late November 1992. However, and in order to bring greater recognition to the Middle East market, Felixstowe would, for the first time, have a strong presence at the Dubai Trade Fair starting November 3rd of 1992. Well before then however, Debbie Coe, daughter of the Suffolk Chief Constable, would join the Marketing group with great application and purpose and she, together with Regional Marketing Director John, and Peter Bennett, General Manager, would be the face of the Port at the Trade Fair. Also now with the Marketing group, again arriving with great purpose, was Christine Wise as the group's Secretary, and to her fell the job of getting the trio safely booked, flying, and hotel booked to, and in, Dubai.

Debbie would sometimes be left in charge of the Port's Stand as Peter and John slipped away for a coffee, or to walk around the many Stands, and on one memorable occasion, they returned to find a long queue of Arab citizens lined up in front of Debbie to receive a pin-on 'Port of Felixstowe' tin badge, some of whom already having had at least two pinned to their National robes! She took it all in good humour and was a clear asset to the Port's presence in Dubai.

The twenty-four years between leaving, and eventual re-joining of the P & O Group had been an extraordinary journey for John and Ankie, travelling together in transit from a challenging sea-going life to the more complex challenges that business life ashore had thrown at them, to include the period that necessitated placing their two sons to Boarding School. Unlike King Canute of Denmark and England who, according to apocryphal legend, sought to prove his vulnerability to any incoming tide, John and Ankie combined to test the deeper water, as perceived to represent business life ashore, to find indeed their allusion as valid, often troubled, but with care, diplomacy, shared Dutch pragmatism, occasional courage, and willingness to learn, nevertheless navigable!

With persistence and determination as their past watchwords, it was now time to recognise that with the Port of Felixstowe under new ownership and management, there could be no let-up in applying both of those guiding nouns, or to be lulled into thinking the water as any shallower! They had settled so happily into Woodbridge and its environs, with John engrossed in, and enjoying, continued career challenges and opportunities, with both he and Ankie enjoying the social contact now brought about by the Port's now advanced application of Public Relations opportunities.

This would continue until the year 2000, but with Derek Harrington's retirement from the Port in 1998, followed by that of Peter Bennett in 1999, there followed a series of disappointing Consultant and Senior Management appointments, some bordering on the bizarre, with some incumbents seemingly lacking in managerial skills, and to all appearances lacking in self-awareness sufficient to recognise their own shortcomings or inadequacies, the Peter Principle in full and unseemly flower.

With his hard-won reputation within the industry under threat John, after discussion and agreement with Ankie, tendered his resignation during year 2000, eleven years after joining as Head of Marketing. He was persuaded to re-phrase his departure as 'early retirement', a euphemism that actually worked, after some hassle, to his financial benefit. His many customers were generous in their expressions of regret at his going, and in their good wishes for the future whatever that should bring, MSC in particular insisting that Ankie and John choose a gratis holiday aboard one of their Cruise ships, such offer being gratefully received. Within some three months of leaving the Port, after golf and several small but relaxing holidays, John found himself sought-after in Consultant roles, which would take him to Bulgaria, Egypt, the USA, Singapore, Hong Kong and Taiwan, as well as several European countries until, at the age of seventy-three, he decided it was time to retire fully, such that he and his beloved Ankie could devote themselves further to enjoy time and travel together, and the wealth of friends that they had been fortunate to accumulate over the years. All of that though, and their further adventures along the way would, as the expression might go, become history in due course!

As an important reference, in June 2007, Anna Petronella Perry, neé Breeschoten, and known as Ankie, took British citizenship, the Dutch Government by then allowing dual nationality – to her two sons, however, she remained in affectionate reference as 'their Dutch mum'!

One solemnly sworn intent between the two of them, however, came to pass. Some three years after setting up home in Woodbridge, a large, wrought iron anchor some one hundred years old was retrieved by fishermen from the seabed off Orford Ness, its purchase and establishment to the front of their property proclaiming silent witness to that sworn intent.

"We ain't bloody moving again."

Or, in Ankie's more pragmatic and diplomatic telling, "We zullen nooit meer huis verhuizen!"

The End!

Appendices

Appendix 1

S.S. "Orcades" Voyage 57 Outward Voyage Itinerary

GMT	PORT	DATE	DEPARTURE TIME SHIP	CLOCK	STEAM TIME	SPEED	RPM @ 10% SLIP	PORT	DATE	ARRIVAL TIME SHIP	HRS IN PORT	SUN RISE	SUN SET	E.T.	L.T.
GMT	LONDON	WEDNESDAY 25th JAN	1600 1800	-1	162			ROTTERDAM	THURSDAY 26th JAN	0200 0500	11	0832	1716	0452	1743 1252
+1	ROTTERDAM	THURSDAY 26th JAN	1600 1800	-1	132½	2639	24.50	126	PIRAEUS	WEDNESDAY 1st FEB	0730 0900	9	0731	1748	H o l i a t s	
+2	PIRAEUS	WEDNESDAY 1st FEB	1800 1900	-1	29	599	20.93	124	PORT SAID	FRIDAY 3rd FEB	0001 0200	5	0642	1728	0552	1231
+2	PORT SAID	FRIDAY 3rd FEB	0700			87		SUEZ	SATURDAY 4th FEB			0639	1729	0743	0112
+2	SUEZ	SATURDAY 4th FEB	0200 0230	-½	60	1305	21.92	129	ADEN	MONDAY 6th FEB	1530 1700	6	0625	1805	2012	1227 70052
+3	ADEN	MONDAY 6th FEB	2300 2330	-½	99½	2052	21.14	124	COLOMBO	SATURDAY 11th FEB	0530 0700	15	0629	1824	1552	0944 2135
+5½	COLOMBO	SATURDAY 11th FEB	2000 2030	-2½	3128	3128	20.70	122	FREMANTLE	SATURDAY 18th FEB	0630 0700	7	0557	1904	1734	043
+8	FREMANTLE	SATURDAY 18th FEB	1500 1600	-1	81	1647	20.12	120	MELBOURNE	WEDNESDAY 22nd FEB	0500 0700	16	0558	1910	1051 23015	055 1755
+10	MELBOURNE	WEDNESDAY 22nd FEB	2300 0200	-1	28	532	19.16	144	SYDNEY	FRIDAY 24th FEB	0300 0600	32	0538	1857	0756 2028 250214	1428 1509
+10	SYDNEY	SATURDAY 25th FEB	1600 1700	-2	59	1232	21.02	124	WELLINGTON	TUESDAY 29th FEB	0606 0800	36	0600	1906	1527 2029	10238 1409
+12	WELLINGTON	WEDNESDAY 1st MARCH	2000 2100	-2	59	1232	21.02	124	SYDNEY	SATURDAY 4th MARCH	0600 0800	104	0545	1830	157 5030 1055 0947	2054

259

Appendix 2

Outward Voyage – Points of Interest

S.S. "ORCADES" VOYAGE 57 OUTWARD

APPROXIMATE TIMES OF PASSING POINTS OF INTEREST

Day	Date	Time	Event
Wednesday	25th January		Depart London
Thursday	26th January	0500	Arrive Rotterdam
Thursday	26th January	1600	Depart Rotterdam
Friday	27th January	0730	Casquets
Friday	27th January	1530	Ushant – Enter Bay of Biscay
Saturday	28th January	0700	Torinana – Leave Bay
Saturday	28th January	1700	Burling Islands
Saturday	28th January	2359	C. St. Vincent
Sunday	29th January	0645	Tarifa – Strait of Gibraltar
Monday	30th January	0645	C. Bengut (Algeria)
Monday	30th January	2000	Ras Engele (Tunesia)
Tuesday	31st January	0115	Pt. Spadillo (Pantelleria Id.)
Tuesday	31st January	0830	C. Spadaro (S. Point of Italy)
Wednesday	1st February	0100	C. Matapan (Morea)
Wednesday	1st February	0200	C. Spathi (Elaphonesis Citannel)
Wednesday	1st February	0730	Embark Piraeus Pilot
Wednesday	1st February	0900	Arrive Piraeus
Wednesday	1st February	1800	Depart Piraeus
Thursday	2nd February	0515	Sidaro – East Coast of Crete
Thursday	2nd February	2359	Embark Port Said Pilot
Friday	3rd February	0200	Arrive Port Said
Friday	3rd February	0700	Depart Port Said – Enter Suez Canal
Saturday	4th February	0200	Arrive/Depart Suez
Saturday	4th February	1030	Shadwan Id – Enter Red Sea
Sunday	5th February	1830	P & O Buoy (GP.Occ.F.Fl)
Monday	6th February	0230	Centre Peak Id.
Monday	6th February	0530	Abu Ail Channel
Monday	6th February	1000	Straits of Perim – Leave Red Sea
Monday	6th February	1530	Embark Aden Pilot
Monday	6th February	1700	Arrive Aden
Monday	6th February	2300	Depart Aden
Tuesday	7th February	1600	Ras Alula
Friday	10th February	0930	Minicoi Id.
Saturday	11th February	0530	Embark Colombo Pilot
Saturday	11th February	0700	Arrive Colombo
Saturday	11th February	2000	Depart Colombo
Saturday	11th February	2359	Pass Galle
Sunday	12th February	1900	Cross Equator
Saturday	18th February	0630	Embark Fremantle Pilot
Saturday	18th February	0800	Arrive Fremantle
Saturday	18th February	1500	Depart Fremantle
Sunday	19th February	0030	C. Leeuwin – Enter Aussie Bight
Tuesday	21st February	2330	C. Otway
Wednesday	22nd February	0300	Port Phillip Heads – Embark Melbourne Pilot
Wednesday	22nd February	0700	Arrive Melbourne
Wednesday	22nd February	2300	Depart Melbourne
Thursday	23rd February	0200	Port Phillip Heads
Thursday	23rd February	1730	Gabo Id.
Friday	24th February	0600	Sydney Heads, Embark Pilot
Friday	24th February	0800	Arrive Sydney
Saturday	25th February	1600	Depart Sydney
Tuesday	28th February	0200	Stepheni Id.
Tuesday	28th February	0400	(N.T)Cook Strait, Twixt N & S. Islands
Tuesday	28th February	0600	Embark Wellington Pilot
Tuesday	28th February	0800	Arrive Wellington
Wednesday	1st March	2000	Depart Wellington
Wednesday	1st March	2200	Cook Strait
Saturday	11th March	0600	Sydney Heads – Embark Pilot
Saturday	11th March	0800	Arrive Sydney

Appendix 3

Outward Voyage Clock Changes

R.M.S. "ORCADES"   VOYAGE 57 OUTWARD

PROPOSED ALTERATIONS OF SHIPS CLOCKS

LONDON - ROTTERDAM

Clocks will be ADVANCED   60 mins @

ROTTERDAM - PIRAEUS

Clocks will be ADVANCED   30 mins @ 0200 on   Sunday, 29th January
Clocks will be ADVANCED   30 mins @ 0200 on   Monday, 30th January.

PIRAEUS - PORT SAID - SUEZ
                                   Nil.

SUEZ - ADEN

Clocks will be ADVANCED   30 mins @ 0200 on   Sunday, 5th February
Clocks will be ADVANCED   30 mins @ 0200 on   Monday, 6th February.

ADEN - COLOMBO

Clocks will be ADVANCED   30 mins @ 0200 on   Wednesday, 8th February.
Clocks will be ADVANCED   60 mins @ 0200 on   Thursday, 9th February
Clocks will be ADVANCED   30 mins @ 0200 on   Friday, 10th February
Clocks will be ADVANCED   30 mins @ 0200 on   Saturday, 11th February.

COLOMBO - FREMANTLE

Clocks will be ADVANCED   30 mins @ 0200 on   Tuesday, 14th February
Clocks will be ADVANCED   30 mins @ 0200 on   Wednesday, 15th February
Clocks will be ADVANCED   30 mins @ 0200 on   Thursday, 16th February
Clocks will be ADVANCED   30 mins @ 0200 on   Friday, 17th February
Clocks will be ADVANCED   30 mins @ 0200 on   Saturday, 18th February.

FREMANTLE - MELBOURNE

Clocks will be ADVANCED   60 mins @ 0200 on   Monday, 20th February
Clocks will be ADVANCED   60 mins @ 0200 on   Tuesday, 21st February

MELBOURNE - SYDNEY
                                   Nil.

SYDNEY - WELLINGTON

Clocks will be ADVANCED   30 mins @ 0200 on   Sunday, 26th February
Clocks will be ADVANCED   60 mins @ 0200 on   Monday, 27th February
Clocks will be ADVANCED   30 mins @ 0200 on   Tuesday, 28th February

WELLINGTON - SYDNEY

Clocks will be RETARDED   60 mins @ 0200 on   Thursday, 2nd March
Clocks will be RETARDED   30 mins @ 0200 on   Friday, 3rd March
Clocks will be RETARDED   30 mins @ 0200 on   Saturday, 4th March.

CRUISE

SYDNEY - DARWIN

Clocks will be RETARDED   30 mins @ 0200 on   Monday, 13th March.

DARWIN - HONG KONG

Clocks will be RETARDED   30 mins @ 0200 on   Saturday, 18th March.

YOKOHAMA - GUAM

Clocks will be ADVANCED   30 mins @ 0200 on   Thursday, 30th March
Clocks will be ADVANCED   30 mins @ 0200 on   Saturday, 1st April.

Appendix 4

Pacific Cruise Itinerary

Appendix 5

Pacific Cruise – Points of Interest

s.s. "ORCADES"

APPROXIMATE TIMES OF PASSING POINTS OF INTERESTS
"CHERRY BLOSSOM CRUISE" 1967

Date	Time	Point of Interest
Wednesday 8th March	1600	Depart Sydney
Thursday 9th March	1530	C. Moreton (Pass Brisbane)
Friday 10th March	1700	Shaw Id. – S. End Whitsunday Passage
Friday 10th March	1800	N. Molle Id. – N. End Whitsunday
		Thence Barrier Reef (Inner Transit) Until
Sunday 12th March	1200	Goods Id. (Torres Strait, Twixt N. Queensland & New Guinea
Sunday 12th March	1630	Carpentaria L/V – Gulf of Carpentaria
Monday 13th March	1900	New Year Id.
Monday 13th March	2215	Vashon Hd. Commence Transit Dundas & Clarence Strts.
Tuesday 14th March	0600	Darwin Fairway
Tuesday 14th March	0900	Arrive Darwin
Tuesday 14th March	1800	Depart Darwin
Wednesday 15th March	0945	Timor Id. – Enter Bandar Sea
Wednesday 15th March	2330	Manipa St. – Leave Bander, Enter Ceram Sea
Thursday 16th March	1930	Enter Celebes Sea
Friday 17th March	0600	Basilan Sarait
Friday 17th March	0730	Clear Strait – Enter Sulu Sea
Friday 17th March	2???	Mindoro Straits
Friday 17th March	2359	Enter China Sea
Sunday 19th March	0700	Embark Hong Kong Pilot
Sunday 19th March	0900	Arrive Hong Kong
Tuesday 21st March	1800	Depart Hong Kong
Tuesday 21st March	2200	Taiwan Strait – S. End
Wednesday 22nd March	1730	Agincourt Id. – Clear Taiwan
Thursday 23rd March	1830	Tanega Sima (Japanese Ids.)
Friday 24th March	0230	Approach Bungo Channel (S. Entrance to Inland Sea of Japan)
Friday 24th March	0330	Embark Inland Sea Pilot
		Thence Inland Sea Transit
Friday 24th March	1800	Arrive Kobe
Sunday 26th March	0700	Depart Kobe
Sunday 26th March	1430	Shiono Misaki – S. Point Honshu Id.
Monday 27th March	0600	Commence Uraga Str. Transit
Monday 27th March	0700	Embark Yokohama Pilot
Monday 27th March	0800	Arrive Yokohama
Wednesday 29th March	1200	Depart Yokohama
Wednesday 29th March	1400	Clear Uraga Channel
Wednesday 29th March	1800	Mikura Id.
Wednesday 29th March	2000	Hachijo Id.
Thursday 30th March	2030	Iwo Id.
Saturday 1st April	0700	Guam Pilot (Marianas or Ladrones Gp. of Ids)
Saturday 1st April	0800	Arrive Guam
Saturday 1st April	1700	Depart Guam
Sunday 2nd April	1545	Latitude of Caroline Ids
Tuesday 4th April	0045	Nusseu Id. N. most Id. Bismark Archipelago
Tuesday 4th April	0345	C. Matanalem (New Hanover)
Tuesday 4th April	0645	Mait Id.
Tuesday 4th April	1245	Makada Id. Commence St. Georges Channel Transit Twixt New Ireland & New Britain
Tuesday 4th April	1530	Clear St. Georges Channel – Enter Solomon Sea
Wednesday 5th April	1200	Rossel Spit, Eastern Extremity New Guinea Enter Coral Sea
Saturday 8th April	0130	Sugarloaf Pt (Coast of N.S.W.)
Saturday 8th April	0600	Embark Sydney Pilot
Saturday 8th April	0800	Arrive Sydney

Appendix 6

Homeward Itinerary – Sydney to London

Appendix 7

Sydney to London Points of Interest

s.s. "ORCADES" — Voyage 57 Homeward

APPROXIMATE TIMES OF PASSING POINTS OF INTEREST

Wednesday 12th April	1100	Depart Sydney
Wednesday 12th April	2330	Gabo Id.
Thursday 13th April	1300	Port Phillip Heads, Embark Pilot
Thursday 13th April	1700	Arrive Melbourne
Friday 14th April	2300	Depart Melbourne
Saturday 15th April	0200	Port Phillip Heads
Saturday 15th April	0515	C. Otway – Enter Aussie Bight
Monday 17th April	2230	C. Leeuwin – Clear Bight
Tuesday 18th April	0515	Rottnest Id.
Tuesday 18th April	0630	Embark Pilot
Tuesday 18th April	0800	Arrive Fremantle
Tuesday 18th April	1900	Depart Fremantle
Monday 24th April	0300	Cross Equator
Tuesday 25th April	0200	Pt. de Galle (Ceylon)
Tuesday 25th April	0530	Embark Colombo Pilot
Tuesday 25th April	0700	Arrive Colombo
Tuesday 25th April	2000	Depart Colombo
Wednesday 26th April	1600	Minikoi Id.
Saturday 29th April	1045	Ras Alula
Sunday 30th April	0430	Embark Aden Pilot
Sunday 30th April	0600	Arrive Aden
Sunday 30th April	1200	Depart Aden
Sunday 30th April	1715	Perim Straits – Enter Red Sea
Sunday 30th April	2130	Abu Ail Channel
Monday 1st May	1000	P & O Buoy
Tuesday 2nd May	1530	Shadwan – Enter Gulf of Suez
Tuesday 2nd May	2359	Arrive Suez Pilot Ground
Tuesday 2nd May	0:00	Anchor Suez Bay
Wednesday 3rd May	0700	Commence Canal Transit
Wednesday 3rd May	2200	Arrive Port Said
Thursday 4th May	0100	Depart Port Said
Friday 5th May	0015	Gavdo Id.
Friday 5th May	2045	dell Armi – Messina Straits
Friday 5th May	2230	Clear Straits
Saturday 6th May	0500	Capri Id.
Saturday 6th May	0600	Embark Naples Pilot
Saturday 6th May	0800	Arrive Naples
Saturday 6th May	1700	Depart Naples
Sunday 7th May	0445	St. Maria Id. Bonifacio Strait Twixt Corsica & Sardinia
Sunday 7th May	1930	Embark Barcelona Pilot
Sunday 7th May	2100	Arrive Barcelona
Monday 8th May	1200	Depart Barcelona
Monday 8th May	2130	C. Nao (Spain – Murcia)
Tuesday 9th May	0130	C. Palos (Spain – Andulusia)
Tuesday 9th May	0545	C. de Gata (Spain – Granada)
Tuesday 9th May	1300	Gibraltar Straits
Tuesday 9th May	2215	C. St. Vincent
Wednesday 10th May	0315	C. Roca
Wednesday 10th May	1500	C. Torinana – Enter Bay of Biscay
Thursday 11th May	0830	Ushant – Enter English Channel
Thursday 11th May	1430	Casquets
Friday 12th May	0400	Embark Pilot Off River Maas
Friday 12th May	0630	Arrive Rotterdam

Appendix 8

Sydney to London Clock Changes

S.S. "ORCADES"   VOYAGE 57 HOMEWARD

PROPOSED ALTERATIONS OF SHIPS CLOCKS

SYDNEY – MELBOURNE

    Nil.

MELBOURNE – FREMANTLE

  Clocks will be RETARDED   60 mins @ 0200 on Sunday, 16th April
  Clocks will be RETARDED   60 mins @ 0200 on Monday, 17th April

FREMANTLE – COLOMBO

  Clocks will be RETARDED   30 mins @ 0200 on Wednesday, 19th April
  Clocks will be RETARDED   30 mins @ 0200 on Thursday, 20th April
  Clocks will be RETARDED   30 mins @ 0200 on Friday, 21st April
  Clocks will be RETARDED   30 mins @ 0200 on Sunday, 23rd April
  Clocks will be RETARDED   30 mins @ 0200 on Monday, 24th April

COLOMBO – ADEN

  Clocks will be RETARDED   30 mins @ 0200 on Wednesday, 26th April
  Clocks will be RETARDED   30 mins @ 0200 on Thursday, 27th April
  Clocks will be RETARDED   30 mins @ 0200 on Friday, 28th April
  Clocks will be RETARDED   60 mins @ 0200 on Saturday, 29th April

ADEN – SUEZ

  Clocks will be RETARDED   30 mins @ 0200 on Monday, 1st May
  Clocks will be RETARDED   30 mins @ 0200 on Tuesday, 2nd May

SUEZ – PORT SAID

    Nil.

PORT SAID – NAPLES

  Clocks will be RETARDED   60 mins @ 0200 on Friday, 5th May

NO FURTHER ALTERATIONS TO CLOCKS NECESSARY AFTER NAPLES.